INDEX TO
Georgia Wills

INDEX TO
Georgia Wills

by

Jeannette Holland Austin

CLEARFIELD

Reprinted for
Clearfield Company, Inc. by
Genealogical Publishing Co., Inc.
Baltimore, Maryland
1998, 2003

Originally published in 1976.
Reprinted in a new and improved format by
Genealogical Publishing Co., Inc.
Baltimore, Maryland 1985
Copyright© 1985 by
Genealogical Publishing Co., Inc.
Library of Congress Catalogue Card Number 84-73074
International Standard Book Number 0-8063-1112-6
Made in the United States of America

Note to the Reader

his is an index to the earliest surviving will books of those Georgia counties formed before the 1832 Land Lottery. The dates given in each entry pertain to the coverage of the respective will books and were assigned by the Clerk in the Ordinary's Office of each county. I did not use the designations *Will Book A, B, C,* etc. because many counties begin their will book series with these letters, then use them again for later time periods. And in the earliest periods there is often more than one *Will Book A,* confusing the situation even further. This way, the researcher should have no difficulty locating the exact book labeled by the Clerk.

This index was not prepared from the original wills themselves, since many of these have been lost or destroyed, but from a microfilm copy of the county will books. More specifically, this index derives from copies of wills made by the Clerk, whose job it was to enter verbatim copies in the large will books. We can but wonder how correct the Clerk was in his spelling and how frequently he made his own interpretations.

The researcher should bear in mind that a good many wills were lost before the State of Georgia commenced its microfilming program, and that some wills, although drawn up, were never officially filed. Therefore, to obtain full satisfaction, the researcher should examine *all* estate records, i.e. returns, divisions, receipts, inventories, and miscellaneous estate records. Please note that this work does not index Chatham County wills. I deliberately omitted these because the Georgia Archives maintains an index to the estate records of Chatham County in its Reading Room.

Jeannette Holland Austin

A LIST OF WILLS INDEXED IN THIS WORK

COUNTY	DATES COVERED
Appling	1877-1925
Baldwin	1806-19A 1819-64B
Bartow	1836-85
Bibb	1823-55A 1851-71B
Burke	1853-70
Butts	1826-41
Camden	1795-1829A 1830-67 (Book B, burned) 1868-1916C
Campbell	1825-1900
Carroll	1852-96
Chattooga	1856-1924
Clarke	1802-42A 1822-42B
Clayton	1859-1921
Cobb	1875-1900 Wills & Administrations
Columbia	
Coweta	1849-93
Crawford	1835-52A 1852-94B
Decatur	1828-38
DeKalb	1840-69A
Dooly	1847-1901
Early	1834-1902 Bonds 1856-89 Admrs Bonds 1856-1927
Effingham	1829-59
Elbert	1791-95A 1803-6B 1809-12C 1816-21D 1829-60E
Emanuel	1815-68
Fayette	1828-97
Floyd	1852-61A 1816-71B
Forsyth	1833-44
Franklin	1786-1813A 1848-67
Gilmer	1836-53
Glynn	1844-53
Greene	1796-1806 1786-95 1817-42
Gwinnett	1852-86
Habersham	1847-1900
Hall	1819-37A 1837-67B
Hancock	1794-1807 Miscellaneous
Harris	1850-75B
Henry	1822-34A 1834-69B
Houston	1827-55A 1855-96B
Irwin	1821-64
Jackson	1802-60
Jasper	1812-39 1825-31
Jefferson	1795-1842
Jones	1812-23 1826-50
Laurens	1809-40
Lee	1854-1955
Liberty	1772-1887
Lincoln	1796-1879
Lowndes	1871-1915
Lumpkin	1833-52 1845-1923
Macon	1856-1909
Madison	1812-41A 1842-96B
Marion	1846-1915
McIntosh	1873-1915
Meriwether	1831-59
Monroe	1824-47
Montgomery	1806-63
Morgan	1830-60
Murray	1840-72
Muscogee	1838-62
Newton	1823-51
Oglethorpe	1793-1807A 1833-66B
Paulding	1850-77
Pike	1823-29A 1844-76B
Polk	1857-1936
Pulaski	1816-50
Putnam	1808-56 1823-56

Rabun	1863-88
Randolph	1845-94
Richmond	1840-53
Screven	1810-1929
Stewart	1831-5A 1837-49B 1850-90C
Sumter	1838-55 Bonds and Wills
Talbot	1828-56
Taliaferro	1826-66
Tattnall	1800-34 Deeds ABC 1836-40 Inventories, etc.
Telfair	1869-1921
Thomas	1826-31 1837-45 Minutes
Troup	1832-48
Union	1877-1942
Upson	1826-1910
Walton	1819-37A 1827-31B 1834-9C
Ware	1879-1915
Warren	1829-60
Washington	1829-71 Divisions 1852-1903 Wills
Wayne	1822-70
Wilkes	1792-1801 1806-08 1818-19 1819-36
Wilkinson	1817-1920

Abbreviations

adm = administration	ind = indenture
admr = administrator	inv = inventory
admx = adminstratrix	gdn = guardian
appr = appraisal	L/A = Letters of Administration
atty = attorney	Mts = Minutes
Col = colored	nunc = nuncupative
declar = declaration	orph = orphan
divs = divisions	retn = return
exor = executor	Rev. = Revolutionary
i = intestate	Sold. = Soldier
illeg = illegible	wid = widow

INDEX TO GEORGIA WILLS

AARON		
Daniel	Madison	1812-41
Daniel	Tattnall	1836-40i
AARONS		
William P.	Forsyth	1833-44
ABBOTT		
Ezekiel	Jasper	1831-39
ABERCROMBIE		
Edmund	Hancock	1833
Gena	Chattooga	1853-1924
H. N.	Union	1877-1942
Isabella	Lumpkin	1845-1923
John	Hancock	1817
Lavinia	Clayton	1858-1929
Rachel	Clayton	1858-1929
Wiley	Putnam	1823-56
William	Lumpkin	1845-1923
Y. B.	Cobb	1931
ABLE		
A. R.	Paulding	1850-77
ACOCK		
Arnold	Walton	1819-37
Jonathan	Walton	1819-37
Redick	Walton	1819-37
ACORD		
John F.	Washington	1852-1903
ACREE		
Joshua L.	Hancock	1821
Starling	Taliaferro	1826-66i
William	Wilkes	1792-1801
ACRES		
William	Greene	1806-16
ADAIR		
Bozeman	Paulding	1850-77i
Edward	Murray	1840-72
James L.	Paulding	1850-77i
John B.	Paulding	1850-77i
M. S.	Paulding	1850-77
Robert J.	Walton	1834-9
Samuel	Bartow	1836-85
William W.	Jackson	1844
ADAMS		
Ahsolom	Carroll	1852-96
Amanda M.	Gwinnett	1852-86
Andrew	Crawford	1852-94
Anna	Harris	1850-75
Arnold L.	Washington	1828-71i
Benjamin	Monroe	1824-47
Benjamin	Upson	1826-1910
Benjamin	Washington	1852-1903
Carter	Upson	1826-1910
Coalson	Thomas	1826-1836i
Coleman	Screven	1810-1929
Daniel	Houston	1855-96
David	Jasper	1844-76
David	Pike	1844-76
E. E. H.	Monroe	1847-

ADAMS (continued)		
Edward	Talbot	1868
Elijah C.	Chattooga	1856-1936
Elizabeth Mrs.	Polk	1856-89 bond
Frances	Henry	1822-34
George	Early	1856-89 bond
George	Muscogee	1838-62
H. M.	Cobb	1913
Hopewell	Washington	1829-1781i
Isaac	Hancock	1811
James	Clayton	1859-1931
James	Hancock	1796
James	Jones	1826-50
James	Upson	1826-1910
James M.	Putnam	1823-56
James W.	Gwinnett	1852-86
Jane	Chattooga	1856-1924
John	Clarke	1822-42
John	Jackson	1802-60
John	Paulding	1850-77
John	Talbot	---
John C.	Thomas	1826-1831i
John Q.	Dooly	1847-1901
Jonathan	Jasper	1831-39
Joseph	Coweta	1848-92
Kate	Chattooga	1856-1924
Levan	Dooly	1847-1901
Mary	Cobb	1912 minor
Mathew	Montgomery	1806-63
May E.	Cobb	1875
Nicholas	Elbert	1829-60
Phillip	Talbot	1858
Wiley	Montgomery	1806-63
William	Elbert	1818
ADAMSON		
A. P.	Clayton	1859-1921
Charles	Polk	1857-1936
Dorothy	Hancock	1794
G. W.	Clayton	1859-1921
L. C.	Clayton	1858-1921
N. C.	Clayton	1859-1921
Sarah V. Mrs.	Polk	1857-1936
Thomas	Polk	1857-1936
ADAY		
Anna	Early	1834-1902 bond
James	Early	1834-1902 bond
ADCOCK		
Edmund	Lincoln	1796-1805
Edward	Paulding	1850-77 bond
Emanuel	Lincoln	1796-1805
G. W.	Paulding	1850-77
ADERHOLD		
Isaac M.	Franklin	1848-67
ADKERSON		
John	Jones	1812-23
ADKINS		
Daniel	Warren	1838
Elizabeth	Dooly	1847-1900
Joel	Polk	1857-1936
John W.	Wilkinson	1861
Joseph C.	Pike	1844-76

ALLEN (continued)
William W.	Jones	1812-23
Willis	Wilkinson	1871
Y. D.	Pike	1823-29
Y. S.	Clayton	1859-1921
Young D.	Pike	1844-76

ALLGOOD
A. P.	Chattooga	1856-1924
Alice L.	Chattooga	1856-1924
Forest Dr.	Chattooga	1856-1924
H. C.	Polk	1857-1936
John W.	Cobb	1897
M. A. Mrs.	Chattooga	1856-1924

ALLISON
Alfred	Greene	1817-42
David	Monroe	1824-47
H. S.	Marion	1846-1915
James	Jackson	1802-60
James W.	Randolph	1845-94
John	Wilkes	1806-08
John	Wilkes	1819-36
Margaret	Warren	1804
Rebecca	Wilkes	1837-77

ALLMAN
| A. A. | Chattooga | 1856-1924 |
| David | Dooly | 1847-1901 |

ALRED
| Jonathan | Clarke | 1822-42 |

ALSTON
Charity	Elbert	1823
Charity	Monroe	1824-47
Henry	Lumpkin	1845-1923
James	Elbert	1814
Susan E.	Habersham	1847-1910
(wid of Col. Thos. Pinkney Alston of S. C.)		
William	Cobb	1909
William	Elbert	1809

ALTHER
| Amelia | Colonial | 1770 |
| Johannes | Colonial | 1755 |

ALVIN
| Joe Sr. | Wilkinson | 1906 |

AMBERCROMBIE
| Nancy | Warren | 1833 |

AMIS
| Thomas | Oglethorpe | 1833-36 |

AMMONS
Jacob	Lincoln	1808-32
James	Lincoln	1831-69
Jesse	Polk	1857-1936
John	Wayne	1824-55
William	Camden	1868-1916

AMMOSS
| Mauldin | Troup | 1832-48 |

AMORY
| Charles L. | Lumpkin | 1845-1923 |

AMOS
| Stephen | Bibb | 1835-52 |
| William M. | Houston | 1855-96 |

ANDERS
| Samuel | Marion | 1846-1915 |

ANDERSON
| A. G. | Lumpkin | 1845-1923 |
| Anne G. | Dooly | 1847-1901 |

ANDERSON (continued)
Augustus	Burke	1853-70
B. M.	Camden	1868-1916
Benjamin	Camden	1868-1916
Benjamin S.	DeKalb	1840-69
Benjamin Simon	DeKalb	1840-69
C. H.	Cobb	1905
Clayborn	Green	1817-42
D. M.	Clayton	1859-1921
David	Liberty	1772-1887
Dudley	Paulding	1850-77
Edward M.	Clayton	1859-1921
Edwin	Paulding	1850-77
Elizabeth	Baldwin	1834
George Capt.	Colonial	1761
George W.	Lumpkin	1845-1923
Gideon	Wilkes	1806-08
H.	Laurens	1809-40
H. S.	Cobb	1891
Hezekiah	Screven	1810-1910
James	Butts	1826-41
James	Colonial	1769
James	Habersham	1847-1900
James	Jefferson	1817
James	Murray	1840-72
James Sr.	Burke	1853-96
Jane	Lee	1854-1955
John	Liberty	1772-1887
John	Lumpkin	1845-1923
John	Taliaferro	1826-66
John	Tattnall	1836-40i
(gdn of Eliza Coursey)		
John	Wilkes	1779-92
John	Wilkes	1810-16
Jordan	Pulaski	1816-50
Joshua	Habersham	1847-1900
Mary	Wilkes	1819-36
Mary J. Miss	Lumpkin	1845-1923
Melvina	Burke	1853-96
Thomas W.	Houston	1826-55
W.	Screven	1810-1910
W. J.	Houston	1855-96
W. P.	Cobb	1885
William	Baldwin	1839
William	Colonial	1772
William	DeKalb	1840-69
William	Lumpkin	1845-1923
William	Morgan	1814-30
William	Pike	1844-76
William	Richmond	1840-53
William	Screven	1810-1910
William	Warren	1819
William H.	Screven	1810-1910
William S.	Washington	1852-1903

ANDREWS
Alexander	Greene	1806-16
C. C.	Cobb	1878
(Julia, wid)		
Emma et al	Cobb	1878i
Garnett Jr.	Union	1877-1942
Gray	Crawford	1852-94
Gray	Hancock	1811
Green	Jasper	1826-31
James	Colonial	1770
Jane	Jefferson	1816
John W.	Upson	1826-1910
Joseph B.	Glynn	1844-53
Martha A.	Ware	1879-1915
Mary	Warren	1838
Micajah	Liberty	1772-1887
Montclaiborne	Warren	1840
Nathaniel	Elbert	1799
Robert	Jasper	1825-31
Samuel	Jefferson	1802
Thomas B.	Early	1856-1889
Thomas R.	Oglethorpe	1833-36
William G.	Upson	1826-1910

ANGLIN

Ann	Jackson	1802-60
David	Wilkes	1806-08
James	Wilkes	1777-78

ANNESLEY

William	DeKalb	1840-69

ANSLEY

Abel	Warren	1822
John H.	Marion	1846-1915
Martin	Crawford	1835-52
Thomas	Warren	1808
Thomas	Warren	1837
W. A.	Marion	1846-1915
W. W.	Ware	1879-1915
William	Lincoln	1808-32

ANTHONY

Alston	Floyd	1852-61i
Ann	Wilkes	1837-77
James	Wilkes	1810-16
Joseph C.	Wilkes	1810-16
M. R.	Wilkes	1837-77
Mary	Jackson	1802-60
Micajah T.	Wilkes	1837-77
Nancy	Carroll	1852-96

ANTONY

James	Jasper	1812-17
Milton	Richmond	1840-53
William H. D.	Burke	1870-96

APPLEBY

Hugh	Floyd	1852-61i

APPLING

Joel	Wilkes	1837-77
Otho O.	Jasper	1813-19
Otto Harmony	Hancock	1821
Thomas	Wilkes	1792-1801

ARCHER

David J.	Screven	1810-1929
Eli A.	Screven	1810-1929
James	Thomas	1837-45 Mts
James K.	Tattnall	1836-40 Mts
John B.	Thomas	1837-45 Mts
L. C.	Clayton	1859-1921
Serenova	Burke	1853-70
William	Washington	1852-1903

ARD

Neil	Pulaski	1816-50

ARMOR (also see Armour)

Amanda E.	Wilkes	1837-77
James	Jasper	1812-17
William C.	Stewart	1850-90

ARMSTEAD

John	Gwinnett	1852-86

ARMSTRONG

Anthony C.	Washington	1852-1903
Edward	Washington	1829-71i divs
Eliza Ann	Washington	1852-1903
Eunice I.	Washington	1852-1903
G. O. Mrs.	Clayton	1859-1921
James	Wilkes	1779-92
Jane	Washington	1852-1903
John	DeKalb	1840-69
John	Jasper	1812-17
John	Wilkes	1779-92
Levice	Marion	1846-1915
Robert	Glynn	1844-53
Thomas	Glynn	1844-53
William	Crawford	1835-52
William	Jasper	1831-39

ARMSTRONG (continued)

William H.	Washington	1852-1903

ARMOUR

James	Jasper	1826-31

ARNALL

Frank M.	Coweta	1849-92

ARNETT

S. A.	Wilkes	1837-77
Samuel	Wilkes	1837-77

ARNOLD

A. A.	Gwinnett	1852-86
Allen J.	Wilkes	1837-77
F. W.	Morgan	1830-60
Hugh P.	Campbell	1825-1900
Jacob	Chattooga	1856-1924
John	Franklin	1848-67
Joshua	Wilkes	1806-08
Moses	Wilkes	1792-1801
Moses	Wilkes	1837-77
Philip L.	Coweta	1849-92
Susan M.	Coweta	1849-92
Susannah	Oglethorpe	1852
Thomas	Oglethorpe	1793-1807
William	Elbert	1812
William	Jasper	1825-31
William	Walton	1834-9
William Sr.	Hancock	1838
William F.	Coweta	1849-92
William L.	Oglethorpe	1833-66
William P.	Madison	1812-41

ARNOW

Joseph L.	Camden	1868-1916

ARP

James T.	Chattooga	1856-1924

ARRINGTON

James	Jefferson	1813
James M.	Polk	1857-1936
John	Jefferson	1827
Silas	Jefferson	1847

ARTHUR

B. K.	Randolph	1845-94
William	Pulaski	1816-50

ARVEN

Francis	Colonial	1769

ARWOOD

Barbay A.	Cobb	1870

ASBURY

Jonathan	Bibb	1823-55
Martha	Greene	1817-42

ASBY

Mary	Bibb	1851-71

ASH

Coleman W.	Lumpkin	1845-1923
H. H.	Lumpkin	1845-1923
Henry	Lumpkin	1833-52
William	Lumpkin	1833-52

ASHFIELD

Frederick	Putnam	1808-22

ASHFORD

William	Troup	1832-48
William	Wilkes	1779-92

ASHLEY

D. Burroughs	Lowndes	1871-1915

ASHLEY (continued)		
Jesse	Decatur	1824-52 Mts
Juliette M. Mrs.	Lowndes	1871-1915
Mary A.	Carroll	1853-96
Stephen	Lincoln	1808-32
ASHMORE		
Clary	Wilkes	1792-1801
John	Lincoln	1831-69
William	Oglethorpe	1793-1807
William	Wilkes	1818-19
ASHURST		
Robert	Putnam	1823-56
ASKEW		
Frederick	Laurens	1809-40
James Sr.	Hancock	1827
John	Hancock	1822
Josiah F.	Bibb	1823-55
Lilly	Greene	1806-16
Thomas	Jefferson	1798i
ASKINS		
Aley	Morgan	1830-60
Nancy	Oglethorpe	1833-36
ASTIN		
Joseph H.	Campbell	1825-1900
Robert	Greene	1817-42
William L.	Coweta	1828-48
ATCHESON		
Campbell	Coweta	1849-92
ATHA		
Susan	Walton	1870-74
ATKINS		
Booker	Floyd	1852-61i
C. B.	Chattooga	1856-1924
Ernest B.	Cobb	1897
Franky	Wilkes	1806-08
Ira	Pulaski	1816-50
James H. et al	Cobb	1889i
ATKINSON		
A. C.	Clarke	1822-42
Abner	Hancock	1820
Alexander W.	Emanuel	1815-68
Armstead	Taliaferro	1826-66
Arthur C.	Butts	1826-41
Dixon	Richmond	1840-53
F. J.	Thomas	1837-45i
George	McIntosh	1873-1915
George P.	Coweta	1849-92
H. D.	Thomas	1837-45
Jemimah	Pike	1844-76
Lemuel	Pike	1823-29
Marion	Franklin	1848-67
Nathan	Greene	1806-16
Thomas	Morgan	1830-60
Tillman J.	Cobb	1882
W. E.	Gwinnett	1852-86
ATTAWAY		
David	Burke	1853-70
Elbert	Burke	1853-70
Elijah	Burke	1853-70
Harley	Burke	1853-70
Joseph	Coweta	1826-1910
ATWATER		
E. B.	Upson	1826-1910
Nancy A.	Upson	1826-1910
AUBREY		
William	Bartow	1836-85

AUGELLY		
Henry	Dooly	1847-1901
AULTMAN		
Solomon	Crawford	1852-94
AUSLEY		
William	Walton	1834-9 orph
AUSTIN		
Harris	Jefferson	1826
Isaac	Walton	1834-9
Joseph	Liberty	1772-1887
Thomas	DeKalb	1840-69
AUTREY		
John	Wilkes	1779-92
AUTRY		
Alexander	Lumpkin	1845-1923
AVANT		
H. H.	Washington	1852-1903
James Ransome	Washington	1852-1903
Jesse W.	Houston	1855-96
AVERA		
Arthur	Putnam	1823-56
Isaac	Lincoln	1796-1805
James A.	Crawford	1852-94
Thomas J.	Lee	1854-1955
AVERETT		
Albert	Stewart	1850-90
D.	Thomas	1837-45i
Thomas	Lincoln	1831-69
AVERY		
Charles	Floyd	1861-71
G. S.	Cobb	--
Herbert	Jasper	1827-31
Holmes M.	Cobb	1893
J. B.	Lumpkin	1845-1923
James	Early	1856-1927i
Lucinda	Cobb	1866
Philip	Jackson	1802-60
Sara	Cobb	1833
Sarah C.	Henry	1822-34
William	Jasper	1826-31
AWLING		
W. H.	Carroll	1852-96
AWTREY		
Absalom	Morgan	1830-60
Merrill C.	Cobb	1890
Sarah	Cobb	1891
AWTRY		
Isaac Q.	Henry	1822-34
Jacob	Carroll	1852-96
AYCOCK		
Burwell	Oglethorpe	1833-66
Irvin	Randolph	1845-94
Houston	Floyd	1852-61i
James	Colonial	1776
James	Wilkes	1777-78
Richard	Lincoln	1808-32
Richard	Wilkes	1779-92
Tabitha	Floyd	1852-61i
AYER		
C. K.	Floyd	1861-71
AYERS		
Gadwell	Hall	1819-37
John	Franklin	1786-1813
Moses	Polk	1859-1936

AYRES		
Thomas	Colonial	1773
William	Lincoln	1796-1805
BABCOCK		
Cecelia M.	Ware	1879-1915
BABB		
Abner	Henry	1834-69
Martha	Baldwin	1819-64
BACCHAUS		
William	Coweta	1828-48i
BACCUS		
John	Walton	1834-9
BACK		
William M.	Lowndes	1871-1915
BACKSHELL		
William	Colonial	1753
BACNEE		
Fidel	Muscogee	1838-62
BACON		
Edmon	Marion	1845-1915
Edmund	Tattnall	1836-40i
John	Liberty	1772-1887
John B.	Laurens	1809-40
Jonathan	Liberty	1772-1887
Joseph	Colonial	1764
Sarah	Tattnall	1836-40i
Thomas Jr.	Liberty	1772-1887
Thomas Sr.	Liberty	1772-1887
BADGER		
Levin	Putnam	1823-56
BAGBY		
George	Jackson	1802-60
George W.	DeKalb	1840-69
BAGETT		
Allen	Walton	1827-31i
Stephen	Walton	1827-31 admr
BAGGETT		
Allen	Walton	1819-37i
Burton	Cobb	1870
BAGLEY		
William	Greene	1806-16
BAGWELL		
Bryant	Cobb	1874i
Parthena	Cobb	1874i
Sarah	Gwinnett	1852-86
Winkfield	Franklin	1786-1813
BAILES		
William	Burke	1853-96
BAILEY		
Azariah	Newton	1823-51
Christopher	Effingham	1829-59
David	Hancock	1817
Ezekiel	Elbert	1812
F. C.	Bartow	1836-85
F. E. Mrs.	Cobb	1906
George	Wilkes	1837-77
Green	Putnam	1823-56
Hannah	Wilkes	1792-1801
J. C.	Wilkinson	1907

BAILEY (continued)		
James	Bibb	1851-71
James	Wilkes	1792-1801
John	Bibb	1851-71
John	Coweta	1842-92
John	Early	1856-89 admr bond
John	Morgan	1814-30
John	Washington	1852-1903
Joseph	Morgan	1814-30
Joshua	Bartow	1836-85
Lewis N.	Gwinnett	1852-86
Martha	Gwinnett	1852-86
Nancy Y.	Bartow	1836-85
Richard A.	Chattooga	1856-1924
Russell Sr.	Wilkes	1837-77
S. T.	Bibb	1851-71
Samuel	Forsyth	1833-44i
Sarah	Fayette	1828-97
Simon	Putnam	1808-22
Thomas	Colonial	1773
Virginia	Crawford	1852-94
William	Carroll	1852-96
William	Early	--
William	Floyd	1852-61i
William	Gwinnett	1852-86
William	Jackson	1802-60
William	Morgan	1808-30
William	Murray	1840-72
BAILLIE		
Kenneth	Colonial	1766
BAIN		
Baldwin	Wilkes	1810-16
John	Cobb	1881i
John	Telfair	1869-1921
BAINE		
Isaac	Jackson	1802-60
BAIRD		
F. T.	Bartow	1836-85
Hannah M.	Floyd	1852-61 orph
Jonathan	Greene	1806-16
Robert	Walton	1834-9
William	Wilkes	1837-77
BAKER		
A.	Cobb	1876i
A.	Forsyth	1833-34i
Barnard	Walton	1819-37
Beal	Hall	1837-67
Charlotte Mrs.	Cobb	1866i
(& children)		
Christopher	Franklin	1786-1813
Edmond	Chattooga	1856-1924
Elijah	Liberty	1772-1887
Fannie M.	Washington	1852-1903
Francis	Cobb	1880
Hugh	Paulding	1850-77
Jane Price	Fayette	1828-97
Jeff	Camden	1868-1916
Jesse	Greene	1806-16
Jessie	Greene	1794-1810
John	Greene	1817-42
John	Liberty	1772-1887
John	Warren	1816
John V.	Cobb	--i
Jonathan	Washington	1829-71i divs
Jordan	Newton	1823-51
Joseph	Baldwin	1817
Mary	Liberty	1772-1887
Mary	Washington	1852-1903
Merril	Harris	1850-75
Nancy	Marion	1846-1915
Patty	Richmond	1840-53
Patty	Warren	1823
Pleasant	Bartow	1836-85

BARFIELD (continued)		
J. S.	Dooly	1847-1901
Jemima	Monroe	1847-
Jesse	Macon	1856-1909
Samuel	Pike	1844-76
William	Morgan	1814-30
BARGE		
J. M.	Washington	1852-1903
Jacob	Campbell	1825-1900
Margaret	Campbell	1825-1900
Richmond Sr.	Campbell	1825-1900
BARKER		
Benjamin B.	Coweta	1849-92
Burwell	Jones	1826-50
John	Upson	1826-1910
Joseph	Houston	1855-96
Lewis	Jackson	1802-60
Thomas	Pike	1844-76
BARKIN		
James	Carroll	1852-96
BARKLEY		
John	Butts	1826-41
William	Morgan	1830-60
BARKSDALE		
Elizabeth F.	Washington	1852-1903
Isaac	Colonial	1757
John	Early	1856-1927
M. J.	Chattooga	1856-1924
William	Washington	1852-1903
BARLOW		
Mary	Laurens	1809-40
BARMORE		
Wiley	Cobb	1867i
(Sarah A. wid)		
BARNARD		
Ann	Liberty	1772-1887
Baxter	Wilkes	1779-92
Edward	Colonial	1755
Fannie E.	Camden	1868-1916
John	Colonial	1747
BARNES		
Allen	Lumpkin	1845-1923
Blanch	Cobb	1897i
Brinsley	Gilmer	1836-53i
Elizabeth	Hancock	1820
Elizabeth J.	Upson	1826-1910
Ephraim	Hancock	1803
Gideon	Pike	1844-76
Henry Montford	Wilkes	1818-19
James	Screven	1810-1929
James P.	Cobb	1884i
James R.	Talbot	1859
Jethro H.	Carroll	1852-96
John	Hall	1837-67
John	Harris	1850-75
John	Lumpkin	1845-1923
John	Morgan	1814-30
John D.	Lowndes	1834
Lewis	Hancock	1804
Linwood	Cobb	1895i
Littleton	Crawford	1835-52
Lucy A.	Lumpkin	1845-1923
M. L. Mrs.	Cobb	1901i
Mary D.	Richmond	1840-53
Mattie	Cobb	1885i
Nathan	Morgan	1814-30
Ransom	Hall	1837-67
Robert G.	Campbell	1825-1900
Thomas	Hancock	1835
W. C.	Coweta	1849-92

BARNES (continued)		
W. L.	Cobb	1909
William	Talbot	1853
William	Wilkes	1779-92
William W.	Lee	1854-1955
BARNETT		
Anna	Clarke	1822-42
David	Madison	1842-96
David	Oglethorpe	1833-66
Eliza. W.	Wilkes	1837-77
Jacob	Lincoln	1808-32
Josiah	Morgan	1830-60
L.	Floyd	1861-71i
Larkin	Floyd	1852-61i
Nathaniel	Elbert	1824
Nelson	Elbert	1801
P. J.	Wilkes	1837-77
Samuel	Jackson	1802-60
Samuel	Wilkes	1837-77
Zadock	Morgan	1814-30
BARNEY		
Simon	Greene	1786-95
BARNHART		
Charles	Greene	1817-42
BARNS		
E. A.	Bartow	1836-85
BARNWELL		
Robert	Cobb	1881i
BARR		
James	Jackson	1802-60
John	Henry	1834-69
John	Houston	1827-55
Jonathan	Franklin	1786-1813
Josiah K.	Carroll	1852-86
Nathan	Jefferson	1815
BARREN		
Sarah J.	Crawford	1852-94
BARRENTINE		
Lucinda	Crawford	1852-94
BARRETT		
George	Cobb	--
(Juda, wid.)		
J. D.	Cobb	1896i
James S.	Cobb	1896i
(Dora, wid)		
John	Cobb	1890
John	Hall	1837-67
Lewis	Wilkes	1819-36
Lewis Y.	Lumpkin	1845-1923
Lucas J.	Macon	1856-1909
Nancy	Richmond	1840-53
Rebecca	Hall	1837-67
Robert T.	Wilkes	1837-77
Vivian	Franklin	1786-1813
W. J.	Floyd	1852-61
William Sr.	Pike	1844-76
BARRON		
James H.	Chattooga	1856-1924
James M.	Upson	1826-1910
Joannah	Jones	1826-50
John	Butts	1826-41
John	Jones	1812-23
Joseph	Troup	1832-48
Sarah J.	Houston	1855-96
Thomas	Talbot	--
William	Houston	1827-55
Willis	Monroe	1824-47

BARROW
Aaron	Burke	1853-70
Francis Rebecca Williams (Mrs.)	Lee	1854-1955
Isaiah	Burke	1853-70
James	Baldwin	1828
James R.	Carroll	1852-96
John	Warren	1809
Nancy	Baldwin	1814
Nancy	Putnam	1823-56
Reuben	Warren	1812
Richard	Warren	1809
Robert	Coweta	1849-92
Samuel	Jones	1826-50
Warren	Monroe	1847-
Wilie	Macon	1856-1909
William W.	Macon	1856-1909

BARRY
Armsted	Franklin	1786-1813

BARTLES
Sarah H.	Cobb	1885i

BARTLETT
H. B.	Carroll	1852-96
H. B.	Clayton	1859-1921
Jackson W.	Early	1856-1927
Thomas J.	Bibb	1851-71
W. A.	Marion	1846-1915

BARTON
B. F.	Cobb	1906i
David	Bartow	1836-85
Elizabeth	Morgan	1830-60
John	Oglethorpe	1793-1807
Matilda	Randolph	1845-94
W. F.	Polk	1857-1936

BASKIN
R. W.	Houston	1855-96

BARWICK
Nathan	Emanuel	1842 deed of gift

BASHALIA
James	Rabun	1863-88

BASKIL
Samuel	Morgan	1814-30

BASKINS
James G.	Houston	1855-96

BASS
Allen	Jasper	1812-17
Eaton	Marion	1838-62
Elizabeth	Newton	1823-51
Ethelred	Wilkes	1779-92
John H.	Putnam	1823-56
Larkin	Upson	1826-1910
Margaret	Cobb	1906i
Martha	Baldwin	1819-64
Mary	Sumter	1838-55i
Mary Ann Mrs.	Lowndes	1871-1915
Mary M.	Floyd	1852-61
Persons	Chattooga	1856-1924
Reddick (Rev. War Sold.)	Warren	1828
Thomas	Walton	1834-9
William A.	Jasper	1820-23

BASSETT
Stephen	Houston	1855-96
W. P.	Houston	1855-96

BASWELL
Alexander	Cobb	1909i

BASWELL (continued)
John C.	Cobb	1887
W. P.	Cobb	1898

BATCHELOR
Cornelius	Wilkinson	1827
Jesse	Putnam	1823-56

BATEMAN
Bryan Sr.	Houston	1827-55
James D.	Pike	1844-76
Mary	Colonial	1772
Mary Ann	Dooly	1847-1901
Seaborn M.	Houston	1855-96
Theophilus	Marion	1846-1915
William	Colonial	1734

BATES
Andrew J.	Murray	1840-72
Anthony W.	Gwinnett	1852-86
J. H.	Cobb	1905
John	Cobb	1910i
John Sr.	Murray	1840-72
Julius Sr.	Murray	1840-72
Mathais	Cobb	1883

BATEY
Catherine	Houston	1827-55

BATTEY
Mary A.	Richmond	1840-53

BATTLE
Andrew	Troup	1832-48
Benjamin G.	Hancock	1809
Henry T.	Sumter	1838-55i
Isaac	Hancock	1835
Jesse	Hancock	1805
Lazarus	Morgan	1814-30
Robert A.	Monroe	1847-
Sarah	Troup	1832-48
T. W.	Stewart	1850-80
William S.	Taliaferro	1826-66

BATTON
Matilda	Macon	1856-1909

BATTS
Ann J.	Lee	1854-1955
George	Washington	1829-71 divs
John	Lee	1854-1955
Julia F.	Lee	1854-1955
Nathan	Washington	1829-71 divs
Nathan J.	Washington	1852-1903
William	Jefferson	1832

BAUGH
Daniel	Putnam	1808-22
David	Franklin	1786-1813
John	Oglethorpe	1833-66
Peter	Greene	1817-42
William	Gwinnett	1852-86

BAUGHAN
Edmond	Meriwether	1831-59

BAXLEY
James W.	Camden	1868-1916
William	Walton	1872-1931

BAXTER
Eliza	Carroll	1852-96
Joseph M.	Gwinnett	1852-86
Reuben	Henry	1834-69
William B.	Cobb	1871i

BAYLE
Peter	Jackson	1802-60

BAYNE

Charles	Henry	1834-69
John	Jones	1826-50

BAYSE

Joseph	Wilkes	1779-92

BAZEMORE

Humphrey	Screven	1810-1929
James P.	Screven	1810-1929
Mary F.	Screven	1810-1929
N. J.	Dooly	1847-1901
Thomas	Jones	1826-50
Thomas Jefferson	Bibb	1851-71

BEACH

Martha A.	Randolph	1845-94

BEACHAM

Lewis	Emanuel	1815-68
Martha A.	Telfair	1869-1921

BEADLES

William	Coweta	1849-92

BEAL

Agathy	Jefferson	1835
Elizabeth	Jasper	1820-23
Elizabeth	Jefferson	1843
Nathaniel	Richmond	1840-53
Selma	Jefferson	1852
Zephaniah	Clarke	1822-42

BEALL

Elias H.	Harris	1850-75
Erasmus T.	Stewart	1850-90
Francis Esq.	Warren	1822
James	Jasper	1823-33
John	Wilkes	1806-08
John W.	Upson	1826-1910
Mannum	Warren	1814
Nathan	Warren	1841
Noble P.	Bartow	1836-85
Robert A.	Bibb	1825-55

BEALLE

Daniel	Franklin	1786-1813
H. Brotcher	Franklin	1786-1813
Irene	Walton	1827-31
James L.	Dooly	1847-1901
William F.	Dooly	1847-1901

BEALLEY

Robert C.	Jasper	1831-9

BEAN

Alexander	Coweta	1849-92
Annie	Carroll	1852-96
William	Henry	1834-69

BEARD

B. T.	Screven	1810-1929
Bainbridge D.	Screven	1810-1929
Catherine C.	Screven	1810-1929
John	Jackson	1802-60
John	Screven	1810-1929
John R.	Madison	1842-96
Mary J.	Lumpkin	1845-1923
William	Walton	1827-31
William	Walton	1834-9
William E.	Lumpkin	1845-1923

BEARDEN

Henry	Lumpkin	1833-52
Richard	Clarke	1822-42
Willabe	Lumpkin	1833-52

BEARDIN

John H. (orph of)	Walton	1827-31

BEARDIN (continued)

Richard (orph of)	Walton	1827-31

BEARFIELD

John	Campbell	1825-1900
Vincent	Burke	1853-96

BEARROW

Aaron	Burke	1853-96

BEASLEY

C. H.	Lee	1854-1955
Charles	Taliaferro	1826-66
David	Crawford	1835-52
J. F.	Cobb	1893i
James	Warren	1799
James	Walton	1827-31
Richard	Camden	1868-1916
Right M.	Emanuel	1847
Robertson	Morgan	1814-30
S. R.	Cobb	1908i
William	Screven	1810-1929

BEATIE

John J.	Greene	1817-42

BEATTY

Joseph	Jefferson	1796

BEATY

Mary	Laurens	1809-40

BEAUCHAMP

William	Meriwether	1831-59

BEAVALL

James	Screven	1810-1929

BEAVERS

James	Jackson	1802-60
Louise	Ware	1879-1915
R. C.	Campbell	1825-1900
Robert	Jackson	1802-60
William	Jackson	1802-60
William A. J.	Campbell	1825-1900
Willis	Clayton	1859-1921

BECK

Francis	Wilkinson	1823
Isaiah Sr.	Carroll	1852-96
Samuel	Rabun	1863-1888
William	Early	--
William R.	Polk	1857-1936

BECKCOME

Charlotte	Baldwin	1818

BECKHAM

Laban	Pike	1844-76
Martha Mrs.	Pike	1844-76
Sherwood	Monroe	1824-47

BEDDINGFIELD

Martha	Walton	1827-31
		gdns retn
Solomon	Laurens	1809-40

BEDELL

Abner	Jones	1810-28
Isaac	Greene	1817-42
John	Greene	1817-42

BEDFORD

J. M.	Lumpkin	1845-1923
James	Lumpkin	1833-52

BEDINGFIELD

Bryan	Stewart	1837-49
John	Baldwin	1810

BIRD		
Buford	Taliaferro	1826-66
Clarissa H. B.	Monroe	1824-47
Ebenezer	Warren	1835
George L.	Morgan	1830-60
George L.	Taliaferro	1826-66
Hiram	Meriwether	1831-59
James	Early	--
(of Decatur Co.)		
James	Madison	1812-41
James R.	Monroe	1824-47
Job	Putnam	1808-22
John L.	Taliaferro	1826-66
Lee	Madison	1812-41
Philemond	Wilkes	1810-16
Pue	Putnam	1823-56
William	Effingham	1829-59
William	Emanuel	1831
William	Warren	1812
Williamson	Taliaferro	1826-66
Williamson	Wilkes	1806-08

BIRDSONG		
B.	Jones	1812-23

BISCOE		
Ann B.	Putnam	1823-56

BISHOP		
Ephraim	Henry	1834-69
Joseph	Campbell	1825-1900
Phillip	Henry	1834-69
S. E.	Cobb	1892i
Simeon	Pulaski	1816-50
W. L.	Cobb	1905i
William	Hancock	1803

BITHED		
William	Early	1834-1902

BIVINS		
Edwin R.	Sumter	1838-55 bonds
Franklin W.	Houston	1855-96
M. L.	Marion	1846-1915
Samuel	Monroe	1824-47
Samuel	Sumter	1838-55 bonds
Theodora	Dooly	1847-1901
Thomas	Marion	1846-1915
William	Wilkinson	1828

BIXLY		
James	Coweta	1849-93

BLACK		
Edward	Wilkes	1792-1801
Edward J.	Screven	1810-1929
George Sr.	Murray	1840-72
George R.	Screven	1810-1929
John	Cobb	1901i
(Sarah wid)		
John	Hall	1819-38
Lemuel	Cobb	1904
Louise J. Mrs.	Lowndes	1871-1915
Matt	Cobb	1904i
Richardson	Putnam	1823-56
Rutha	Upson	1826 1910
Silvey	Henry	1834-69
Thomas	Campbell	1825-1900
Thomas	Oglethorpe	1793-1807
Thomas J.	Madison	1842-96
W. W.	Monroe	1824-47

BLACKBURN		
David H.	Screven	1810-1929
John L.	Meriwether	1831-59
Rachael	Screven	1810-1929

BLACKER		
B. M.	Burke	1853-70

BLACKMAN		
William K.	Harris	1850-75

BLACKMORE		
Thomas	Wilkes	1779-92

BLACKMORIS		
---	Carroll	1852-96

BLACKSHEAR		
A. M.	Bibb	1851-71
Edward	Thomas	1826-1836
Elijah	Laurens	1809-40
James J.	Thomas	1837-45i
Joseph	Laurens	1809-40
Mary L.	Ware	1879-1915
Thomas	Thomas	1837-45i

BLACKSTOCK		
W. F.	Paulding	1850-77 bond

BLACKWELL		
Blackwell	Banks	1835
Elizabeth	Cobb	1895i
J. B.	Cobb	1894i
Joseph	Elbert	1804
Joseph	Elbert	1819
Joseph	Elbert	1829-60
Ralph	Elbert	1829-60
Randolph	Bibb	1823-55

BLAIR		
Andrew	Walton	1819-37
James	Franklin	1786-1813
John	Franklin	1786-1813
Rachel	Jefferson	1802
William	Walton	1834-9

BLAKE		
Allen	Hall	1837-67
Eleanor Mrs.	Bibb	1851-71
Ezekiel	Pike	1844-76
John	DeKalb	1840-69
Mary	DeKalb	1840-69
Mary A.	Bibb	1823-55
William	Elbert	1796
William	Lumpkin	1845-1923

BLAKEY		
Churchwell	Wilkes	1837-77
Judith C.	Wilkes	1837-77

BLALOCK		
Allidea	Jones	1810-28
C. N. Mrs.	Clayton	1859-1921
David	Lincoln	1796-1805
J. L.	Jackson	1802-60
J. O.	Clayton	1859-1921
James	Jones	1826-50
James	Upson	1826-1910
John Sr.	Wilkes	1792-1801
Richard	Macon	1856-1909
Zadoc	Fayette	1828-97

BLANCE		
Josephine Mrs.	Polk	1857-1936

BLANCHARD		
Thomas	Harris	1850-75

BLAND		
Elisha	Washington	1852-1903
Micajah	Washington	1852-1903
Simeon	Washington	1829-71 divs
Simeon	Washington	1852-1903
W. E.	Lumpkin	1845-1923

BLANDFORD		
Francis	Jones	1826-50

BLANKENSHIP		
William	Cobb	1882i

BLANTON		
Benjamin	Oglethorpe	1833-66
Charles	Lincoln	1796-1805
Christopher	Lincoln	1796-1805
P.	Bartow	1836-85

BLASINGAME		
James	Walton	1834-9
James G.	Crawford	1852-94
Jane E.	Forsyth	1833-44
Louisa	Crawford	1852-94

BLASSENGAME		
Clara	Cobb	1902i
Philip	Greene	1817-42

BLAYLOCK		
John	Meriwether	1831-59

BLEDSOE		
Aaron	Greene	1806-16
Gilmore	Hancock	1821
Miller	Oglethorpe	1833-66
Peggy	Troup	1832-48
Robert	Putnam	1823-56

BLENFIELD		
John	Colonial	1747

BLESSET		
Elisha	Butts	1826-41
George	Butts	1826-41
Polly	Butts	1826-41
William	Butts	1826-41

BLITCH		
Benjamin	Effingham	1829-59
Ellen J. Mrs.	Screven	1810-1929
Speir	Effingham	1829-59
Thomas Sr.	Effingham	1829-59
William M.	Screven	1810-1929

BLIZZARD		
Brinkley	Baldwin	1819-64

BLOCKER		
B. M.	Burke	1853-96

BLOODWORTH		
David M.	Carroll	1852-96
Miles M.	Wilkinson	1873
W. L.	Carroll	1852-96
William	Wilkinson	1851
Willis	Wilkinson	1895

BLOOM		
A. E.	Bibb	1851-71

BLOUNT		
Daniel	Washington	1829-71 divs
Elizabeth	Jones	1826-50
Henry N. S.	Jones	1826-50
James	Jones	1826-50
John	Jasper	1825-31
Philip	Decatur	1824-52 Mts
R. A.	--	1819-64
Richard	Baldwin	1843

BLOW		
John	Jones	1826-50
Miriam	Jones	1826-50

BLUE		
Simeon	Marion	1846-1915

BLUET		
James	Greene	1796-1806

BLUNT		
Edmund	Putnam	1823-56
Thomas	Jones	1826-50

BLYTH		
James M.	Marion	1846-1915
Sarah (nee Hirsh)	Cobb	1874i
William C.	Cobb	1871i

BOATWRIGHT		
John	Washington	1852-1903
Rolly	Dooly	1847-1901
Ruben	Emanuel	1866 gdn

BOBBETT		
Martha	Greene	1817-42

BOBERSON		
William	Clarke	1802-22

BOBO		
Benjamin	Floyd	1852-61i
Callabat E.	Cobb	1872i
Lester	Polk	1857-1936
Lewis	Floyd	1852-61i
Lewis	Franklin	1786-1813
Martin	Floyd	1852-61i
Mary	Franklin	1786-1813
Willis	Floyd	1852-61i

BODDIE		
Bennett V. N.	Harris	1850-75

BOGER		
Elijah	Cobb	1906

BOGGS		
Elizabeth P.	Harris	1850-75

BOHANNON		
Duncan P.	Lincoln	1808-32
J. V.	Cobb	1903
John D.	Coweta	1849-92
Joseph	Coweta	1849-92

BOHRMAN		
Michael	Colonial	1771

BOLAN		
M. C. Miss	Cobb	--

BOLDEN		
William	Cobb	1881i

BOLES		
Jesse	Oglethorpe	1793-1807
William	Burke	1853-70

BOLING		
Manning	Putnam	1808-22
S. H.	Chattooga	1856-1924

BOND		
Daniel	Elbert	1829-60
Elizabeth	Elbert	1824
H. C.	Clayton	1859-1921
J. R.	Madison	1842-96
Joel	Bibb	1851-71
Joseph	Bibb	1851-71
Joseph M.	Campbell	1825-1900
Joseph T.	DeKalb	1840-69
Leonard	Franklin	1848-67
Nathan	Elbert	1829-60
Nathan Sr.	Elbert	1815
Penelope Mrs.	Bibb	1851-71

BOND (continued)
Seth	Jones	1812-23
Silas	Coweta	1849-92
Thomas	Cobb	1896i
Thomas	Wilkes	1810-16
Washington	Campbell	1825-1900
William	Bibb	1851-71

BONE
Bailey	Paulding	1850-77i
Bailey Jr.	Cobb	Mt. Book O.
(Bailey Sr. gdn)		

BONEFIELD
Harriett Mrs.	Burke	1853-96

BONER
Allen	Walton	1834-9 orph
Frances E.	Walton	1834-9
		orph of Allen
Lucy	Walton	1834-9

BONERS
Philemond Sr.	Stewart	1850-90

BONES
William H.	Clarke	1822-42

BONN
Henry	Walton	1834-9

BONNELL
Anthony	Emanuel	1825
Anthony	Screven	1810-1929
John	Screven	1810-1929

BONNER
Claborn	Cobb	1876
Fanny	Henry	1834-69
James	Baldwin	1841
Jane	Talbot	--
John	Carroll	1852-96
Sanders W.	Carroll	1852-96
Thomas	Morgan	1830-60
Whitmel	Jasper	1820-23
Zadock	Carroll	1852-96

BOOKER
Esther	Wilkes	1837-77
Gideon	Wilkes	1806-08
Richerson	Wilkes	1837-77
William	Walton	1828 return
William S.	Wilkes	1837-77

BOOLES
Jesse	Greene	1817-42
Permelia	Greene	1817-42
William	Greene	1817-42

BOON
Benjamin H.	Morgan	1830-60
Exum	Jasper	1812-17
G. W.	Forsyth	1833-44
Gilly	Morgan	1830-60
Jacob	Jasper	1813-19
Jesse	Carroll	1852-96
Rebecca F.	Morgan	1814-30
Sion	Morgan	1814-30
Stephen F.	Sumter	1835-55 bonds
William R.	Carroll	1852-96

BOONE
J. M.	Wilkinson	1908
R. W.	Cobb	1910i

BOOTH
Gabriel	Elbert	1829-60
George	Elbert	1818
John Sr.	Elbert	1802

BOOTHE
Edward	Warren	1831
James	Jackson	1802-60
John M.	Pulaski	1816-60
Thomas D.	Taliaferro	1826-66

BORANN
Alexander	Dooly	1847-1901

BORDEN
Benjamin O.	Hancock	1806

BORDERS
Isaac	Jackson	1802-60
Michael	Jackson	1802-60
Stephen L.	Jackson	1802-60

BOREN
Alfred D. L.	Bibb	1851-71
James	Wilkes	1810-16

BORING
Mary M.	Cobb	1890i

BORN
Daniel	Clarke	1802-22
J. A. L.	Cobb	1908
John A.	Gwinnett	1852-86

BOROM
Peggy	Wilkes	1819-36

BORUM
Elizabeth A.	Oglethorpe	1833-66

BOSHAN
Matthew	Jackson	1802-60

BOSOMWORTH
Adam	Colonial	1757

BOSTIC
Wade	Lincoln	1808-32

BOSTICK
David D.	Jones	1826-50
John	Jefferson	1840
John	Lincoln	1796-1805
Nathan Sr.	Jefferson	1817
Rebecca	Clarke	1822-42
William	Wilkes	1810-16

BOSTON
Green	Burke	1853-70

BOSTWICK
A. C.	Dooly	1847-1901
Ann M.	Muscogee	1838-62
Azariah B.	Morgan	1830-60
C. C.	Cobb	1873i
Floyd C.	Burke	1853-70
Littleberry Sr.	Jefferson	1823
Mary	Pulaski	1816-50

BOSWELL
Henry	Jasper	1831-39
John C.	Floyd	1852-61i
Susannah	Jones	1810-28

BOSWORTH
Wiley W.	Fayette	1828-97

BOTHWELL
David	Jefferson	1801
David E.	Dooly	1847-1901
Samuel	Jefferson	1828
Sarah	Jefferson	1828
William C.	Lee	1854-1955

BOTTOMS

Joseph	Fayette	1828-97

BOURQUIN

Henry Lewis	Colonial	1774

BOWDEN

Jesse	Henry	1834-69

BOWDER

Isham	Morgan	1830-60

BOWEN

Ephraim	Hancock	1800
Giles	Coweta	1849-92
Horatio C.	Coweta	1849-93
James	Campbell	1825-1900
John, gdn	Tattnall	1836-40i
John	Wilkes	1779-92
Jonathan	Campbell	1825-1900
Levi	Tattnall	1836-40i
Mark	Tattnall	1836-40i
Martha A. E.	Coweta	1849-93
Mary	Tattnall	1836-40 orph
Robert C.	Greene	1794-1810
Seaborn	Tattnall	1836-40i orph
Samuel	Colonial	1774
Thomas C.	Jackson	1802-60
Susan	Coweta	1849-92

BOWER

Benaniel	Baldwin	1843
James C.	Wilkinson	1886

BOWERS

David	Crawford	1852-94
David	Stewart	1850-90
Matilda	Baldwin	1819-64

BOWIE

James H.	Screven	1810-1929
Langston	Floyd	1861-71
W. C.	Screven	1810-1929

BOWIN

Charles S. B.	Jones	1826-50

BOWLES

Benjamin B.	Taliaferro	1826-66
John	Colonial	1776
John J.	Taliaferro	1826-66
Judith	Wilkes	1819-36
Martin D.	Butts	1826-41

BOWLING

John	Coweta	1828-48i

BOWMAN

H. B.	Cobb	1904i
Joel H.	Chattooga	1856-1924
John	Bibb	1851-71
John M.	Lumpkin	1833-52
Levi	Tattnall	1836-40i
Martha H.	Bibb	1851-71
Vincent	Bartow	1836-85

BOWYER

T. S.	Montgomery	1806-63

BOX

Richard	Liberty	1772-1887

BOYCE

Meshack	Gwinnett	1852-86

BOYD

Allen	Burke	1853-96
Benjamin	Burke	1853-96
David	Cobb	1877

BOYD (continued)

Elijah	Emanuel	1856
Israel	Cobb	1867i
J. J.	Screven	1810-1929
James	Fayette	1828-97
John H.	Campbell	1825-1900
Kezia	DeKalb	1840-69
L. Roberts	Lumpkin	1845-1923 minor
M. G.	Lumpkin	1845-1923
Richard	Jasper	1823-33
Robert	Jefferson	1811
Robert	Meriwether	1831-59
Robert M.	Cobb	1865
Samuel	Glynn	1844-53
Samuel C.	Jefferson	1833
Weir	Lumpkin	1845-1923 gdn
William	Lumpkin	1845-1923

BOYET

Arthur	Emanuel	1866
Elizabeth	Emanuel	1867
Harriett R.	Emanuel	1867 minor
J. V.	Emanuel	1867 minor
James	Emanuel	1867 minor
Thomas L.	Emanuel	1867 minor

BOYKIN

Elizabeth	Richmond	1840-53
Francis	Jasper	1822-26
James	Muscogee	1838-62
Jesse W.	Jasper	1826-31
John	Screven	1810-1929
John B.	Screven	1810-1929
S. L. Mrs.	Screven	1810-1929
Samuel	Muscogee	1838-62
Solomon	Colonial	1770

BOYNKIN

William P.	Jasper	1822-26

BOYNTON

Stewart	Jasper	1825-31
Willard	Stewart	1850-90

BOYT

James	Emanuel	1857

BOZEMAN

Reddick	Houston	1855-96

BRABANT

Isaac	Colonial	1763

BRACEWELL

James	Pulaski	1816-50

BRACEWOOD

James	Gwinnett	1852-86

BRACK

Benjamin	Burke	1853-70
James	Gilmer	1836-53i
Richard	Houston	1855-96

BRACKER

Amos	Franklin	1786-1813

BRACKETT

B. W.	Gilmer	1836-53i

BRADDY

John	Washington	1852-1903

BRADFIELD

Nancy	Coweta	1849-92

BRADFORD

Edward	Jasper	1826-31
Ella T.	Cobb	1887i

BRAYNARD		
A.	Forsyth	1833-34i
BRAZEAL		
Britton	Campbell	1825-1900
BRAZELL		
Daniel	Screven	1810-1929
James (nunc)	Camden	1868-1916
BRAZIEL		
Frederick	Jackson	1802-60
BRAZIER		
Anna	Stewart	1850-90
Elijah W.	Stewart	1850-90
BRAZIL		
Elizabeth	Jackson	1802-60
BRAZLETON		
Jacob	Jackson	1802-60
BRAZZELL		
James	Fayette	1828-97
William	Fayette	1828-97
Willis	Fayette	1828-97
BREEDLOVE		
Moses	Talbot	1863
Nathan	Jones	1826-50
BRENEN		
J. L.	Madison	1842-96
BRETTON		
John Peter	Colonial	1770
BREWER		
Benjamin I.	Madison	1842-96
Drury	Morgan	1830-60
E.	Jasper	1825-31
E. E.	Bibb	1851-71
George	Greene	1796-1806
George	Putnam	1808-22
Hopkins	Wilkes	1819-36
J. L.	Madison	1842-96
J. N.	Cobb	1901i
James	Wilkes	1818-19
Jesse T.	Houston	1855-96
Joel	Polk	1857-1936
John	Elbert	1818
John	Franklin	1786-1813
John	Hancock	1802
John	Walton	1827-31
John	Walton	1834-9
John H.	Elbert	1813
N. T.	Screven	1810-1929
Nathan	Morgan	1814-30
Sackville	Elbert	1811
T. A.	Screven	1810-1929
Thomas H.	Effingham	1829-59
BREWSTER		
Hugh	Polk	1857-1936
J. S.	Polk	1857-1936
BRIANT		
Braxton E.	Oglethorpe	1833-36
BRICE		
Richard T.	Muscogee	1838-62
BRIDEWELL		
Jesse	Wilkes	1779-92
BRIDGE		
Mary	Madison	1842-96

BRIDGES		
David	Wilkes	1779-92
J. A.	Union	1877-1942
James M.	Carroll	1852-96
John	Stewart	1837-49
Jonathan F.	Jones	1826-50
Jonathan F.	Stewart	1837-49
Joseph	Dooly	1847-1901
Mary	Stewart	1850-90
Nathaniel	Wilkes	1779-92
Sarah	Randolph	1845-94
Thomas	Wilkes	1779-92
William	Dooly	1847-1901
BRIDGEWELL (see Bridewell)		
BRIERS		
Lawrence	Jasper	1813-19
BRIGGS		
Della P.	Clayton	1859-1921
H. C.	Lowndes	1871-1915
John (col)	Gwinnett	1852-86
Matt Ashley	Lowndes	1871-1915
BRIGHTWELL		
John	Clarke	1822-42
BRIMSON		
Josiah	Lincoln	1831-69
BRINKLEY		
A. H.	Cobb	1909i
E. F. Mrs.	Cobb	1896
William	Upson	1826-1910
BRINLE		
Henry	Franklin	1786-1813
BRINLER		
Frederick	Franklin	1786-1813
BRINNETT		
A. G.	Paulding	1850-77
Oliver	Paulding	1850-77
Sarah	Paulding	1850-77
BRINSON		
A. J.	Screven	1810-1929
Jason	Thomas	1837-45i
Jeremiah	Pulaski	1816-50
Laren	Thomas	1837-45
Lucy	Burke	1853-70
M. F.	Early	--
Sarah E. Mrs.	Lowndes	1871-1915
Shepard	Burke	1853-70
Simon	Burke	1853-70
BRISBANE		
William	Colonial	1771
BRISCOE		
Elizabeth	Oglethorpe	1833-66
John	Oglethorpe	1833-66
John	Walton	1834-9
orph of M. O.		
BRITT		
John J.	Sumter	1838-55 bonds
John R.	Randolph	1845-94
William G.	Pike	1844-76
BRITTON		
John C.	Lumpkin	1845-1923
T.	Union	1877-1942
Thomas	Clarke	1802-22
BRITTS		
Joel W.	Polk	1857-1936

BROWN (continued)

John D.	Washington	1829-71 divs
John E.	Coweta	1849-92
John T.	Sumter	1849-92
John W.	Early	1834-1902
John W.	Jasper	1826-31
Jonathan	Franklin	1786-1813
Joseph	Franklin	1786-1813
Joseph	Walton	1834-39
L. Mrs.	Polk	1857-1936
L. S.	Wilkes	1837-77
Lemuel	Jackson	1802-60
Lucinda	Pike	1844-76
Lucy	Pike	1844-76
Lyman	Early	1834-1902
M. L.	Cobb	1882i
Martha	Newton	1823-51
Mary	Emanuel	1841
		deed of gift
Mary	Talbot	--
Mary A.	Randolph	1845-94
Matilda	Cobb	1880i
Matilda	Washington	1852-1903
Nancy E.	Burke	1853-70
Nepsey	Pulaski	1816-50
P. A.	Cobb	1882i
P. E.	Cobb	1893i
Philip C.	Camden	1868-1916
Phillip	Irwin	1821-64
Reuben	Greene	1794-1810
Reuben	Monroe	1847-
Robert et al	Cobb	1890i
Robert	Harris	1850-75
Robert	Jones	1826-50
Robert	Lincoln	1796-1805
Robert	Meriwether	1831-59
Robert	Morgan	1814-30
Robertson B.	Houston	1855-96
Russell	Jefferson	1813
Samuel	Burke	1853-70
Samuel	Carroll	1852-96
Samuel	Early	1834-1902
Sarah	Washington	1852-1903
Sarah A.	Wilkes	1837-77
Sarah A. F.	Houston	1855-96
Shelldrake	Greene	1796-1806
S. M.	Cobb	1890i
Silas	Cobb	1869
Solomon	Washington	1829-71 divs
Stephen	Houston	1855-96
Stephen J.	Pike	1844-76
Strap	Chattooga	1856-1924
T. W.	Gwinnett	1852-86
Thomas	Clarke	1802-22
Thomas A.	Talbot	--
Thomas E.	Washington	1852-1903
Thomas H.	Washington	1852-1903
Thomas R.	Oglethorpe	1833-66
Turner	Bibb	1851-71
W.	Henry	1834-69
W. M.	Cobb	1895i
W. R.	Dooly	1847-1901
W. S.	Cobb	1879i
W. S.	Cobb	1887i
W. S.	Cobb	1908i
William	Houston	1855-96
William	Jefferson	1807
William	Pike	1844-76
William	Wilkes	1779-92
William	Wilkes	1818-19
William	Wilkinson	1845
William B.	Coweta	1849-92
William F.	Hancock	1821
William F. M.	Wilkinson	1857
William G.	Cobb	1890i
Winnie	Cobb	1891i

BROWNE

George H.	Stewart	1850-90

BROWNFIELD

John	Jasper	1820-23
John	Wilkes	1779-92

BROWNING

George Sr.	Tattnall	1800-35 deeds
George W.	Telfair	1869-1921
John	Greene	1796-1806
Joshua	Clarke	1802-22
Radford	Thomas	1837-45i
Susannah	Greene	1806-16
William	Morgan	1814-30
William	Walton	1819-37

BROWNLEE

Vinson	Gwinnett	1852-96

BROWNSON

Elizabeth	Colonial	1775

BRUCE

Abe	Cobb	1903
John N.	Talbot	--
Marcenia	Union	1877-1942

BRUMBY

T. M.	Cobb	1900i

BRUMBALOW

Jackson	Cobb	1868i

BRUMFIELD

Charlotte	Henry	1834-69
James	Baldwin	1823

BRUNDAGE

A. R.	Wilkinson	1887

BRUNER

Lewis	Sumter	1838-55
		gdn bond
Wyatt A.	Lumpkin	1845-1923

BRUNSON

Simeon	Burke	1853-96
Thomas	Muscogee	1838-62
William Sr.	Houston	1855-96

BRUNT

Richard	Sumter	1838-55 bond
Sarah	Sumter	1838-55 bond

BRUTON

E.	Floyd	1852-61

BRYAN

Absolom	Glynn	1844-53
Agnes	Colonial	1775
Angeline	Thomas	1837-45 minor
David	Talbot	1864
David C.	Stewart	1850-90
Elizabeth	Franklin	1786-1813
Elizabeth	Houston	1855-96
Ely	Franklin	1786-1813
F. M.	Macon	1806
Henry	Hancock	1806
James	Effingham	1829-59
James	Hancock	1807
Jason	Washington	1829-71 divs
Jasper N.	Macon	1856-1909
John	Franklin	1786-1813 retn
John	Screven	1810-1929
John H.	Thomas	1826-30
John R.	Macon	1856-1909
Joseph	Thomas	1826-36
Joseph	Thomas	1837-45i
Josiah	Colonial	1774
L. A.	Stewart	1850-90
Lucius	Thomas	1837-45i

BRYAN (continued)		
M.	Glynn	1844-53
M. L.	Screven	1810-1929
Mary	Colonial	1776
Nathan	Macon	1856-1909
Paul Allen	Screven	1810-1929
Permelia C. Mrs.	Lee	1854-1955
R. C. Dr.	Houston	1855-96
Robert	Hancock	1799
Royal	Franklin	1786-1813
S. C.	Macon	1856-1909
S. O.	Wayne	1822-70
Sally	Franklin	1786-1813
Sarah	Thomas	1837-45 minor
Silvanus	Early	1856-89
W. T. O.	Wayne	1822-70
William B.	Early	1856-89 adm bond
William B.	Franklin	1786-1813

BRYANT		
J. W.	Chattooga	1856-1924
Jason	Washington	1852-1903
John	Carroll	1852-96
John	Houston	1855-96
John Sr.	Jasper	1825-31
Mary	Putnam	1823-56
Patrick	Morgan	1808-13
R. R.	Cobb	1874i
Silvanus S.	Early	1856-89 adm bonds
Sophie	Burke	1853-70
T. J.	Cobb	1877i
W. C.	Houston	1855-96
Wiley	Jones	1826-50
William Sr.	Campbell	1825-1900

BRYCE		
James	Carroll	1852-96

BRYSON		
William	Upson	1826-1910

BUCHANAN		
Benjamin	Baldwin	1847
Benjamin	Jasper	1820-23
F. P.	Gwinnett	1852-86
George	Talbot	--
George H.	Marion	1846-1915
James	Early	1856-1927
James	Jasper	1831-39
Joseph	Morgan	1808-13
Margaret	Newton	1823-51
Mary Ann	Baldwin	1848
Robert	Baldwin	1807
Sarah	Baldwin	1825

BUCK		
William	Washington	1852-1903

BUCKEHEER		
James	Dooly	1847-1901

BUCKHALTER		
Isaac	Pulaski	1816-50
Nancy	Floyd	1852-61i

BUCKHOLTZ		
Mary	Dooly	1847-1901
Peter	Dooly	1847-1901

BUCKHOUN		
William F.	Morgan	1814-30

BUCKINGHAM		
Charles G.	Stewart	1837-49

BUCKNER		
Avery	Monroe	1847-

BUCKNER (continued)		
Charles	Putnam	1808-22
John	Jones	1812-23
John	Putnam	1808-22

BUFFINGTON		
Henderson	Fayette	1828-97
William H.	Floyd	1852-61i

BUFFORD		
W. D.	Wilkes	1837-77

BUFORD		
A. W.	Bartow	1836-85
John	Screven	1810-1929

BUGG		
Charles A.	Richmond	1840-53
Elizabeth	Oglethorpe	1833-66

BUICE		
Allie	Cobb	1901i
James D.	Cobb	1889i
Louie	Cobb	1899i

BUIE		
Malcolm	Decatur	1828-38

BUIST		
George L.	Habersham	1847-1900

BULL		
Martha Mrs.	Troup	1832-48
Mary E.	Talbot	1860

BULLARD		
J. M.	Cobb	1906i
James	Jasper	1831-39
Jesse	Jasper	1813-19
John	Franklin	1786-1813
Lewis	Washington	1852-1903
Micajah	Cobb	1866i
Needham	Burke	1853-70
Phereby	Burke	1853-70
R. R.	Dooly	1847-1901
Robert	Cobb	1845
Ruby	Cobb	1897i
Sarah	Jasper	1831-39
Thomas Sr.	Elbert	1823
William	Cobb	1874i
William	Lee	1854-1955

BULLEN		
Andrew G.	Early	1834-1902

BULLOCH		
Ann Graham	Colonial	1762

BULLOCK		
A. G.	Paulding	1850-77
admr est N. A. Lester		
Alexander G.	Madison	1842-96
Edward	Greene	1817-42
Irwin	Dooly	1847-1901
John	Madison	1812-41

BUNCH		
Austin	Greene	1817-42
Doctrine	Richmond	1840-53
William H.	Richmond	1840-53
William J.	Richmond	1840-53

BUNKLEY		
Jesse	Warren	1823
Joshua	Greene	1817-42
Macharine	Upson	1826-1910
Rebecca	Talbot	--
William R.	Camden	1868-1916

BUNN			
Catharine Mrs.	Polk	1857-1936	
M. H.	Cobb	1884	
Mattie	Polk	1857-1936	
William C.	Polk	1857-1936	

BUNTZ		
Barbara	Colonial	1775
Henry Ludwig	Colonial	1774
Urban	Colonial	1774

BURAN		
Drucilla	Campbell	1825-1900
Lorenzo D.	Campbell	1825-1900

BURCH		
Edward	Pulaski	1816-50
Elizabeth	Elbert	1829-60
John	Gilmer	1836-53i
John	Hancock	1818
William S.	Elbert	1817
William S.	Elbert	1822

BURDEN		
Clareyca	Elbert	1829-60
Thomas	Elbert	1829-60

BURDETT		
John	Wilkes	1819-36
Thomas	Wilkes	1818-19

BURDINE		
John	Wilkes	1818-19

BURELL		
John L.	Gwinnett	1852-86

BURFORD		
Amelia	Putnam	1808-22
Thomas	Hall	1819-37
William	Greene	1794-1810

BURGAMY		
John	Fayette	1828-97

BURGAY		
John	Houston	1827-55
Leven	Monroe	1847-

BURGE		
Adolphus G.	Polk	1857-1936
J. B.	Cobb	1900i
Jackson	Bartow	1836-85
Wilie	Newton	1823-51
Willie	Morgan	1814-30

BURGES		
Rebecca	Dooly	1847-1901

BURGESS		
Elias	Franklin	1786-1813
Elijah	Walton	1819-37
James	Wilkes	1779-92
Josiah	Putnam	1823-56
Sarah	Crawford	1852-94
Thomas	Elbert	1804-9
William	Crawford	1852-94

BURGSTINER		
Ann C.	Effingham	1829-59
Matthew	Effingham	1829-59

BURK		
John	Fayette	1828-97
Jordan T.	Sumter	1835-55 bond
Myles	Taliaferro	1826-66

BURKE		
David	Screven	1810-1929

BURKE (continued)		
David Sr.	Screven	1810-1929
Ella A.	Cobb	1906i
Eugenia M.	Carroll	1852-96
J. N.	Wilkinson	1907
John	Burke	1853-70
Martha	Cobb	1902i
William M.	Floyd	1852-61

BURKETT		
John	Upson	1826-1910

BURKHALTER		
Ann E.	Marion	1846-1915
John	Marion	1846-1915

BURKHOLDER		
Michael	Colonial	1762

BURKS		
C. C.	Clayton	1859-1921
Henry	Clayton	1859-1921
Wiley	Clayton	1859-1921

BURN		
Hugh	Colonial	1767

BURNAM		
Elijah	Houston	1855-96
G. A. Mrs.	Macon	1856-1909
William	Randolph	1845-94

BURNAP		
G. C.	Cobb	1896
George S.	Cobb	1891i

BURNES		
John W.	Wilkes	1806-08

BURNETT		
A.	Carroll	1852-96
Jeremiah	Bibb	1823-55
John	Bibb	1823-55
John	Upson	1826-1910
Mary Anne Mrs.	Upson	1826-1910
S. M.	Glynn	1844-53
Thomas	Pike	1844-76
John	Glynn	1844-53

BURNEY		
Green B.	Wilkinson	1866
J. H.	Cobb	1889i
Janet E.	Wilkinson	1915
Simon	Wilkes	1792-1801
Susan	Wayne	1822-70

BURNLEY		
Israel	Wilkes	1779-92
Richard	Colonial	1771
Samuel	Colonial	1767
Stephen	Warren	1837
Thomas	Liberty	1772-1887

BURNS		
Cenitha	Floyd	1852-61i
D. S.	Washington	1852-1903
J. M.	Screven	1810-1929
John Jr.	Glynn	1844-53
Robert L.	Floyd	1852-61
Samuel H.	Franklin	1848-67
Virgil H.	Screven	1810-1929

BURNSIDES		
James	Houston	1827-55

BURROUGHS		
Bazel	Madison	1812-41
Henry H.	Franklin	1848-67
James	Madison	1842-96

BURROUGHS (continued)		
Lemuel	Wayne	1822-70i
Peggy	Wilkes	1819-36

BURROW		
John	Jasper	1812-17

BURROWS		
Jennie Mrs.	Lowndes	1871-1915

BURRUS		
Catherine	Muscogee	1838-62

BURSON		
David	Walton	1827-31
G. W.	Carroll	1852-96
Isaac	Jackson	1802-60
James	Campbell	1825-1900
Mary	Baldwin	1810

BURT		
James	Putnam	1823-56
Jesse	Putnam	1823-56
William J.	Lumpkin	1845-1923

BURTCHELL		
Marian Blackey	Gwinnett	1852-86

BURTON		
Abraham	Elbert	1810
Henry	Elbert	1822
Robert	Bibb	1823-55
Robert	Effingham	1829-59
Robert	Elbert	1813
Thomas	Elbert	1828
Thomas J.	Burke	1853-70

BUSBEE		
W. R.	Bibb	1851-71

BUSE		
E. W.	Cobb	1888i
W. F.	Cobb	1870i

BUSENDINE		
Isaac	Floyd	1852-61i

BUSH		
Asa	Cobb	1881
Bartlett	Pulaski	1816-50
Daniel	Franklin	1786-1813
Elizabeth	Franklin	1786-1813
F. A.	Stewart	1850-90
Frankie	Cobb	1890i
Henry et al	Cobb	1882i
Hezekiah	Franklin	1848-67
Isaac	Bibb	1823-55
James	Early	1834-1902
James	Early	1856-1889
Jasper	Oglethorpe	1833-66
John	Wilkes	1806-08
Malinda	Cobb	1904
Martha	Cobb	1902i
Priscott	Stewart	1837-49
Robert N.	Franklin	1848-67
Silas	Stewart	1837-49
Thomas	Warren	1804
W. R.	Franklin	1786-1813
Wilie	Oglethorpe	1833-66
William	Early	1834-1902
William W. Jr.	Oglethorpe	1833-66

BUSSEY		
Benjamin	Muscogee	1838-62
Harris et al	Cobb	1892i
Hezekiah	Lincoln	1796-1805
J. C.	Pike	1844-76
Joshua	Lincoln	1831-69
M. L.	Cobb	1895i

BUSSEY (continued)		
Malachi	Pike	1844-76
Nathan	Talbot	--
Nathan Sr.	Talbot	--
Thomas	Lincoln	1808-32
Thomas L.	Cobb	1895i

BUSTIAN		
John	Elbert	1859

BUSWELL		
Daniel	Tattnall	1836-40i

BUTLER		
Edward	Wilkes	1810-16
Elizabeth	Floyd	1852-61i
Ezekiel	Dooly	1847-1901
Francis	Taliaferro	1826-66
Francis W.	Wilkes	1819-36
J. C.	Early	1856-1927
J. W.	Pike	1844-76
James	Oglethorpe	1833-66
Joel	Wilkinson	1861
John	Early	1856-1927
John C.	Early	1856-1927
John M.	Morgan	1814-30
Joseph	Colonial	1773
Joseph Jr.	Colonial	1760
Malachi	Wilkinson	1850
Mary A.	Randolph	1845-94
Massey R.	Putnam	1823-56
Matthew	Dooly	1847-1901
P. W.	Ware	1879-1915
Tarlton Brown	Burke	1853-70
Thomas	Jasper	1813-19
William	Colonial	1759
William	Randolph	1845-94
William E.	Wilkinson	1885
Zacheus	Putnam	1823-56

BUTNER		
J. C.	Cobb	1906i

BUTT		
E.	Marion	1846-1915
Eugene W.	Union	1877-1942
Henry	Washington	1852-1903
J. A.	Union	1877-1942
Jeremiah	Warren	1840
John E.	Morgan	1830-60
John G.	Union	1877-1942
Jonathan	Greene	1796-1806
Moses	Muscogee	1838-62
N. L.	Union	1877-1942
Willis	Jasper	1823-33
Zachri	Meriwether	1831-59

BUTTER		
Edmond	Hancock	1801

BUTTOLPH		
David L.	Cobb	1905
Laura E.	Cobb	--
W. S.	Cobb	1890

BUTTRELL		
Thomas	Warren	1825

BUTTS		
Eldridge	Morgan	1814-30
Elijah	Dooly	1847-1901
George	Hancock	1813
James	Hancock	1835
Lewis	--	1819-64
Moses	Warren	1800
Samuel	Jasper	1812-17
Sarah	Hancock	1803
Thomas Clements	Hancock	1799

BUYERS		
John	Carroll	1852-96

BYARS		
John	Jasper	1812-17

BYERS		
John	Jasper	1813-19

BYINGTON		
James L.	Wilkinson	1911
Joseph	Coweta	1849-93

BYNAM		
Turner L.	Washington	1829-71 bond

BYNE		
Thomas A.	Burke	1853-70

BYRAM		
Beverly	Pike	1844-76

BYRD		
Daniel M.	Gwinnett	1852-86
James et al	Cobb	1866i
Phillip M.	Hall	1837-67
S. N. Mrs.	Cobb	1895
W. J.	Cobb	1889i
William	Hall	1837-67
William D.	Gwinnett	1852-86
Willie	Cobb	1890i
Willie et al	Cobb	1892i

BYROM		
Seymour	Jasper	1820-23
Seymour	Jasper	1825-31

CABANISS		
Sarah	Jones	1826-50
William D.	Stewart	1850-90

CABBELL		
Robert J.	Clarke	1822-42

CABINESS		
Elizabeth	Floyd	1852-61
William B.	Stewart	1837-49

CABLE		
John	Colonial	1762

CABOT		
F. M.	Lumpkin	1833-55

CADE		
James	Wilkes	1837-77
Robert	Wilkes	1819-36
Wineford	Wilkes	1818-19

CADY		
M. W.	Macon	1856-1909

CAGLE		
George	Henry	1822-34

CAHOON		
David	Wilkes	1779-92

CAILE		
James	Madison	1811-40

CAIN		
Jacob	Wilkes	1819-36
John	Gwinnett	1852-86
John	Paulding	1850-77

CALDWELL		
Charles Y.	Pike	1844-76
Curtis C.	Paulding	1850-77
David	Talbot	--
Eliza M.	Pike	1844-76
Henry George	Jefferson	1802
Hiram	Meriwether	1831-59
John	Greene	1806-16
John H.	Talbot	--
Littleton	Greene	1817-42
Mathew	Bartow	1836-85
McG.	Union	1877-1942
Oscar A.	Bibb	1851-71
Robert	Meriwether	1831-59
W. J.	Camden	1868-1916

CALHOUN		
Adam	Jefferson	1813
Amelia A.	Upson	1826-1910
Elbert	Bibb	1823-55
John	Jones	1812-23
Phillip	Baldwin	1812
Rachael	Wilkinson	1831
Sally	Wilkes	1810-16
Thomas B.	Montgomery	1806-63
W. D.	Early	1856-89
W. H.	Houston	1855-96
Wesley	Dooly	1847-1901
William	Early	1856-89
William	Jefferson	1849
William D.	Polk	1857-1936

CALKINS		
Mary L.	Ware	1879-1915

CALLAHAN		
Mary J.	Polk	1857-1936
William	Oglethorpe	1833-66

CALLAWAY		
Chenoth	Wilkes	1837-77
Enoch	Wilkes	1837-77
Frances	Wilkes	1779-92
Isaac	Wilkes	1819-37
Job Sr.	Wilkes	1806-08
John	Wilkes	1819-36
Margaret	Walton	1870-74
Mary Ann	Wilkes	1837-77
Matthew	Oglethorpe	1807-26
Parker	Wilkes	1837-77
S. W.	Wilkes	1837-77
Seaborn	Wilkes	1837-77
William	Wilkes	1819-36
Woodson	Wilkes	1837-77

CALLOWAY (see Caloway, Callaway)		
Frances	Franklin	1786-1813
J. L.	Paulding	1850-77 bond
John	Sumter	1838-55 bond
Joshua	Walton	1834-9
Louiza J.	Wilkinson	1880
William A.	Walton	1834-9

CALOWAY		
John	Gwinnett	1852-86
William J.	Henry	1834-69

CALVIN		
John	Henry	1834-69

CALWELL		
John	Thomas	1837-45

CAMBELL		
Henderson D.	Union	1877-1942

CAMBRON		
Amanda	Polk	1857-1936

CAMERON

Alexander	Lincoln	1796-1805
Elizabeth	Floyd	1861-71
George S.	Lincoln	1831-69
James	Troup	1832-48
John	Clarke	1802-22
John A.	Talbot	--
Nancy	DeKalb	1840-79

CAMICAL

Abram	Coweta	1849-92

CAMMEL

Smith	Franklin	1786-1813

CAMP

Abner	Clayton	1859-1921
Abner	Coweta	1849-92
Alfred J.	Campbell	1825-1900
Benjamin	Campbell	1825-1900
Benjamin T.	Cobb	1866i
Claibourn	Paulding	1850-77i
Ed & Freddie	Cobb	1887i
Edmond	Walton	1827-31
Edmond	Walton	1834-9
F. M.	Carroll	1852-96
George H.	Cobb	1907
George T.	Campbell	1825-1900
Gillis	Gwinnett	1852-86
Harrison	Floyd	1852-61
Hiram	Coweta	1849-92
Hosea	Polk	1857-1936
Ida H.	Screven	1810-1929
John	Clayton	1859-1921
Joseph	Campbell	1825-1900
Joseph	Clayton	1859-1921
Lutitia L.	Cobb	1869i
Maud	Cobb	1886i
Paul et al	Cobb	1892i
Rufus C.	Polk	1857-1936
Thomas	Campbell	1825-1900
T. A.	Cobb	1900i
Thomas	Cobb	1867i
W. B.	Cobb	1908i
Wesley	Carroll	1852-96
Westley	Henry	1822-34

CAMPBELL

Alice & Porter	Cobb	1880i
Alice S. et al	Cobb	1867i
Andrew Jr.	Campbell	1825-1900
Archibald	Telfair	1869-1921
Charles	Morgan	1814-30
Charter	Morgan	1830-60
D. C.	--	1819-64
Daniel	Paulding	1850-77
G. B.	Cobb	1895i
George	Morgan	1830-60
James L.	Campbell	1825-1900
John	Cobb	1873i
(Mary A. wid)		
John	Wilkes	1779-92
Joseph	Taliaferro	1826-66
M. M. Mrs.	Telfair	1869-1921
Maggie E. Mrs.	Lowndes	1871-1915
Major	Floyd	1852-61i
Margaret	Telfair	1869-1921
N. E. Mrs.	Cobb	1905i
Porter F.	Morgan	1830-60
Robert	Colonial	1776
Robert	Polk	1857-1936
Robert B.	Hall	1837-67
S. E. Mrs.	Cobb	1902i
Sarah D.	Morgan	1814-30
Sterling	Butts	1826-41
W. J.	Fayette	1828-97
W. L.	Clayton	1859-1921
Watson	Bibb	1851-71
William	Oglethorpe	1833-66

CAMPHER

Christian	Colonial	1774

CAMUSE

Joseph	Colonial	1764

CAN

John	Coweta	1849-93

CANADA

H. C.	Habersham	1847-1900

CANADAY

Henry	Stewart	1837-49

CANDLER

Betty	Union	1877-1942
W. E.	Union	1877-1942

CANNADY

Mary	Sumter	1838-55 bond
Wright	Sumter	1838-55 bond

CANNING

John	Elbert	1832

CANNON

Frank A.	Wilkinson	1915
James	Floyd	1852-61
James N.	Sumter	1838-55 bonds
Nathaniel	Wilkinson	1842
Richard	Colonial	1735
Richard C.	Ware	1879-1915
Roger	Wilkes	1779-92
Samuel	Coweta	1849-93
Tebeck	Sumter	1838-55 bond
W. F.	Wilkinson	1901
Wiley	Muscogee	1838-62

CANTER

William R. S.	Washington	1852-1903

CANTILOU

Alice	Lincoln	1831-69
Lucinda M.	Lincoln	1831-69
William B.	Lincoln	1831-69

CANTRELL

Harris	Lumpkin	1845-1923
James	Lumpkin	1833-55
R. C.	Polk	1857-1936
Stephen	Lumpkin	1845-1923

CANTY

Abram	Washington	1852-1903

CAPE

J. R.	Cobb	1882i

CAPEL

Sterling	Jones	1826-50

CARDELL

N. T.	Macon	1856-1909

CARDEN

Charles (col)	Polk	1857-1936
Charles F.	Houston	1855-96
Thomas M.	Houston	1855-96
William	Jasper	1823-33

CARDIN

James	Henry	1834-69
William	Jasper	1826-31

CARDWELL

John W.	Morgan	1830-60

CAREY
Jesse	Laurens	1809-40
Martha Ann	Bibb	1851-71

CARGILE
George	Jasper	1826-31
John	Butts	1826-41
John	Jasper	1823-33
John	Jasper	1831-9
Thomas	Jasper	1820-23

CARIKER
John	Pike	1844-76

CARITHERS
Cary	Madison	1842-96
Mary	Madison	1842-96
Robert G.	Muscogee	1838-62
William C.	Madison	1842-96

CARLETON
Robert	Wilkes	1792-1801
Stephen	Elbert	1829-60

CARLISLE
Edmund	Morgan	1814-30
James	Cobb	1877-
James	Dooly	1847-1901
Sarah	Bartow	1836-85
Mathew	Talbot	--

CARLTON
George E.	Wilkinson	1892
Henry	Morgan	1806-13
Jacob	Franklin	1786-1813
Robert	Franklin	1786-1813
Sarah	Franklin	1786-1813
Thomas J.	Morgan	1814-30
W. M.	Polk	1857-1936

CARMACK
James W.	Dooly	1847-1901

CARMICHAEL
John	Jackson	1802-60
John	Richmond	1840-53

CARN
J. T.	Carroll	1852-96

CARNEGIE
Thomas	Camden	1868-1916

CARNELISON
Sarah	Lincoln	1831-69

CARNES
Eli	Henry	1834-69
Harriet	Polk	1857-1936
John	Appling	1877-1925
John	Polk	1857-1936
Nancy E.	Clayton	1859-1921
Stephen	Clayton	1859-1921
Thomas	Carroll	1852-96
Thomas P.	Clarke	1822-42
W. B.	Clayton	1859-1921

CARNEY
Arthur	Bibb	1851-71

CARPENTER
John	Burke	1853-70
James	Elbert	1829-60
Thomas D.	Bartow	1836-85

CARR
Henry	Oglethorpe	1833-66
J. N.	Houston	1855-96
James H.	Jefferson	1816

CARR (continued)
John T.	Carroll	1852-96
Joseph	Hancock	1809
Kenchen	Richmond	1840-53
Mark	Colonial	1767
Mary	Floyd	1852-61 orph
Robert C.	Floyd	1861-71
William	Floyd	1861-71
William B.	Wilkinson	1899

CARREKER
Jacob	Talbot	--

CARRELL
Edward	Franklin	1786-1813
James	Jackson	1802-60
John	Elbert	1821
Mary	Elbert	1821

CARRINGTON
John P.	Coweta	1828-48 gdn

CARROLL
Arthur B.	Sumter	1838-55 bond
Benjamin	Paulding	1850-77
Elisha	Henry	1822-34
Francis A.	Marion	1846-1915
J. B. W.	Chattooga	1856-1924
Mary	Elbert	1821
Solomon	Forsyth	1833-44
Thomas	Fayette	1828-97

CARRUTH
Robert K.	Madison	1842-96

CARSON
Adam	Jones	1826-50
Elizabeth	Jones	1812-23
J. T.	Macon	1856-1909
J. W.	Carroll	1852-96
J. W.	Macon	1856-1909
John	Jones	1812-23
John C.	Franklin	1848-67
Joseph	Coweta	1828-48
Samuel	Wilkes	1779-92
Sarah	Coweta	1828-48
Sarah	Bartow	1836-85
Thomas	Greene	1786-95

CARSWELL
James A.	Jefferson	1841
James A.	Stewart	1850-90
Jasper E.	Burke	1853-70
John W.	Burke	1853-70
Sara	Wilkinson	1838
William E.	Wilkinson	1887

CARTER
Abner	Sumter	1838-55 bonds
Amelia	Henry	1834-69
Anna Matilda	Muscogee	1838-62
Charles	Oglethorpe	1833-66
D. J. W.	Macon	1856-1909
Dock	Washington	1852-1903
Edward J.	Burke	1853-96
Elizabeth	Elbert	1826
Ezekiel	Polk	1857-1936
Francis	Baldwin	1813
Francis	Coweta	1849-92
H. D.	Bartow	1836-85
Harriett	Appling	1877-1925
Isabella	Washington	1852-1903
Isaiah	Burke	1853-96
James	Bartow	1836-85
James	Elbert	1829-60
James	Franklin	1848-67
James	Polk	1857-1936
James	Warren	1807
James W.	Rabun	1863-88

CAVENAH (continued)
Nicholas (of Burke Co.)	Jefferson	1794

CAVENDER
Jesse J. (nunc)	Carroll	1852-96

CAWDELL
John	Franklin	1848-67

CAWDERY
Charles F.	Houston	1855-96

CAWOOD
R. C. Mrs.	Lee	1854-1955

CAWTHON
James	Pike	1844-76
Rhoda	Franklin	1786-1813
William	Franklin	1786-1813
William	Franklin	1848-67

CELLA
Christopher	Muscogee	1838-62

CELLUM
Samuel	Madison	1842-96

CHABNER
John	Franklin	1786-1813

CHADWICK
Susan	Richmond	1840-53

CHAFFIN
Isham	Wilkes	1819-36
Lemuel	Morgan	1830-60

CHALKLEY
Alfred A.	Marion	1846-1915

CHALMERS
John	Franklin	1786-1813

CHAMBERS
Bricy	Washington	1829-71 divs
Bricy	Washington	1852-1903
Henry	Greene	1796-1806
Henry Greenfield	Wilkinson	1853
John	Hancock	1794
John G.	Hancock	1812
Joseph S.	Clayton	1859-1921
Mary A.	Union	1877-1942
Maxa B.	Wilkinson	1905
Rebecca	Cobb	1873 minor
William	Wilkinson	1836
William P.	Carroll	1852-96

CHAMBLEE
John	Forsyth	1833-34 admr

CHAMBLISS
Christopher	Bibb	1840i
Henry	Bibb	1823-55
Jeptha C.	Stewart	1850-90
Powell	Talbot	--

CHAMPION
Cynthia	Marion	1846-1915
Daniel	Floyd	1861-71
Elizabeth	Bibb	1851-71
Elizabeth G.	Bibb	1851-71
George M.	Marion	1846-1915
John	Hancock	1805
Phileman	Harris	1850-75
William	Floyd	1852-61i

CHANCE
Drury	Burke	1853-96

CHANCE (continued)
George W.	Carroll	1852-96
Henry	Burke	1853-70
Jacob	Burke	1853-70
Simpson	Houston	1827-55
Warren	Carroll	1852-96

CHANDLER
Abraham	Bartow	1836-85
Asa	Fayette	1828-96
B. C.	Madison	1842-96
Edmund	Franklin	1786-1813
James	Franklin	1786-1813
Joseph	Franklin	1786-1813
Joseph	Franklin	1848-67
Joseph	Pike	1844-76
Mary O.	Madison	1842-96
Sarah	Early	--
Sarah M.	Talbot	--
Shadrick	Franklin	1786-1813
Sterling	Jackson	1802-60
Tabitha	Jackson	1802-60
Thomas	Carroll	1852-96
W. E.	Ware	1879-1915
W. K.	Polk	1857-1936

CHAPMAN
Ambrose	Bibb	1851-71
Ambrose	Marion	1846-1915
Asa	Jasper	1825
B. F.	Lumpkin	1845-1923
Benjamin	DeKalb	1840-69
Britton	Henry	1834-69
Deborah S.	Carroll	1852-96
Edmond	Jasper	1813-19
Edward	Jasper	1813-19
Eli T.	DeKalb	1840-69
Elizabeth	Clayton	1859-1921
Fannie M. Mrs.	Lee	1854-1955
George	Hall	1837-67
Grace	Jones	1826-50
J. M.	Bartow	1836-85
J. T.	Wayne	1822-70
James H.	Clayton	1859-1921
James L.	Marion	1846-1915
John	Jasper	1822-26
John	Taliaferro	1826-66
Milly	Baldwin	1830
Philip R.	Hall	1837-67
Randal	Greene	1817-42
Thomas	Taliaferro	1826-66
William	Jones	1810-28
William H. J.	Randolph	1845-94

CHAPPEL
Robinson	Walton	1827-31

CHAPPELL
Christopher	Colonial	1774
John (Arena, wid)	Cobb	1866i
John	Hancock	1807
Nancy	Cobb	1871 minor
Robert	Morgan	1814-30
Wiley	Jones	1826-50

CHARLTON
John	Effingham	1828-59

CHARY
John	Early	1856-1889 adm bonds
John	Early	1856-1927

CHASE
John D.	Wilkes	1837-77
Mary O.	Cobb	1881i

CHURCH

Giles	Colonial	1771
Mary B.	Clayton	1859-1921
Rodman E.	Bibb	1823-55

CHURCHILL

Catharine H.	Gwinnett	1852-86
Mary	Burke	1853-96
Samuel	Newton	1823-51

CLACK

Sterling	Gwinnett	1852-86

CLARK

Ann M.	McIntosh	1873-1915
Calphacy	Montgomery	1806-63
Christopher	Burke	1853-70
Christopher	Elbert	1803
Christopher Sr.	Elbert	1819
Daniel	Colonial	1757
David	Elbert	1829-60
David	Franklin	1786-1813
David	Houston	1827-55
David Sr.	Houston	1827-55
E. A. Mrs.	Screven	1810-1929
Elijah	Lincoln	1796-1805
Henry	Montgomery	1806-63
Hugh	Colonial	1771
J. Wesley	Telfair	1869-1921
James	Elbert	1829-60
Jane	Cobb	1885
John	Franklin	1786-1813
John	Muscogee	1838-62
John B.	Chattooga	1856-1924
John T.	Randolph	1845-94
Joshua	Lee	1854-1955
Joshua B.	Jones	1826-50
Julia	McIntosh	1873-1915
L. B.	Fayette	1828-97
Larkin	Elbert	1829-60
Lawrence	Colonial	1770
Lewis J.	Muscogee	1838-62
Major B.	Coweta	1849-93
Nathaniel	Colonial	1761
Patrick	Colonial	1756
Samuel	Montgomery	1806-63
Sarah F.	Camden	1868-1916
Sevier	Hall	1837-67
Susan A.	Sumter	1838-55 bonds
William	Hall	1837-67
William	Walton	1834-9

CLARKE

Christopher	Burke	1853-96
Daniel F.	Bibb	1851-71
Dempsey Sr.	Houston	1855-96
Edward	Lincoln	1808-32
George C. Rev.	Houston	1855-96
James	Houston	1827-55
John	Warren	1838
John H.	Houston	1855-96
Johnston	Jackson	1802-60
Mark D.	Bibb	1823-55
William	Jefferson	1827
William H.	Camden	1868-1916

CLAY

A. S.	Cobb	1910
Edward W.	Wilkinson	1897
Henry	Wilkinson	1897
Jesse Sr.	Jasper	1825-37
Jesse C.	Jasper	1831-9
Mariam	Jasper	1826-31
Nathan	Greene	1796-1806
Thomas C.	Cobb	1899
William	Washington	1852-1903

CLAYTON

Alexander	Lincoln	1796-1805

CLAYTON (continued)

Augustine S.	Clarke	1822-42
Charles	Franklin	1786-1811
George R. Sr.	Baldwin	undated
James	Butts	1826-41
James	Stewart	1850-90
John	Bartow	1836-85
Robert B.	Bibb	1851-71
Sampson	Walton	1819-37
Thomas	Pulaski	1816-50

CLEATON

Austin	Butts	1826-41

CLECKLER

Elijah	Campbell	1825-1900
Henry	Campbell	1825-1900
Hillary	Fayette	1828-97

CLEGG

Virgil A.	Lee	1854-1955

CLEGHORN

John	Chattooga	1856-1924

CLEM

Frederick	Jefferson	1806

CLEMENS

L. N.	Telfair	1869-1921

CLEMENT

A.	Forsyth	1833-44i
Janet	Screven	1810-1929

CLEMENTS

Austen	Morgan	1814-30
David	Hancock	1812
David	Henry	1834-69
David L. D.	Henry	1822-34
Ellis W.	Polk	1857-1936
G. M. O.	Montgomery	1806-63
Jacob A.	Marion	1846-1915
Jacob W.	Montgomery	1806-63
James D.	Montgomery	1806-63
John	Wayne	1822-70
Nelson	Stewart	1850-90
W. N.	Union	1877-1942
William A.	Stewart	1850-90
William J.	Early	--

CLEMMONS

John C.	Dooly	1847-1901
John R.	Chattooga	1856-1924
Robert	Chattooga	1856-1924
William J.	Early	1856-89
		admrs bonds

CLEMONT

Stephen	Wilkes	1792-1801

CLERVIS

Elizabeth Ann	Dooly	1847-1901

CLEVELAND

A. A.	Wilkes	1837-77
A. M. Mrs.	Crawford	1852-94
Benjamin	Stewart	1850-90
Catharine	Franklin	1786-1813
David	Franklin	1786-1813
J.	Franklin	1786-1813
Jacob	Elbert	1791
Jacob	Henry	1834-69
John	Franklin	1786-1813
Washington C.	Crawford	1852-94
Wiley	Pike	1844-76
William	Crawford	1835-52

CLIATT

Isaac	Lincoln	1831-69
Isaac	Stewart	1850-90

CLIETT

Alfred M.	Houston	1855-96
John	Houston	1855-96

CLIFTON

Curtis	Greene	1817-42
George	Clarke	1822-42
John Sr.	Emanuel	1846
Levin	Tattnall	1836-40i

CLINCH

Duncan L.	Camden	1795-1829
Mary L.	Habersham	1847-1900
Sophie	Habersham	1847-1900

CLINGAN

George	Greene	1806-16

CLINTON

John P.	Campbell	1825-1900
William P.	Campbell	1825-1900

CLOSE

Gideon P.	Chattooga	1856-1924

CLOUD

Carroll A.	Screven	1810-1929
Ezekiel	Henry	1834-69
Joel	Warren	183-
Reuben	Decatur	1828-38
Reuben	Decatur	1824-52 Mts.

CLOWER

Morgan	Meriwether	1831-59
Peter	Jones	1826-50
Stephen	Jones	1826-50

CLOYED

Nancy E.	Chattooga	1856-1924

CLUBB

John	Colonial	1771
Sarah F.	Camden	1868-1916

COAL

William	Paulding	1850-77

COALSON

E.	Thomas	1837-45 minor
Mary	Thomas	1837-45 minor
Paul	Thomas	1826-36i
Rebecka	Pulaski	1816-50
Sanders	Pulaski	1816-50

COATS

J. G.	Laurens	1809-40
John	Marion	1846-1915
John G.	Clarke	1822-42
Nathaniel	Wilkes	1810-16
Robert	Laurens	1809-40

COBB

A. A.	Floyd	1852-61i
Catherine	Upson	1826-1910
E. P.	Forsyth	1833-44
Howell	Bibb	1851-71
Howell	Houston	1855-96
Howell	Jefferson	1818
John	Walton	1819-37
Mary	Carroll	1852-96
N. H.	Polk	1857-1936
Seth	Muscogee	1838-62
Thomas W.	Oglethorpe	1830
W. W.	Carroll	1852-96
William A.	Upson	1826-1910

COCHRAN

Abner	Greene	1817-42
Banister	Jackson	1802-60
Benjamin	Morgan	1814-30
Berry W.	Campbell	1825-1900
Dora Mrs.	Polk	1857-1936
Eli	Carroll	1852-96
G. W.	Lumpkin	1845-1923
George L.	Burke	1853-96
James	Jasper	1812-17
John	Burke	1853-70
Karen Mrs.	Lee	1854-1955
Maggie M.	Polk	1857-1936
Matthew	Morgan	1830-60
N. Mrs.	Polk	1857-1936
Newton	Polk	1857-1936
R. Lee	Cobb	1879 minor
S. R.	Cobb	1894
Samuel	Oglethorpe	1833-66
Samuel	Wilkes	1779-92
Thomas	Chattooga	1856-1924
Virginia A.	Campbell	1825-1900
W. B.	Cobb	1880i
William W.	Floyd	1852-61i

COCK

J. P.	Lee	1854-1955

COCKE

Henry	Baldwin	1807
Jack F.	Clarke	1802-22

COCKRAN

John A.	Upson	1826-1910
John M.	Bartow	1836-85

COCKRELL

Mary	Fayette	1828-97
Thomas	Newton	1823-51

CODE

John	Muscogee	1838-62

CODONE

Frank	McIntosh	1873-1915

CODY

Edmund	Warren	1831
James	Warren	1825
Michael	Warren	1831

COFER

J. B.	Wilkes	1837-77
John	Wilkes	1837-77

COFFEE

John	Colonial	1759
Peter	Hancock	1803

COGGINS

John	Pike	1844-76

COGLAN

Mollie	McIntosh	1873-1915

COGLAND

Edward	Burke	1853-70

COHEN

Mary H.	Camden	1868-1916

COHRON

John	Wilkes	1806-08
Joseph	Wilkes	1819-36

COILE

James	Madison	1812-41

COKER

Abraham	Fayette	1828-97
James	Clayton	1859-1921
Sylvia	Washington	1829-71 divs
William	Henry	1822-34

COLBERT

B. F.	Habersham	1847-1900
Frederick	Bibb	1851-71
John	Wilkes	1779-92
John G.	Crawford	1852-94
John G.	Morgan	1830-60
Jonathan	Crawford	1852-94
L. G.	Madison	1842-96
M. S.	Floyd	1852-61
Philip P.	Madison	1821-41
Richard	Elbert	1820
Richmond	Hancock	1832
S. W.	Madison	1842-96
Thomas	Elbert	1829-60
William	Hancock	1797

COLE

Alis	Liberty	1772-1887
Austin W.	Gwinnett	1852-86
Duke	Greene	1817-42
Duke	Jasper	1822-26
Grovey	Putnam	1823-56
Henry G.	Cobb	1875
Jacob	Pike	1844-76
James A.	Liberty	1772-1887
James D.	Clarke	1822-42
Jesse	Henry	1822-34
John	Greene	1817-42
John Sr.	Lincoln	1831-69
Josiah	Oglethorpe	1793-1807
William	Jasper	1825-31
William	Wilkes	1806-08

COLELOUGH

Charity	Taliaferro	1826-66

COLEMAN

Daniel	Putnam	1808-22
Daniel	Wilkes	1779-92
David	Walton	1834-39
Eden	Greene	1817-42
Elijah	Franklin	1786-1813
Elizabeth	Newton	1823-51
Elliott	Baldwin	1814
Harris	Wilkes	1818-19
Hobson J.	Screven	1810-1929
Irene A.	Polk	1857-1936
Isham	Washington	1852-1903
J. S. C.	Early	1856-1927
John	Greene	1817-42
John	Jackson	1802-60
John	Jefferson	1836
John	Wilkes	1777-78
Jonathan	Emanuel	1841
Jonathan	Randolph	1845-94
Levi	Muscogee	1846
Malcum C.	Emanuel	1841 gdn
Matthew	Greene	1817-42
Nancy	Greene	1817-42
Perry	Emanuel	1867i
Robert	Bibb	1851-71
Samuel	Meriwether	1831-59
Sarah	Meriwether	1831-59
Theophilis	Laurens	1809-40
Thomas	Randolph	1845-94
Thompson	Wilkes	1819-36
W. E.	Chattooga	1856-1924
Willis	Putnam	1823-56

COLEY

Philip	Early	1834-1902

COLLARS

Elizabeth	Lincoln	1831-69
Isaiah	Lincoln	1831-69

COLLEY

John	Wilkes	1810-16
Spain	Wilkes	1837-77
Thomas	Oglethorpe	1793-1807
Zachariah	Elbert	1799
Zacharies	Oglethorpe	1793-1807

COLLIER

Ambrose	Early	1856-97 gdns bonds
Benjamin	Crawford	1835-52
Benjamin	Early	1834-1902 adm bonds
Benjamin	Early	1856-89 adm bonds
Elizabeth	Upson	1826-1910
Henry	Early	1834-1902 adm bonds
Henry G.	DeKalb	1840-69
Isaac	Upson	1826-1910
James	Early	1834-1902 adm bonds
James W. (nunc)	Pike	1844-76
Jesse	Early	1834-1902 adm bonds
John	DeKalb	1840-69
John	Early	1834-1902 adm bonds
John	Laurens	1809-40
John W.	Early	--
Merrel	DeKalb	1840-69
Robert	Henry	1822-34
Robert M.	Upson	1826-1910
Thomas	Laurens	1809-40

COLLIN

John	Jasper	1825-31
William	Morgan	1830-60
William L.	Jasper	1826-31

COLLINS

Albert R.	Cobb	1873 minor
(Cynthia, gdn)		
Ann	Richmond	1840-53
C. P.	Lumpkin	1845-1923
Charles	Bibb	1851-71
Charles H. &	Cobb	1867 minors
Richard (Cynthia, gdn)		
Elba	Madison	1842-96
Ernest L.	Cobb	1890 minors
Gibson	Wilkes	1837-77
Henry	Dooly	1847-1901
Henry	Tattnall	1836-40i
J. D.	Union	1877-1942
Jacob	Tattnall	1800-35 deeds
James A.	Cobb	1866i
Jesse E.	Cobb	1889 minor
John	Decatur	1824-52 Mts.
John	Decatur	1828-38
John	Madison	1840-60
John	Madison	1842-96
John	Richmond	1840-53
John	Washington	1829-71 divs
Joseph	Tattnall	1836-40i
(est Isaac K. Baldwin)		
Lois & Josephine	Cobb	1904 minors
Martha C.	Campbell	1825-1900
Mayer C. Sr.	Wilkinson	1846
Parker	Forsyth	1833-44
Polly (Mary)	Wilkinson	1858
Robert	Baldwin	1823
Robert	Bibb	1851-71
Stephen	Marion	1846-1915
William	Bibb	1851-71
Willis S.	Talbot	--

COLLINS (continued)		
Zachariah	Jackson	1802-60
COLLINSWORTH		
John	Putnam	1823-56
COLLUM		
Thomas	Oglethorpe	1793-1807
COLLY		
Demsy C.	Wilkes	1837-77
Francis	Wilkes	1837-77
Henry F.	Wilkes	1837-77
COLQUITT		
Henry	Hancock	1819
James	Oglethorpe	1833-66
John	Upson	1826-1910
W. E.	Early	1856-1927
Walter T.	Muscogee	1838-62
William E.	Early	1856-1889 L/A
COLSON		
Elizabeth	Sumter	1838-55 bonds
G.	Tattnall	1836-40i
gdn heirs of James Stephens		
Jacob	Wilkes	1777-78
COLT		
John	Greene	1817-42
COLTON		
James G.	Harris	1850-75
Smith	Harris	1850-75
COLVIN		
Caroline	Upson	1826-1910
COLYER		
Sallie L.	Houston	1855-96
COMBS		
James	Wilkes	1818-19
COMER		
Ann	Jones	1826-50
James	Jones	1826-50
Nancy	Jones	1826-50
COMMANDER		
Samuel	Crawford	1835-52
COMPTON		
John	Campbell	1825-1900
John Sr.	Jasper	1820-23
N.	Forsyth	1833-44
Pleasant	Jasper	1822-26
Polly	Jasper	1826-31
Richard	Paulding	1850-77
CONCH		
Matthew	Coweta	1849-93
CONDON		
John	Oglethorpe	1833-66
CONE		
Ezekiel	Greene	1817-42
J. B.	Macon	1856-1909
Jeremiah	Floyd	1861-71
Mary L.	Floyd	1852-61i
W. B.	Dooly	1847-1901
William	Greene	1817-42
CONEY		
Andrew W.	Floyd	1852-61 orph
Henry L.	Chattooga	1852-61
Jane C.	Floyd	1852-61 orph
John E.	Floyd	1852-61i

CONEY (continued)		
Nancy	Floyd	1852-61 gdn
Samuel	Floyd	1852-61
William C.	Floyd	1852-61 orph
William G.	Floyd	1852-61i
CONLEY		
Bettie	Union	1877-1942
Davie Colwell	Union	1877-1942
Frank E.	Union	1877-1942
Sarah	Union	1877-1942
CONN		
John	Franklin	1786-1813
CONNALLY		
Patrick	DeKalb	1840-69
CONNELL		
Jesse	Hancock	1805
CONNELY		
William	Eamnuel	1868 bond
CONNER		
Boby	Franklin	1786-1813
C. H. Mrs.	Screven	1810-1929
Charles	Franklin	1786-1813
Henry	Lincoln	1796-1805
James	Screven	1810-1929
John	Franklin	1786-1813
Lewis	Screven	1810-1929
Simon D.	Screven	1810-1929
Thomas	Franklin	1886-1813
Thomas	Montgomery	1806-63
William L.	Screven	1810-1929
CONYERS		
Bennett H.	Bartow	1836-85
John	Screven	1810-1929
Sarah	Screven	1810-1929
COOGLE		
Minnie Arminta	Lee	1854-1955
COOK		
B. W.	Carroll	1852-96
Benjamin	Elbert	1800
Benjamin	Elbert	1803
Benjamin	Pike	1844-76
Berry	Pike	1823-29
Beverly O.	Elbert	1829-60
Ezekiel	Henry	1822-34
Francis	Cobb	1872
Francis	Elbert	1804
Frederick W.	Oglethorpe	1833-66
George	Elbert	1829-60
Harbard	Fayette	1828-97
Henry	Effingham	1829-59
Henry J.	Chattooga	1856-1924
James	Jones	1826-50
James C.	Muscogee	1844
James M.	Union	1877-1942
John	Campbell	1825-1900
John	Talbot	--
John D.	Burke	1853-96
Jones E.	Floyd	1852-61i
Joshua	Elbert	1822
Judith	Wilkes	1779-92
Judith N.	Newton	1823-51
Lydia	Effingham	1829-59
Lydia	Washington	1852-1903
Nellie S. Mrs.	Polk	1857-1936
Neverson	Hall	1837-67
P.	Stewart	1837-49
Philip	Sumter	1838-55i
Samuel	Henry	1834-69
Samuel	Houston	1827-55
Samuel	Jones	1826-50

COOK (continued)

Shun	Carroll	1852-96
Smith	Elbert	1829-60
Theodosius	Henry	1822-34
Thomas	Laurens	1809-40
Thomas Sr.	Hall	1819-37
W. C.	Early	1856-97
William	McIntosh	1873-1915

COOKE

Eugene D.	Richmond	1840-53
Mary	Sumter	1838-55i

COOKSEY

Hezekiah	Warren	1817
John W.	Wilkes	1819-36

COOLEY

Elizabeth	Floyd	1861-71
Hollis	Floyd	1852-61

COON

Isaac S.	Lowndes	1871-1915
Issockah	Henry	1834-69

COOPER

A. J.	Paulding	1850-77 bond
Adam	Pike	1844-76
Betsy	Greene	1806-16
Charles C.	Glynn	1844-53 minor
Cornelius	Franklin	1786-1813
E. E.	Cobb	1910
Edmund	Baldwin	1816
Elizabeth	Paulding	1850-77 appr
George	Screven	1810-1929
George	Warren	1802
Henry	Putnam	1823-56
James	Baldwin	1812
James	Greene	1806-16
Jesse	Paulding	1850-77 retn
Jesse	Paulding	1850-77
adm Elizabeth Cooper		
John Thornton	Houston	1855-96
Jonathan	Madison	1842-96
Joseph	Putnam	1808-22
Levi M.	Gwinnett	1852-86
Lozie Mrs.	Screven	1810-1929
Martha	Putnam	1823-56
Mary Mrs.	Houston	1855-96
Millie	Lee	1854-1955
Peter	Stewart	1837-49
Richard	Liberty	1772-1887
Samuel	Muscogee	1841
Stacy	Paulding	1850-77
Thomas	Coweta	1849-93
Thomas	Hancock	1793
Thomas	Putnam	1823-56
W. C.	Screven	1810-1929
William	Paulding	1850-77 bond
William	Screven	1810-1929
William	Wilkes	1779-92
Willoby	Wayne	1822-70

COPE

Elizabeth	Effingham	1829-59

COPELAND

Comfort A.	Talbot	1859
Mary Dasher Mrs.	Lowndes	1871-1915
Pinkney A.	Harris	1850-75
R.	Thomas	1826-1836i
Richard	Putnam	1823-56
Robert	Thomas	1837-45i
W.	Bartow	1836-85
William	Carroll	1852-96
William	Stewart	1850-90
William Sr.	Harris	1850-75
William B.	Harris	1850-75

COPELEN

Anna	Meriwether	1831-59

COPP

Andrew	Polk	1857-1936
David T.	Polk	1857-1936
J. M.	Polk	1857-1936

COPPEDGE

Charles	Pike	1844-76

CORAM

Anne	Warren	1829
John Jasper	Randolph	1845-94
William	Warren	1821
Rev. Soldier		

CORBET

Hansford	Morgan	1814-30

CORBETT

Eleanor	Wilkes	1837-77
James	Wilkes	1818-19
William	Wilkes	1810-16

CORBIN

B. H.	Lumpkin	1845-1923
Jane A.	Lumpkin	1845-1923
M. L. Mrs.	Lumpkin	1845-1923
Napoleon B.	Crawford	1852-94

CORCERAN

Thomas	Coweta	1849-92

CORDLE

Abraham	Floyd	1852-61i

CORDRAY

Daniel	Muscogee	1838-62

CORKER

Dancy	Burke	1853-70
Stephen	Burke	1853-70

CORLEY

Louise	Coweta	1849-93

CORNEALISON

Conrad	Wilkes	1792-1801

CORNECK

James	Colonial	1773

CORNELIUS

M. M.	Polk	1857-1936

CORNETT

George	Putnam	1823-56

CORNINE

Richard	Putnam	1823-56

CORNWELL

Elijah	Jasper	1826-31

CORRY

Alexander	Greene	1817-42
William	Greene	1817-42

CORTELYOU

P. R.	Cobb	1902

CORYELL

Sophronia W.	Campbell	1825-1900
Thomas	Campbell	1825-1900

COSE

William	Washington	1829-71 divs

CRARE		
Benjamin	Hancock	1803
CRATIC		
Dommie	Bibb	1851-71
CRATIN		
Silvester	Taliaferro	1826-66
CRATON		
John	Wilkes	1819-36
CRAUSTON		
C. B.	Morgan	1814-30
CRAVEN		
Lewis M.	Floyd	1852-61
CRAWFORD		
Alice S.	Upson	1826-1910
Arthur	Hall	1819-37
B. E.	Gwinnett	1852-86
E. S.	Madison	1842-96
Joah F.	Union	1877-1942
Joel	Early	1856-97
John	Elbert	1814
John	Pulaski	1816-50
John	Thomas	1826-36i
John	Thomas	1837-45 minor
John M.	Jackson	1802-60
Lucy	Elbert	1831
Mathew	Franklin	1848-67
Robert	Lincoln	1796-1805
S. E.	Thomas	1826-36i
Samuel H.	Marion	1846-1915
Sarah P. Mrs.	Houston	1855-96
Shadrack	Sumter	1838-55
Silas E.	Thomas	1837-45i
Starling O.	Lumpkin	1845-1923
Stephen W.	Habersham	1847-1900
Thomas	Greene	1817-42
Uriah P.	Talbot	--
William	Elbert	1831
William	Greene	1796-1806
William	Henry	1822-34 bond
William	Henry	1834-69
William H.	Lincoln	1831-69
William L.	Wilkes	1819-36
Willson	Glynn	1844-53
CRAWLEY		
Charles Jr.	Morgan	1830-60
Charles Sr.	Morgan	1830-60
G.	Clayton	1859-1921
John	Morgan	1830-60
Thomas	Floyd	1852-61i
W. F.	Ware	1879-1915
CRAY		
B. G.	Montgomery	1806-63i
Mary L. Mrs.	Bibb	1851-71
CRAYNE		
Benjamin	Morgan	1814-30
CREECH		
T. P.	Lowndes	1871-1915
CREEL		
George	Clayton	1859-1929
J. T.	Ware	1879-1915
CREIGHTON		
Andrew	Wilkes	1810-16
CREMIN		
Celia	Hancock	1809
John	Hancock	1815

CRENSHAW		
Benjamin	Taliaferro	1826-66
Jarrel W.	Jasper	1823-33
Jesse	Franklin	1848-67
CRESSWELL		
Samuel	Wilkes	1779-92
CREWS		
Benedictine	Wilkes	1837-77
Etheldred	Putnam	1823-56
Isham	Liberty	1772-1887
John	Clarke	1822-42
Lucretia	Wayne	1822-70i
R. J.	Harris	1850-75
CRICHTON		
Eleanor A.	Camden	1868-1916
CRIDDLE		
Abigail	Henry	1822-34
CRIDER		
David	Franklin	1848-67
CRISBY		
Thomas	Wayne	1822-70i
CRITTENDON		
John	Fayette	1828-97
Lemuel	Putnam	1823-56
CROCKER		
John	Stewart	1850-90
CROCKETT		
David	Bibb	1823-55
Floyd	Richmond	1840-53
James W.	DeKalb	1840-69
John	Henry	1834-69
Louisa	Cobb	1909
M. E.	Cobb	1901
Robert	Carroll	1852-96
CROFTON		
Lydia	Jefferson	1839
CROLL		
James	Jasper	1812-17
CRONAN		
Hiram	Lumpkin	1845-1923
CROOK		
Elizabeth R.	Muscogee	1838-62
John	Oglethorpe	1833-66
Osborn	Harris	1850-75
Robert	Jefferson	1836
CROOKE		
Heriot	Colonial	1756
Heriot Jr.	Colonial	1774
CROOKER		
Lemuel	Emanuel	1825
(of Laurens Co.)		
CROOM		
Jesse	Washington	1852-1903
CROSBY		
D. W.	Appling	1877-1925
Sarah Mrs.	Appling	1877-1925
CROSS		
Ann	Jasper	1826-31
Edward	Houston	1855-96
George	Jasper	1823-33
John	Jasper	1823-33

CROSS (continued)

Leonard	Sumter	1838-55
Rhoda	Jasper	1826-31
Robert	Henry	1822-34
Thomas	Colonial	1768
William	Colonial	1737
William	Hall	1837-67

CROUCH

George	Muscogee	1838-62
George Sr.	Muscogee	1844
Nancy	Talbot	--
Shadrack	Putnam	1823-56

CROW

Amos	Walton	1834-9
Barbary	Franklin	1848-67
Didama Mrs.	Polk	1857-1936
Elizabeth	Bartow	1836-85
M.	Clayton	1859-1921
Moore H.	Franklin	1848-67
Stephen	Clarke	1822-42

CROWDER

Edmond	Hancock	1796
James	Meriwether	1831-59
John	Hancock	1819
Lucy L.	Oglethorpe	1833-66
Thomas S.	Baldwin	1835
William B.	Oglethorpe	1833-66

CROWELL

William	DeKalb	1840-69

CROWLY

James	DeKalb	1840-69

CROXSON

John	Hancock	1796

CROXTON

James	Clarke	1822-42

CRUMBLEY

J. J.	Polk	1857-1936

CRUMBLY

Anthony	Henry	1822-34

CRUMLEY

Matthew	Henry	1822-34

CRUMLY

F.	Henry	1834-69

CRUMP

Charles	Elbert	1821
Philip	Richmond	1840-53
Robert	Franklin	1848-67
Wesley	Henry	1822-34

CRUMPLER

Matilda	Dooly	1847-1901

CRUMPTON

R.	Paulding	1850-77 admr
Sarah	Paulding	1850-77 admx
Thomas	Paulding	1850-77
William	Paulding	1850-77 admr

CRUN

James T.	Effingham	1829-59

CRURERS

John	Coweta	1849-92

CRUSE

Stephen	Coweta	1849-92

CRUTCHFIELD

John	Greene	1806-16

CRUTHERS

Robert	Jones	1826-50

CUBBAGE

George	Colonial	1758

CUDDY

Margaret	Jefferson	1815 probate
(will gone)		

CUGH

Robert	Henry	1822-34

CULBERSON

Isaac	Troup	1832-48

CULBERTSON

Isaac N.	Floyd	1852-61
Wade	Floyd	1852-61

CULBRAITH

Daniel	Emanuel	1815

CULLAFER

Henry	Putnam	1823-56

CULLER

Anna C.	Macon	1856-1909
Mary S.	Houston	1855-96

CULLIN

John	Oglethorpe	1793-1807
Vines	Oglethorpe	1793-1807

CULP

David	Greene	1817-42

CULPEPPER

Charles	Houston	1827-55
Daniel	Crawford	1835-52
Daniel	Warren	1819
Joel	Dooly	1847-1901
John	Stewart	1850-90
Joseph	Houston	1827-55
Joseph	Jackson	1802-60
Nancy	Coweta	1849-92
Rachel	Houston	1827-55
Sampson	Laurens	1809-40
William	Warren	1806

CULVERSON

Samuel	Jasper	1812-17

CUMMING

Ann Mrs.	Richmond	1840-53
David	Washington	1829-71 divs
Eli	Washington	1829-71 divs
Francis	Greene	1817-42
M. E.	Forsyth	1833-44
Maggie Jane	Polk	1857-1936
Ridley W.	Stewart	1837-49
W. H.	Cobb	1893

CUMMINGS

Robert	Washington	1852-1903

CUNGAS

Henry	Houston	1855-96

CUNIE

Daniel S.	Montgomery	1806-63

CUNNADY

Wright	Sumter	1838-55

CUNNINGHAM

Andrew	Jackson	1802–60
Ansel	Jackson	1802–60
Charles	Richmond	1840–53
Elizabeth	Jackson	1802–60
Gabriel	Lee	1854–1955
Henry	Colonial	1770
J. T.	Jackson	1802–60
James	Greene	1806–16
James	Randolph	1845–94
Jesse H.	Oglethorpe	1833–36
John	Floyd	1852–61
M.	Madison	1842–96
Mary	Jackson	1802–60
R. E.	Jefferson	1841
Robert Eve	Jefferson	1838 & 1841 Codicil
Robert S.	Gilmer	1836–53i
William	Elbert	1799

CUNYERS

| Henry | Bartow | 1836–85 |
| William | Bartow | 1836–85 |

CURD

| Richard | Henry | 1822–34 |

CURDEN

| Martha | Jackson | 1802–60 |

CURETON

Richard	Hancock	1797
T.	Newton	1823–51
William	Jackson	1802–60
William B.	Talbot	––

CURRY

Cary	Baldwin	1819
David	Washington	1829–71 divs
Eliza	Carroll	1889
James	Lincoln	1808–32
James W.	Bartow	1836–85
Nathaniel	Lincoln	1831–69
Peter	Wilkes	1819–36
Polly	Putnam	1823–56
Rebecca	Cobb	1889
Thomas	Lincoln	1808–32
Whitmell	Sumter	1838–55i

CURTIS

Alexander	Camden	1868–1916
Caleb	Pike	1844–76
Caldwell	Paulding	1850–77
(Lindsey Elsberry admr)		
Robert	Troup	1832–48

CUSHMAN

| Ira | Early | 1834–1902 adm bonds |

CUTHBERT

| George | Colonial | 1767 |
| James | Colonial | 1770 |

CUTTER

| Henry S. | Bibb | 1823–55 |

CUTTS

| Joseph | Houston | 1827–55 |

CUYLER

| Telaman | Colonial | 1772 |

CYE

| James P. | Marion | 1846–1915 |

D'VAUGHN

| Catherine | Fayette | 1828–97 |
| John | Fayette | 1828–97 |

DABEY

| J. C. | Henry | 1822–34 |

DABNEY

Anderson	Jasper	1822–26
Elizabeth	Jasper	1822–26
Garland	DeKalb	1840–69
Hannah	Jasper	1822–26

DABRIMPLE

| Isaac | Lumpkin | 1833–52 |

DAFOUR

| Louis | Camden | 1795–1829 |
| Mary M. | Camden | 1795–1829 |

DAGGETT

| John | Jasper | 1812–17 |

DAHLER

| Thomas | Bartow | 1836–85 |

DAILEY

John	Henry	1834–69
John Sr.	Henry	1834–69
Richard	Henry	1834–69
Sarah Miss	Montgomery	1806–63
William	Glynn	1844–53

DAILY

| Georgia | McIntosh | 1873–1915 |

DALE

| Robert | Greene | 1806–16 |
| Seaborn | Randolph | 1845–94 |

DALEY

| Frances Henrietta Mrs. | Screven | 1810–1929 |
| John M. | Pike | 1823–29 |

DALLIS

Dennis B.	Lincoln	1808–32
Edwin	Upson	1826–1910
Lavina	Lincoln	1808–32
Thomas Jr.	Lincoln	1808–32
Thomas Sr.	Lincoln	1808–32
William	Camden	1796–1829

DALTON

| John | Jackson | 1802–60 |

DAMMON

| Charles | Jackson | 1802–60 |

DAMOUN

| John H. | Bibb | 1851–71 |

DAMPIER

| Daniel | Effingham | 1829–59 |

DAMSON

D. W.	Appling	1877–1925 affidavit
Henry	Burke	1853–96
Washington N.	Jones	1826–50

DANFORTH

| Richard | Richmond | 1840–53 |

DANIEL

Addison E.	Clayton	1859–1921
Anna	Wilkes	1806–08
Augustus	Cobb	1878i
Benjamin	Laurens	1809–40

DANIEL (continued)

E. P.	Pike	1823-29
Echols	Floyd	1852-61
Frederick	Pike	1823-29
G. B. & S. N.	Cobb	1878 minors
H. V.	Cobb	1876i
Henrietta V. Mrs.	Cobb	1873i
Henry A.	Taliaferro	1826-66
Isaac	Dooly	1847-1901
Isaac R.	Pike	1844-76
Isham	Houston	1855-96
James	Clayton	1859-1921
James	Henry	1834-69
James	Wilkes	1819-36
James K.	Sumter	1838-55
Jane E.	Wilkes	1837-77
John	Hancock	1821
John	Pulaski	1816-50
John M.	Morgan	1830-60
John T.	Taliaferro	1826-66
Joseph	Marion	1846-1915
Joseph	Washington	1852-1903
Levi	Jasper	1825-31
Lucretia	Laurens	1809-40
Manson	Talbot	--
Mitchell Sr.	Lee	1854-1955
Moses	Jasper	1826-31
Noah	Dooly	1847-1901
Robert K.	Marion	1846-1915
Samuel	Greene	1817-42
Sarah	Greene	1806-16
Sarah	Wilkes	1818-19
Silas L.	Washington	1829-71 divs
Stephen	Troup	1832-48
Thomas	Greene	1806-16
Thomas	Sumter	1838-55 bonds
W. R.	Cobb	1878i
William	Bibb	1823-55
William	Clayton	1859-1921
William	Greene	1806-16
William	Morgan	1830-60
William	Wilkes	1779-92
William Sr.	Clarke	1822-42
William W.	Clayton	1859-1921
Woodson	Oglethorpe	1833-66

DANIELL

Curtis	Houston	1827-55
Neoma & Dora	Cobb	1903 minors
Robert	Cobb	1881
S. N.	Cobb	1890i
Stephen	Cobb	1907i

DANIELLE

James	Hancock	1797

DANIELLY

Andrew	Warren	1822
M. D.	Crawford	1852-94

DANIELS

R. Y. B.	Houston	1855-96
William B.	Early	1834-1902 qdn bonds

DANIELSON

William	Early	1834-1902

DANSON

George	Bartow	1836-85

DANVER

David	Wilkes	1837-77

DANVILLE

Levi	Hancock	1800

DARBY

A. C.	Cobb	1904 minor

DARBY (continued)

John	Cobb	1880
Mary F.	Cobb	1886

DARDEN

Abner	Taliaferro	1826-66
Elbert	Sumter	1838-55 bond
Jesse	Taliaferro	1826-66
John	Jasper	1820-23
William	Taliaferro	1826-66

DARK

Daithy	Meriwether	1831-59

DARLEY

Sarah	Montgomery	1806-63

DARLING

Andrew	Colonial	1767
Mary	Richmond	1840-53

DARLINGTON

Hortie	Screven	1810-1929

DARNELL

David	Campbell	1825-1900

DARRACOTT

Francis	Wilkes	1818-19
James B.	Taliaferro	1826-66
Thomas	Wilkes	1792-1801

DARRAUGH

Archibald	Bibb	1823-55

DARRAWAY

Garland W.	Wilkes	1819-36

DARSEY

Benjamin	Liberty	1772-1887

DART

Cyrus	Glynn	1844-53

DARTIN

Isaac	Lumpkin	1845-1923

DASHER

Christian	Effingham	1829-59
James A. Sr.	Lowndes	1871-1915
Samuel	Effingham	1829-59

DAUGHERTY

Dennis	Carroll	1852-96
James B.	Forsyth	1833-34i

DAUGHERY

Benjamin	Emanuel	1867 gdns bond
Bryant (est of Berren)	Emanuel	1866 L/A
Elizabeth	Emanuel	1867 minors
Jacob	Emanuel	1867 minor

DAUGHTRY

J. H.	Screven	1810-1929
Joseph	Early	1856-1927
Joseph	Screven	1810-1929
W. V.	Screven	1810-1929

DAVENPORT

B. M.	Polk	1857-1936
Burkett	Greene	1817-42
Dicey	Campbell	1825-1900
Francis	Clarke	1822-42
James	Oglethorpe	1793-1807
John	Harris	1850-75
Marcus L.	Cobb	1867i
Sanford H.	Cobb	1870 minors
William	Morgan	1814-30

DAVID

Berry	Madison	1840-60
Fielding C.	Stewart	1850-90
Isaac	Madison	1812-41
Isaac	Madison	1842-96
J.	Early	1856-1927
John M.	Madison	1842-96
John W.	Troup	1832-48
Joseph	Washington	1829-71 divs
Lewis M.	Madison	1842-96
Morasset Jr.	Madison	1842-96
Morasset Sr.	Madison	1842-96
Pertee	Madison	1842-96
William	Campbell	1825-1900
William	Madison	1812-41

DAVIDSON

Charles	Clarke	1802-22
David W.	Stewart	1850-90
E. J.	Wilkinson	1906
John	Harris	1850-75
John	Wilkinson	1818
John	Wilkinson	1841
William	Jones	1812-23

DAVIE

Randolph	Lincoln	1831-69
Sarah	Lincoln	1831-69
William	Lincoln	1808-32

DAVIES

William	Pulaski	1816-50

DAVIS

A. H.	Chattooga	1856-1924
Abner	Henry	1834-69
Absolom	Elbert	1814
Absolom Sr.	Elbert	1807
Allatia Westbrook	Lee	1854-1955
Arthur	Walton	1834-9
Arthur L.	Morgan	1830-60
Augustine	Wilkes	1779-92
Benjamin	Elbert	1796
Benjamin	Wilkes	1792-1801
Crispan	Pike	1844-76
Daniel Sr.	Lumpkin	1845-1923
David	Warren	1787
Delilah	Lumpkin	1845-1923
Dioclipion	Washington	1852-1903
Dodson	Washington	1829-71 divs
Dolphina	Crawford	1852-94
Duncan	Early	1856-1889
		admr bonds
E. R.	Cobb	1868
(Temperance S., wid)		
Edward A.	Hancock	1823
Eli	Harris	1850-75
Eli A.	Polk	1857-1936
Elisha	Bibb	1851-71
Elizabeth	Gwinnett	1852-86
Elizabeth	Muscogee	1828
Elizabeth	Washington	1852-1903
Elizabeth Mrs.	Clayton	1859-1921
Emma M. Mrs.	Upson	1826-1910
Enos A.	Washington	1829-71 divs
Ephraim	Camden	1795-1829
Frances	Upson	1826-1910
Gardner	Jones	1812-23
Gary	Cobb	1875
Gehaze	Warren	1795
George H.	Fayette	1828-97
Grant	Morgan	1830-60
H. L.	Forsyth	1833-44
Harriet	Forsyth	1833-34i
Ichabod	Macon	1856-1909
Isabel	Morgan	1814-30
Isham	Oglethorpe	1833-66
Israel P.	Polk	1857-1936
J.	Polk	1857-1936

DAVID (continued)

J. C.	Polk	1857-1936
J. L.	Paulding	1850-77 appr
J. N. Sr.	Camden	1868-1916
J. W.	Harris	1850-75
James	Hancock	1803
James	Harris	1850-75
James	Putnam	1823-56
James J.	Henry	1822-34 bond
James W.	Gwinnett	1852-86
Jane	Troup	1832-48
Jesse H.	Henry	1822-34
Jeptha V.	Coweta	1849-92
John	Colonial	1761
Christ Church Parish		
John	Colonial	1773
St. Philips Parish		
John	Crawford	1835-52
John	Elbert	1829-60
John	Morgan	1808-13
John	Wilkes	1779-92
John	Wilkinson	1808
John Sr.	Washington	1829-71 divs
Joseph	Harris	1850-75
Joseph	Jackson	1802-60
Julia M.	Macon	1856-1909
Kiziah	Marion	1846-1915
L.	Lumpkin	1845-1923
L. D.	Lumpkin	1845-1923
Lewis	Greene	1794-1810
M. M.	Bibb	1851-71
Malinda P.	Paulding	1850-77
Margaret	DeKalb	1840-69
Mary Ann	Harris	1850-75
Mary O.	Houston	1855-96
Maxa M.	Wilkinson	1812
Nancy	Sumter	1838-55
Nancy	Wilkinson	1854
Nathan	Warren	1807
Paschal	Fayette	1828-97
Pelina	Jackson	1802-60
Phebby	Walton	1834-9
Polly	Morgan	1814-30
Ransom	Lincoln	1831-69
Rebecca	Bibb	1823-55
Richard	Franklin	1786-1813
Richard	Morgan	1814-30
Richard	Wilkes	1818-19
Robert	Colonial	1773
S. A. K. Mrs.	Burke	1853-96
Salley	Taliaferro	1826-66
Samuel	Burke	1853-96
Samuel	Lincoln	1796-1805
Stafford	Ware	1879-1915
Susan	Lumpkin	1845-192
Thomas	Lumpkin	1845-1923
Thomas	Morgan	1808-13
Thomas B.	Jasper	1825-31
Thomas G.	Forsyth	1833-44
W. B.	Crawford	1852-94
Wiley S.	Bartow	1836-85
William	Baldwin	1829
(of Chatham Co.)		
William	Camden	1795-1829
William	Jones	1812-23
William	Washington	1852-1903
William	Wilkes	1818-19
William	Wilkes	1819-36
William A.	Walton	1834-9
William D. Sr.	Chattooga	1856-1924
William H.	Walton	1827-31
William W.	Houston	1855-96
Zadoc	Fayette	1828-97

DAVISON

James	Jones	1826
John S.	Polk	1857-1936
Paul	Taliaferro	1826-66
Talbot	Pike	1844-76

DENMEADY		
Tolbott	Cobb	1877i

DENNARD		
H. L.	Houston	1855-96
F. S. A. Mrs.	Houston	1855-96
Shadrack	Houston	1827-55
T. C.	Wilkinson	1910

DENNING		
Nathan	Jones	1826-50

DENNIS		
Horace	Sumter	1838-55 bond
Jacob	Jones	1812-23
John	Butts	1826-41
John	Jones	1826-50
Joseph	Putnam	1808-22
Samuel J.	Crawford	1835-52
William Jr.	Putnam	1823-56
William Sr.	Putnam	1823-56
William B.	Coweta	1849-92
William B.	Warren	1837

DENNISON		
Isaac	Crawford	1835-52

DENNY		
Robert	Elbert	1829-50
Samuel	Jefferson	1824

DENSON		
Elkanal	Fayette	1828-97
James	Jones	1812-23
John E.	Hancock	1821

DENT		
George	Bartow	1836-85
Mary M.	Wilkes	1819-36
Michael L.	Muscogee	1847
Peter	Hancock	1821
Samuel	Jones	1812-23
William B. M.	Coweta	1849-92

DENTON		
J. W.	Screven	1810-1929
Mary	Hancock	1837
Mary Ann	Baldwin	1849

DEOS		
Alexander	Montgomery	1806-63

DERIZOUS		
Daniel	Colonial	1766

DESCLEAUX		
Joseph	Camden	1795-1829

DESHAZA		
Martha	Greene	1817-42
Richard	Pulaski	1816-50

DESHEIL		
George	Hancock	1807

DESOME		
A. A.	McIntosh	1873-1915

DeTREVILLE		
Eliza Mrs.	Cobb	1862i
Robert	Cobb	1862 minor
Ruth	Cobb	1872 minor

DEUPREE		
Daniel	Oglethorpe	1833-66
William H.	Oglethorpe	1833-66

DEVALL		
Thomas	Colonial	1758

DEVANEY		
Mary	Polk	1857-1936

DEVAUGHN		
Eliza B.	Clayton	1859-1921

DEVEAUX		
Archibald M.	Baldwin	1816
John	Colonial	1759
Samuel	Hancock	1839

DEWBERRY		
Henry	Taliferro	1826-66
Irby	Talbot	--
James	Warren	1836
Mariah	Talbot	--

DEWER		
William S.	Richmond	1840-53

DEWOLF		
D. F.	Cobb	--

DEWRY		
Edwin	Pike	1844-76

DICKENS		
Ephraim	Jones	1810-28

DICKENSON		
James	Bartow	1836-85
Paynter	Colonial	1767

DICKERSON		
Calvin	Morgan	1830-60
Edmond	Walton	1827-31
Ellen	Cobb	1878i
Emma A.	Houston	1855-96
James	Bartow	1836-45
John	Cobb	1874
Lewis	Bartow	1836-85
Nancy F.	Chattooga	1856-1924

DICKEY		
George	Gilmer	1836-53i
John	Upson	1826-1910
John B.	Gilmer	1836-53i
Patrick	Putnam	1823-56
Tolley	Elbert	1829-60
William	Clayton	1859-1921

DICKINSON		
Winburn	Upson	1826-1910

DICKSON		
D. W.	Cobb	1864
David	Fayette	1828-97
E. A.	Cobb	1869 minor
George M.	Muscogee	1838-62
J.	Coweta	1828-48i
J. W.	Lowndes	1871-1915
Jacob	Hancock	1799
James	Talbot	--
John	Coweta	1828-48
Mary E. & David	Cobb	1866 minors
Michael	Hancock	1803
Michael	Lincoln	1831-69
R. D.	Clayton	1859-1921
Robert H.	Talbot	--
Thomas	Bibb	1823-55
Thomas	Hancock	1823
W. W.	Coweta	1849-92

DIEHH		
John J.	Richmond	1840-53
Zachariah	Elbert	1831

DIGBY		
Joseph	Baldwin	1816

DOOLEY

John M.	Lincoln	1808-32

DOOLY

John	Wilkes	1779-92
Thomas	Wilkes	1792-1801

DOORS

John	Colonial	1777

DORAN

Andrew	Clarke	1822-42

DOREAUZEAUX

Stevens	Jefferson	1833

DORMAN

L. P.	Sumter	1838-55 bond

DORMANY

John	Irwin	1821-64

DORMER

James	Colonial	1747

DOROUGH

Sarah	Oglethorpe	1833-66

DORRIS

John	Carroll	1852-96

DORRUS

Winifred	Camden	1795-1829

DORSE

Stephen	Wilkes	1806-08

DORSETT

Elijah	Chattooga	1856-1924

DORSEY

Bassel	Franklin	1786-1813
Benjamin	Laurens	1809-40
E. A. Mrs.	Stewart	1850-90
Jared	Wilkes	1819-36
John	Franklin	1786-1813
John	Henry	1836-69
John	Stewart	1850-90
S. G.	Clayton	1859-1921

DORTCH

James	Franklin	1848-67
Lewis	Franklin	1848-69
Speed D.	Franklin	1848-67

DOSS

Edward	Gwinnett	1852-86

DOSSEY

Elias	Oglethorpe	1793-1807
Sally	Oglethorpe	1833-66
Seaborn	Taliaferro	1826-66
William	Taliaferro	1826-66

DOSTER

Benjamin	Stewart	1837-49

DOUD

Amos	Glynn	1844-53

DOUGHERTY

Bryant	Houston	1855-96
Charles	Jackson	1802-60

DOUGLAS

Alexander	Appling	1877-1925
C. T.	Sumter	1838-55 bonds
David	Colonial	1759
Elisha	Early	1856-1889

DOUGLAS (continued)

George L.	Sumter	1838-55 bonds
Heath	Sumter	1838-55 bond
John R.	Sumter	1838-55 bonds
Joseph	Meriwether	1831-59
Joseph	Sumter	1838-55
Laura F.	Macon	1856-1909
M.	Sumter	1838-55 bonds
Martha	Wilkes	1819-36
Thomas	Wilkes	1819-36
William A.	Emanuel	1867 minors
for Elizabeth F., Mary A. & Wm. P.		

DOUGLASS

John	Talbot	1861

DOUTHIL (?)

William	Bartow	1836-85

DOVE

Thomas	Warren	1801

DOVEN

Francis M.	Bartow	1836-85

DOWD

Joseph J.	Stewart	1850-90

DOWDELL

James	Harris	1850-75

DOWDLE

James	Hancock	1796

DOWDY

Martin	Oglethorpe	1833-66

DOWNING

George	Hall	1819-37
Hannah	Wilkinson	1819
Thomas	Henry	1822-34

DOWNS

Andrew H.	Madison	1842-96
Mary	Washington	1852-1903
Shely	Henry	1822-34
William	Camden	1795-1829
William	Effingham	1829-59
William	Morgan	1814-30

DOWSE

Gideon	Liberty	1772-1887

DOWSING

William	Lincoln	1808-32

DOZIER

Agnes	Pike	1844-76
Catharine E.	Talbot	--
Elias	Camden	1795-1829
Elizabeth	Wilkes	1837-77
James	Warren	1804
James	Wilkes	1837-77
James C.	Houston	1827-55
Lovet R.	Sumter	1838-55 bonds
Richard	Muscogee	1838-62
Thomas J.	Talbot	--

DRAKE

Archibald	Oglethorpe	1833-66
Cargill	Cobb	1881
Epaphraditus	Hancock	1831
F. A.	Coweta	1849-92
Francis	Bibb	1823-55
John Calvin	Upson	1826-1910
Thomas	Jefferson	1794-1808
(of Warren Co.)		
Thomas	Warren	1794

DRAN		
Thomas W.	Madison	1842-96
DRANE		
William	Talbot	--
DRAWDY		
Levi	Lowndes	1871-1915
William	Wayne	1822-70
DRENNAN		
Clarissa	Fayette	1828-97
Hugh	Fayette	1828-97
DREW		
J. B.	Crawford	1835-52
Samuel (Col)	Chattooga	1856-1924
DRIGGAN		
John H.	Washington	1827-71 divs
DRISCALL		
Dennis	Lee	1854-1955
DRISKELL		
George P.	Carroll	1852-96
Wulliam M.	Carroll	1852-97
DRIVER		
Anny (Amey)	Henry	1834-69
Giles	Jones	1826-50
Giles	Pike	1844-76
John	Pike	1844-76
DRUMMOND		
Daniel	Murray	1840-72
David	Colonial	1761
Edwin C.	Morgan	1814-30
Henry	Polk	1857-1936
William H.	Polk	1857-1936
DRUMRIGHT		
W. P.	Macon	1856-1909
DRURY		
Humphrey	Stewart	1837-49
Humphrey	Sumter	1838-55
Towns	Elbert	1818
DUBOURG		
Anderson	Baldwin	1834
Virginia	Baldwin	1848
DUCKET		
M. E.	Murray	1840-72
DUCKETT		
J. M.	Lumpkin	1845-1923
DUCKWORTH		
F. M.	Union	1877-1942
G. J.	Union	1835
Joseph	Jones	1826-50
Joseph	Sumter	1838-55 bonds
DUDLEY		
E.	Early	1856-1927
Elam	Washington	1829-71 divs
Samuel	Madison	1842-96
DUFFEY		
D. L.	Clayton	1859-1921
Daniel	Crawford	1835-52
John	Henry	1834-69
DUGAS		
Lewis	Wilkes	1806-08

DUGGAN		
Archelas	Washington	1852-1903
Asa	Washington	1852-1903
Jesse J.	Campbell	1825-1900
John C.	Washington	1852-1903
John H.	Washington	1852-1903
John M.	Washington	1852-1903
Martha C.	Washington	1852-1903
S.	Pike	1823-29
Thomas G.	Washington	1852-1903
DUGGER		
Esther	Effingham	1829-51
John	Effingham	1829-51
DUHART		
David	Pulaski	1816-50
DUHIGNON		
C. P.	Glynn	1844-53
DUKE		
Aristotle G.	Butts	1826-41
Elliott & Mary	Tattnall	1836-40i
George	Sumter	1838-55 bonds
Henry	Wilkes	1779-92
Henry	Wilkes	1781-83
John	Jones	1826-50
John T.	Newton	1823-51
Sarah	Sumter	1838-55 bonds
Stephen	Upson	1826-1910
Thomas	Carroll	1852-96
Thomas	Coweta	1849-92
Welcome	Polk	1857-1936
DUKES		
F. A.	Marion	1846-1915
J. R.	Bartow	1836-85
James	Marion	1846-1915
James	Wilkes	1779-92
John R.	Thomas	1837-45i
Nancy Caroline	Washington	1852-1903
DUMAS		
Jeremiah	Jones	1826-59
Jeremiah J.	Houston	1855-96
DUNAGAN		
Abner J.	Harris	1850-75
Sarah	Lumpkin	1833-55
DUNAWAY		
John	Dooly	1847-1901
Robert L.	Dooly	1847-1901
Samuel	Wilkes	1837-77
DUNCAN		
Alexander	Lumpkin	1845-1923
Alexander B. Sr.	Lee	1854-1955
Edmund	Jones	1826-50
Ellis	Laurens	1809-40
George Sr.	Jones	1826-50
John A.	Newton	1823-51
M. B.	Floyd	1861-71
Martha B.	Cobb	1899
Matthew	Putnam	1823-56
Robert	Talbot	1857
Thomas	Laurens	1809-40
Thomas	Wilkinson	1880
William W.	Gwinnett	1852-86
DUNHAM		
Andrew J.	Camden	1868-1916
James H.	Marion	1846-1915
John	McIntosh	1873-1915
William	Colonial	1769
DUNKIN		
Miles	Wilkes	1779-92

DUNLAP		
James	Campbell	1825-1900
Joseph	Meriwether	1831-59
DUNMAKER		
Daniel	Bartow	1836-1885
DUNN		
Benjamin	Troup	1832-48
D. D.	Cobb	1868 minor
John	Montgomery	1806-63
John L.	Lincoln	1831-69
Mary	Randolph	1845-94
Nehemiah	Jones	1812-23
Sarah	Sumter	1838-55 bonds
Thomas	Oglethorpe	1833-66
DUNNING		
Timothy	Muscogee	1851
DUNNINGTON		
William	Screven	1810-1929
DUNSON		
C. C. Mrs.	Clayton	1858-1921
DUNTON		
Frances P.	Cobb	1874i
DUNWOODY		
Ellen C.	Cobb	1895
Henry M.	Early	1856-1889 admr bonds
James	Houston	1855-96
DUPREE		
Ann	Cobb	1866
D. D.	Cobb	1867i
E. M.	Cobb	1864i
J. H.	Dooly	1847-1901
Jeremiah	Houston	1827-55
John	Jefferson	1807
Lewis Sr.	Stewart	1837-49
Mary	Meriwether	1831-59
Thomas	Paulding	1850-77 gdn
Thomas W.	Wilkinson	1884
William	Sumter	1838-55 bonds
William H.	Houston	1827-55
DURDAN		
Jesse	Sumter	1838-55 bonds
Lewis	Washington	1852-1903
Mathew	Washington	1852-1903
DURDEN		
Jesse	Warren	1826
DURHAM		
Abner Sr.	Meriwether	1831-59
Abram	Clarke	1822-42
Charlot	Cobb	1875 minor
J. S. Mrs.	Cobb	1907
Lucy W.	Cobb	1866 minor
Matthew	Monroe	1833
Nathan	Cobb	1907
Samuel D.	Clarke	1822-42
Thomas	Monroe	1826
Thomas K.	Camden	1795-1829
William	Bartow	1836-85
DURLOO		
Hattie C.	Washington	1852-1903
DURRETT		
Louise B.	Bibb	1823-55
DUSE		
Adriene	Bibb	1851-71

DUSKIN		
Michael	Stewart	1837-49
DUTTON		
D. S.	Cobb	1865i
R.	Cobb	1866i
DWIGHT		
S. B.	Murray	1840-72
DYE		
Jane	Elbert	1829-60
Martin	Franklin	1786-1813
William	Wilkes	1837-77
DYELS		
John	Tattnall	1836-40i
DYER		
Ann	Baldwin	1826
B. E.	Union	1877-1942
John	Carroll	1852-96
John	Tattnall	1836-40
Thomas Sr.	Coweta	1828-48
Thomas J.	Coweta	1849-92
DYERS		
C. Hodo	Talbot	1862
Herbert Laughtry	Lowndes	1871-1915
John B.	Talbot	--
William	Macon	1856-1909
DYKES		
Henry	Sumter	1838-55
James	Pulaski	1816-50
Jesse	Effingham	1829-59
George	Sumter	1838-55
DYNNATTE		
Reuben	Putnam	1808-22
DYPART		
John	Hancock	1804
Moses	Hancock	1805
DYSART		
Charity	Greene	1817-42
DYSON		
J. C. et al	Cobb	1878i
EADS		
Eliza	Oglethorpe	1833-66
George	Oglethorpe	1793-1807
John	Oglethorpe	1793-1807
EADY		
Allen H.	Wilkinson	1864
John	Wilkinson	1880
EAGERTON		
Charles	Jasper	1823-33
EAGLE		
Artimus	Campbell	1825-1900
EAKIN		
Samuel	Putnam	1808-22
EALEY		
Jesse	Greene	1817-42
EARLE		
Samuel	Cobb	1872

ENGRAM		
Ann E.	Houston	1855-96
Edward	Houston	1827-55

ENLOW
| Deason | Meriwether | 1831-59 |

ENNETT
| Elizabeth | Washington | 1852-1903 |

ENNIS
| Nathaniel | Hancock | 1819 |

ENZOR
| M. D. | Lee | 1854-1955 |
| R. H. | Lee | 1854-1955 |

EPPERSON
| Daniel | Franklin | 1786-1813 |
| John | Franklin | 1848-67 |

EPPINGER
| John | Colonial | 1777 |
| Robert | Pike | 1844-76 |

EPPS
| J. W. | Marion | 1846-1915 |

ERECKS
Catherine Miss	Screven	1810-1929
J. D. A.	Screven	1810-1929
Mary	Screven	1810-1929
T. J.	Screven	1810-1929
W. W.	Screven	1810-1929
William F. R.	Screven	1810-1929

ERNEST
| Asa E. | Bibb | 1851-71 |

ERVIN
| Elizabeth | Wilkes | 1810-16 |

ERWIN
Alexander	Chattooga	1856-1924
Alice M.	Union	1877-1942
Alse	Wilkes	1792-1801
James L.	Bartow	1836-85
Robert H.	Union	1877-1942

ESHAM
| William Columbus | Meriwether | 1831-59 |

ESKEW
| Richard N. | DeKalb | 1840-69 |

ESLER
| Sara | Cobb | 1881 |

ESPEY
| James | Putnam | 1823-56 |

ESTE
| William M. | Cobb | 1900 |

ESTER
| James | Hancock | 1816 |

ESTES
A. T.	Clayton	1859-1921
Catherine	Jasper	1831-39
G. B.	Clayton	1859-1921
Joel	Clayton	1859-1921
L. B.	Clayton	1859-1921

ESTICE
| Cleveland | Bartow | 1836-85 |

ETHERIDGE
| Elijah | Houston | 1855-96 |

ETHERIDGE (continued)
| J. H. | Early | 1856-1927 |
| Meret | Wilkinson | 1849 |

EUBANKS
Elijah	Crawford	1852-94
John	Hall	1819-37 Mts
John	Hancock	1833
Joseph	Cobb	1898
Nancy T.	Crawford	1852-94
W. J.	Cobb	1907

EULOW
| Nannie Mrs. | Polk | 1857-1936 |

EUTREKIN
| Samuel | Carroll | 1852-96 |
| William | Carroll | 1852-96 |

EVANS
A. M. Mrs.	Clayton	1859-1921
Amos Floyd	Burke	1853-96
Arden Sr.	Wilkes	1837-77
Beverly D.	Washington	1852-1903
Catharine	Dooly	1847-1907
David	Madison	1842-96
Elijah	Taliaferro	1826-66
Elvira J. H.	Morgan	1830-60
George	Clarke	1802-22
Henry T.	Madison	1842-96
Henry W.	Jasper	1812-17
Hugh	Clayton	1859-1921
I. W.	Washington	1852-1903
Isham	Jefferson	1842
J. H.	Screven	1810-1929
J. J.	Lumpkin	1845-1923
J. W.	Clayton	1859-1921
James	DeKalb	1840-69
Jesse McKinney	Houston	1855-96
John	Franklin	1786-1813
John	Morgan	1814-30
John	Oglethorpe	1833-66
John R.	Screven	1810-1929
Mary	Oglethorpe	1833-66
Nelly C.	Fayette	1828-97
Pleasant	Henry	1834-69
Rebecca J.	Taliaferro	1826-66
Rufus K.	Bibb	1851-71
S. J. Mrs.	Crawford	1852-94
William	Lincoln	1808-32
William	Wilkes	1819-36
William Sr.	Taliaferro	1826-66
William T.	Morgan	1830-60
Zachus	Early	1856-1927

EVE
| Oswell B. | Floyd | 1852-61 |

EVERET
| Samuel H. | Franklin | 1786-1813 |

EVERETT
Aaron	Thomas	1837-45
Alexander	Polk	1857-1936
Anna A.	Burke	1853-70
C. C.	Hancock	1842
Emma C. Mrs.	Polk	1857-1936
J. C.	Union	1877-1942
James A.	Houston	1827-55
Josiah	Tattnall	1836-40i
admr for Jas Archer		
Manervie	Ware	1879-1915
Sherrod G.	Walton	1870-74
Thomas H.	Stewart	1850-90
William	Decatur	1824-52 Mts
William	Decatur	1828-38

EWEN
| William | Colonial | 1776 |

EWING
William	Campbell	1825-1900

EXLEY
John	Effingham	1829-59
John W.	Effingham	1829-59

EXUM
James	Wilkinson	1844

EZELL
John	Jasper	1831-39
Levi	Houston	1855-96
William	Early	1834-1902 bonds

FAGALIE
William	Warren	1823

FAGAN
Edward	Randolph	1845-94
Henery	Houston	1827-35

FAIN
John	Gilmer	1836-53 bond
Matthew	Early	1834-1902
Thomas	Decatur	1828-38

FAIR
Peter Sr.	Baldwin	1824

FAIRCHILD
Cader	Decatur	1828-38

FAIRCLOTH
Charles	Emanuel	minor
E. J.	Emanuel	gdns bond
Peter	Thomas	1826-1836i

FAIRFAX
Robert	Houston	1855-96

FALKNER
John	Elbert	1817

FALL
C. J.	Coweta	1849-92
Milton B.	Fayette	1828-97

FALLEGANT
M. C. Mrs.	Screven	1810-1929

FALLIN
Charles B.	Taliferro	1826-66

FAMBRO
Urban C.	Polk	1857-1936

FAMBROUGH
Anderson	Clarke	1802-22
Anderson	Oglethorpe	1833-66
Mary	Pike	1844-76
Thomas	Greene	1817-42

FAMIS
Ann Francis	McIntosh	1873-1915

FANN
Thomas	Decatur	1824-52 Mts

FANNIN
Benjamin	Cobb	1890
Isham S.	Morgan	1814-30
James	Greene	1796-1806
Joseph D.	Putnam	1808-22

FARGUSON
Johnson	Henry	1834-69

FARLESS
Abigail	Houston	1827-55

FARLEY
Benjamin	Colonial	1765
James	Jasper	1825-31
John	Colonial	1763
John	Jasper	1825-31

FARMBY
Nathan	Walton	1834-9

FARMER
J. W.	Paulding	1850-77 gdn retn
James	Taliaferro	1826-66
John	Elbert	1859-1921
John	Muscogee	1845
John M.	Paulding	1850-77
L. W.	Elbert	1859-1921
S.	Floyd	1861-71
Thomas	Laurens	1809-40
Thomas J.	Lumpkin	1845-1923
William T.	Wilkinson	1901

FARNSWORTH
J. Clark	Chattooga	1856-1924
John G.	Chattooga	1856-1924

FARR
Martha D.	Talbot	--
R. S.	Houston	1855-96

FARRALL
John Sr.	Wilkes	1819-36

FARRELL
Elizabeth	Hancock	1834
J. H.	Bibb	1851-71

FARRER
Abel	Putnam	1823-56

FARROW
Mary	Lincoln	1831-69

FATMER
Henry	Coweta	1849-92

FAUL
George	Colonial	1767

FAULKNER
A. M.	Paulding	1850-77
James	Elbert	1808
John Sr.	Elbert	1806
Peter	Campbell	1825-1900
Thomas F.	Fayette	1828-97
William	Elbert	1829-60

FAUST
George W.	Oglethorpe	1833-66
Peter	Sumter	1838-55 bonds
William	Sumter	1838-55 bonds

FAVER
Columbus	Carroll	1852-96
Isaiah	Putnam	1823-56
Reuben	Meriwether	1831-59
Oliver	Fayette	1828-97

FAW
Enoch	Cobb	1902

FAYIL
John	Morgan	1814-30
Mary	Morgan	1814-30

FEAGIN
Missouri	Houston	1855–96
R. C.	Bibb	1851–71
Richardson	Jones	1812–23
William Sr.	Morgan	1830–60

FEARS
James	Morgan	1830–60
William	Greene	1817–42
Zachariah	Morgan	1830–60

FEATHERSTONE
| G. W. | Polk | 1857–1936 |

FELDER
| Samuel | Houston | 1855–96 |

FELPS
| David D. | Putnam | 1808–22 |

FELTON
John R.	Macon	1856–1909
L. M.	Macon	1856–1909
S. R.	Macon	1856–1909
Samuel H.	Macon	1856–1909
William	Macon	1856–1909

FELTS
| John | Putnam | 1823–56 |

FENN
Elizabeth	Dooly	1847–1901
Henry	Dooly	1847–1901
S. E.	Cobb	1890
Zacharias	Jefferson	1799

FENNIS
| Luna | Screven | 1810–1929 |

FERGUSON
C. M.	Lumpkin	1845–1923
Daniel	DeKalb	1840–69
Elizabeth	Thomas	1837–45i
George P.	Polk	1857–1936
Henry G.	Hancock	1811
John	Lincoln	1831–69
Joshua	Colonial	1777
Lewis H.	Henry	1822–34
Lewis M.	Henry	1822–34
Marteen	Thomas	1826–36
Mary Ann Elizabeth	Talbot	--
Niel	Butts	1826–41
W.	Polk	1857–1936
William H.	Campbell	1825–1900

FERRELL (Ferrill)
Barton	Thomas	1837–45i
Benjamin	Screven	1810–1929
Byrd	Screven	1810–1929
George W.	Polk	1857–1936
Hutching	Thomas	1837–45
Thomas A.	Campbell	1825–1900
William	Thomas	1837–45

FEW
| John | Ware | 1879–1915 |
| Leonidas | Jackson | 1802–60 |

FICKLIN
| Fielding | Wilkes | 1837–77 |

FIELD
| Boling W. | Lumpkin | 1845–1923 |
| Emily | Lumpkin | 1845–1923 adm |

FIELDER
| John | Morgan | 1808–13 |
| Samuel | Morgan | 1814–30 |

FIELDER (continued)
Sarah An	Newton	1823–51
Thomas	Morgan	1830–60
William L.	Morgan	1814–30

FIELDS
George W.	Clayton	1859–1921
Harmon	Washington	1852–1903
James	Stewart	1850–90
Thomapson	Houston	1855–96

FIFE
| Samuel | Henry | 1834–69 |

FIGG
| John D. R. | Jefferson | 1818 |

FIGGS
| William H. | Greene | 1817–42 |

FINCH
Charles	Oglethorpe	1793–1807
Charles	Oglethorpe	1833–66
William	Clarke	1802–22
William	Oglethorpe	1833–66

FINCHER
| John | Newton | 1823–51 |
| Joseph | Pike | 1844–76 |

FINDLEY
James	Greene	1817–42
James J.	Lumpkin	1845–1923
Thomas	Greene	1796–1806

FINISHA
| Jonathan | Paulding | 1850–77 bond |

FINLEY
Elizabeth	Houston	1827–55
John	Greene	1796–1806
Mary	Jackson	1802–60
Robert	Clarke	1802–22
Samuel	Chattooga	1856–1924

FINNEY
Benjamin	Jones	1812–23
Euphrema	Washington	1829–71 divs
Ezekiel	Washington	1829–71 divs
Henry	Jones	1826–50
James	Wilkes	1806–08

FINNIE
| John | Jones | 1812–23 |

FISH
George W.	Macon	1856–1909
Thomas J.	Macon	1856–1909
William	Washington	1852–1903

FISHBURNE
| Edward B. | Muscogee | 1836–62 |

FISHER
Metcalf	Washington	1829–71 divs
Metcalf	Washington	1852–1903
Nicholas	Colonial	1769

FITCH
| John | Colonial | 1762 |

FITTEN
| Isaiah C. | Greene | 1806–16 |

FITZGERALD
Ann	Fayette	1828–97
Catherine	Baldwin	1819–69
David	Pulaski	1816–50
James	Stewart	1850–90

FITZGERALD (continued)
Philip	Clayton	1859-1921

FITZJAMS
Blake	Jones	1826-50

FITZPATRICK
Benjamin	Morgan	1814-30
Bennett	Crawford	1852-94
C. Perkins	Morgan	183-60
Jackson	Murray	1840-72
James	Madison	1842-96
Joseph	Greene	1806-16
Mary	Morgan	1830-60
Sarah	Morgan	1814-30
Susan	Camden	1795-1829
William	Jasper	1812-17

FITZSIMMONS
Catherine	Richmond	1840-53
James	Colonial	1769
Sally	Greene	1796-1806

FITZWALTER
Joseph	Colonial	1742
Penelope	Colonial	1765

FLAG
Chandler	Jackson	1802-60

FLAKE
Michael	Richmond	1840-53

FLANDERS
A. C.	Emanuel	1866 gdns bond
Mandania	Putnam	1823-56

FLANIGAN
Kenion	Stewart	1850-90

FLANNIKEN
James	Greene	1786-95

FLATCHESSON
Rosa A.	Polk	1857-1936

FLEEMAN
Harriet Eleanor	Oglethorpe	1833-66

FLEETING
Margaret	Jefferson	1836
Richard	Jefferson	1817

FLEMING
Francis F.	Lincoln	1831-69
Henery	Elbert	1824
John	Jefferson	1837
John	Pulaski	1816-50
Robert	Jefferson	1826
Robert	Warren	1839
Samuel	Jefferson	1834
Thomas	Muscogee	1843
W. B.	Liberty	1772-1887

FLERYL
Charles	Colonial	1764
John	Colonial	1776
Mary	Colonial	1764

FLETCHER
E.	Henry	1822-34
Indiana	Lee	1854-1955
J. D.	Henry	1822-34
John W.	Sumter	1838-55 bonds
Still	Henry	1822-34
Thomas Franklin	Ware	1879-1915
Ziba	Merlwether	1831-51

FLEWELLEN
Abner	Baldwin	1812
Ann	Bibb	1823-55
Archelaus	Warren	1821
Elvira	Muscogee	1838-62
Louisa	Butts	1826-41
William	Jones	1826-50

FLINT
Ira H.	Houston	1827-55
Ira H.	Walton	1819-37
William	Paulding	1850-77

FLINTHON
Clement	Morgan	1814-30

FLOOD
John	Chattooga	1857-1924

FLORENCE
Jenny	Lincoln	1808-32
John	Lincoln	1808-32
Juda	Lincoln	1808-32
L. O. Mrs.	Cobb	1907
Obediah	Paulding	1850-77
Thomas	Lincoln	1831-69
William	Cobb	1884
William	Lincoln	1796-1805

FLOURNOY
Eliza	Jackson	1802-60
Gibson	Hancock	1811
Gibson	Jasper	1813-19
John F.	Putnam	1808-22
John M.	Muscogee	1838-62
Josiah	Chattooga	1856-1924
Josiah	Jasper	1825-31
Josiah	Putnam	1823-56
William	Putnam	1823-56
William F.	Jasper	1825-31

FLOWERS
Edward	Jasper	1820-23
James	Gwinnett	1852-86
John	Jones	1810-28
Rhoda	Houston	1827-55
Theophilus	Troup	1832-48

FLOYD
Elizabeth Ann	Liberty	1772-1887
Garland	Hall	1837-67
George J.	Stewart	1850-90
John	Morgan	1830-60
John G.	Camden	1829-68
John T.	Early	1834-1902
Joseph J. J.	Early	1834-1902
Maranda	Randolph	1845-94
Maria	Camden	1868-1916
Mary A. Mrs.	Washington	1852-1903
Mittie Mrs.	Washington	1852-1903
Shadrack	Greene	1817-42

FLUKER
Baldwin	Bibb	1823-55
Owen	Wilkes	1819-36
Robert	Washington	1852-1903
Robert T.	Washington	1829-71 divs
William	Wilkes	1806-08

FLYNN
James O.	Upson	1826-1910

FLYNT
John	Wilkes	1819-36
Tarpley	Oglethorpe	1793-1807

FOARD
Baxter	Baldwin	1823
Jane S.	Baldwin	1839

FOARD (continued)		
Thomas	Baldwin	1841
FOKES		
Elizabeth L. D.	Macon	1856-1909
William Sr.	Jefferson	1807
FOLGUT		
william	Walton	1834-9
FOLLY		
Thomas	Jasper	1812-17
FOLSOM		
Mary C.	Wilkinson	1861
FONTAINE		
Ghomas	Warren	1808
FORARD		
A. J.	Baldwin	1819-64
FORBES		
George N.	Talbot	--
John	Colonial	1775
FORBIS		
Hattie C. Mrs.	Lee	1854-1955
FORCE		
Samuel F.	Chattooga	1856-1924
FORD		
John	Elbert	1803
Keziah	Talbot	--
Sarah Jane	Chattooga	1856-1924
Thomas J.	Floyd	1861-71
William B.	Early	1856-1927
FOREMAN		
James	Stewart	1850-90
Martin	Jefferson	1815
Reuben	Greene	1796-1806
FOREST		
Mickle J.	Stewart	1850-90
FORESTER		
Sarah	Polk	1857-1936
FORISTER		
William	Walton	1834-9
FORMBY		
Catherine Rogers	Lee	1854-1955
Nancy	Wilkes	1837-77
FORRESTER		
Eleanor	Franklin	1786-1813
Elizabeth T.	Lee	1854-1955
Julian J.	Lee	1854-1955
Mary E.	Lee	1854-1955
Owen	Franklin	1786-1813
FORSYTH		
James	Paulding	1850-77
Martin	Paulding	1850-77 bond
FORT		
A. S.	Clayton	1859-1921
Caroline E.	Ware	1879-1915
George W.	Bibb	1823-55
Mary F.	Stewart	1850-90
Miranda	Talbot	--
Owen	Jefferson	1818
Robert W.	Bibb	1823-55
Tomlinson	Baldwin	1819-64
Tomlinson	Stewart	1837-49
Z. C.	Clayton	1859-1921

FORTSON		
Easton	Elbert	1829-60
Edwin K.	Clayton	1858-1921
Thomas	Elbert	1824
FOSKEY		
C. W.	Ware	1879-1915
FOSSET		
Peter E.	Pike	1844-76
FOSTER		
Adam R.	Houston	1855-96
Andrew S.	Campbell	1825-1900
Arthur	Greene	1817-42
Henry	Polk	1857-1936
James A.	Talbot	--
James M.	Henry	1822-34 bond
John	Clarke	1822-42
John	Henry	1822-34
John	Jasper	1822-26
John Harden	Wilkes	1792-1801
Kimmie	Morgan	1814-30
Mary A.	Campbell	1825-1900
Phelemon	Hancock	1816
R.	Chattooga	1856-1924
Thomas J.	Chattooga	1856-1924
W. L.	Chattooga	1856-1924
William	Liberty	1772-1887
William S.	Carroll	1852-96
William S.	Wilkes	1819-36
FOUCH		
Daniel	Wilkes	1818-19
FOUCHE		
Daniel	Wilkes	1837-77
FOULK		
Jared	Lincoln	1831-69
FOUNTAIN		
Henry	Jefferson	1826
Israel	Wilkinson	1848
Israel J.	Wilkinson	1898
James H.	Wilkinson	1864
Jonathan	Jefferson	1803
Magdalene	Colonial	1754
Sarah	Gwinnett	1852-86
William	Emanuel	1829
to Eleanor		deed of gift
William	Jefferson	1814 "very old"
William T.	Wilkinson	1881
FOWLER		
D. C.	Chattooga	1856-1924
Elbert	Washington	1852-1903
Elliot	Carroll	1852-96
George	Jefferson	1832
George T.	Cobb	1888
James	Chattooga	1856-1924
Jeremiah	Early	1834-1902
Joel	DeKalb	1840-69
John	Franklin	1848-67
Nathan	Crawford	1852-94
Nathan	Jackson	1802-60
Sarah	DeKalb	1840-69
Syntha, admr	Henry	1822-34
FOX		
Ann	Richmond	1840-53
Benjamin	Colonial	1773
Benjamin A.	Troup	1832-48
David	Colonial	1766
David Sr.	Colonial	1760
Francis C.	Morgan	1830-60
James	Colonial	1773
Richard	Colonial	1771
Richard	Muscogee	1846

FUDGE		
Elizabeth	Crawford	1835-52
Jacob	Crawford	1835-52
Solomon	Houston	1855-96
FULCHER		
John C.	Burke	1853-70
Valentine	Burke	1853-70
William	Richmond	1840-53
FULFORD		
Stephen	Macon	1856-1909
FULGHUM		
Elizabeth D.	Washington	1852-1903
James	Washington	1852-1903
Lunean	Washington	1852-1903
Mathew	Washington	1852-1903
William	Washington	1852-1903
FULLER		
Amos E.	Fayette	1828-97
Elijah	Greene	1817-42
George W.	Morgan	1830-60
Jacob	Paulding	1850-77
Jacob Jr.	Paulding	1850-77
James A.	Cobb	1872i
James A.	Meriwether	1831-59
John	Early	1856-1889
Jones L.	Paulding	1850-77
Jacob admr of		
Laura	Cobb	1872 minors
Nancy B.	Talbot	--
Solomon	Bartow	1836-85
W. G.	Cobb	1871
Walton	Sumter	1838-55 bonds
FULLERS		
W. A.	Clayton	1859-1921
FULLERTON		
Thomas	Henry	1834-69
FULLILOVE		
F. M.	Bartow	1836-85
FULLINGTON		
Caleb	Dooly	1847-1901
FULMER		
A. C.	Polk	1857-1936
Jacob F.	Chattooga	1856-1924
FULSOM		
Benjamin	Wilkes	1779-92
FULTON		
Samuel	Colonial	1775
FURGUSON		
Isabella	Lowndes	1871-1915
Marshall	Gwinnett	1852-86
FURLOW		
Charles	Walton	1834 9
David	Greene	1817-42
William	Greene	1796-1806
FURMAN		
George	Walton	1819-37
Martin	Walton	1819-37
FURR		
James	Bartow	1836-85
FURRY		
Martha	Richmond	1840-53

FUSSELL		
Jacob	Telfair	1869-1921
Morris	Marion	1846-1915
FUTCH		
Moses	Thomas	1837-45i
FUTRELL		
Abraham	Crawford	1835-52
Micajah	Effingham	1829-59
FYFFE		
Alexander	Colonial	1756
GAAR		
Joel	Morgan	1814-30
Lewis	Morgan	1814-30
William	Elbert	1829-60
GABLE		
Elizabeth	Cobb	1869i
(minors of)		
GACHET		
Ann	Stewart	1837-49
Benjamin	Pike	1823-29
Charles C.	Stewart	1831-5
GAFFORD		
Martha	Crawford	1852-94
Stephen	Jones	1812-23
GAINES		
E. P.	Chattooga	1856-1924
Hiram	Elbert	1815
Isaac Sr.	Ware	1879-1915
James	Bartow	1836-85
James M.	Cobb	1869i
Livingston P.	Elbert	1824
Margaret	Bartow	1836-85
William	Elbert	1829-60
William	Paulding	1850-77
GAINEY		
Francis Sr.	Wilkinson	1825
John	Wilkinson	1855
Margaret J.	Wilkinson	1895
GAINS		
George G.	Decatur	1828-38
Gustavus	Putnam	1808-22
GAITHER		
Brice	Putnam	1823-56
E. C.	Murray	1840-72
GALAWAY		
James	Franklin	1786-1813
GALBREATH		
Hugh	Montgomery	1806-63
GALLACHE		
John	Colonial	1755
GALLMAN		
Harry	Henry	1834-69
GALLOWAY		
William	Gwinnett	1852-86
GALPHIN		
Hattie	Burke	1853-70

GAMBELL

Richard	Colonial	1770

GAMBLE

John	Lincoln	1796-1805
John W. Sr.	Talbot	--
Roger L.	Jefferson	1838
William B.	Bibb	1851-71

GAMBLIN

Rubin W.	Lumpkin	1833-55

GAMISON

Caleb	Paulding	1850-77

GAMMAGE

James	Dooly	1847-1901

GANER

Sarah	Early	1834-1902

GANEWAY

Ann	Jefferson	1810

GANLEY

Zilphy	Stewart	1850-90

GANN

Edward	Cobb	1867i
Francis Seaborne	Paulding	1850-77 admr
John	Cobb	1881i
John & Seaborn (est Nathan)	Paulding	1850-77 admrs
Selina (Seaborn, gdn)	Paulding	1850-77 orph

GANNON

John	Lumpkin	1845-1923

GANNT

Joseph	Cobb	1884

GANT

Brittain	Putnam	1823-56

GAPPING

John B.	Elbert	1829-60

GAPPINS

Jordan (col)	Cobb	--

GARBUT

Gasper	Colonial	1772

GARDINER

Pryor	Warren	1827

GARDNER

Andrew	DeKalb	1840-69
Elizabeth	Morgan	1830-60
Ethelred	Jasper	1820-23
Ethelred	Jasper	1823-33
James	Richmond	1840-53
John M.	Upson	1826-1910
Nancy G.	Lee	1854-1955
Robert	Polk	1857-1936
Sterling	Upson	1826-1910
Thomas	Henry	1834-69
Thomas	Madison	1812-41 power of atty
Verlinda	Wilkes	1819-36
William	Jasper	1823-33

GARLAND

Henry	Upson	1826-1910
Henry Jr.	Upson	1826-1910
Patrick C.	Stewart	1850-90
Sarah F.	Morgan	1830-60

GARLINGTON

James	Jasper	1826-31

GARMON

Mary A. Mrs.	Polk	1857-1936

GARNER

Benjamin	Morgan	1814-30
Benjamin	Walton	1827-31
Elisha K.	Chattooga	1856-1924
Elizabeth	Henry	1822-34
George H.	Clayton	1859-1929
J. L.	Washington	1852-1903
Jail	Clarke	1822-42
James	Gwinnett	1852-86
James Sr.	Richmond	1840-53
Joanna	Richmond	1840-53
John	Henry	1822-34
Lucretia	Gwinnett	1852-86
Peggy	Clarke	1822-42
Thomas W.	Henry	1822-34
Thomas W.	Newton	1823-51
W. Thomas (may be Thomas W.)	Henry	1822-34
Wash. M.	Washington	1852-1903

GARNET

Elias	Lincoln	1831-69
Elizabeth	Lincoln	1831-69
Wilks B.	Lumpkin	1845-1923

GARNETT

Samuel M.	Richmond	1840-53

GARR

Michael	Wilkes	1779-92
R. W.	Carroll	1852-96

GARRARD

John	Wilkes	1837-77

GARRETT

Charles	Meriwether	1831-59
Christopher	Franklin	1786-1813
Ellen E.	Ware	1879-1915
Jacob	Putnam	1808-22
James	Greene	1786-95
James	Oglethorpe	1807-26
John	Elbert	1807
John	Greene	1817-42
John	Jones	1810-28
Mariah S.	Henry	1834-69

GARRISON

Baxter M.	Coweta	1849-92
Christopher	Franklin	1786-1813
James	Coweta	1849-92
Michael	Coweta	1849-92
William	Carroll	1852-96

GARTRELL

Joseph Sr.	Wilkes	1818-19

GARVEY

James	Colonial	1772

GARVIN

A. L.	Lumpkin	1845-1923

GARY

Hartwell	Newton	1823-51

GASCOIGNE

Richard A.	Camden	1795-1829

GASAWAY

Eliza	Harris	1850-75
J. L. N.	Harris	1850-75

GASSAWAY

Thomas	Franklin	1848-67
(of Pickens Co., S. C.)		

GASTON

Alexander	Meriwether	1831-59
George M.	Jasper	1831-9
Thomas	Jasper	1831-9

GATES

Benjamin	Meriwether	1831-59
Bennet H. H.	Meriwether	1831-59
Samuel	Meriwether	1831-59

GATEWOOD

Betty	Elbert	1807
John	Franklin	1786-1813
Larkin	Elbert	1802
Richard	Elbert	1794

GATHWITE

H. Milton	Lumpkin	1833-52

GATHWRIGHT

William M.	Jackson	1802-60

GATLIN

Gilbert	Taliaferro	1826-66
John	Pulaski	1816-50
Zachariah	Morgan	1814-30

GATLING

Levi	Morgan	1814-30

GATRELL

Francis	Lincoln	1808-32

GAULIN

James	Greene	1817-42

GAULT

Edward N.	Cobb	1866i
Emma	Cobb	1880 minor
William	Cobb	1880i
William L.	Cobb	1866i

GAUSEY

C. R. Mrs.	Houston	1855-96

GAUTER

Benedict	Richmond	1840-53

GAUTIER (Gotere)

Anthione	Colonial	1772

GAY

Allen	Coweta	1828-48
Allen J.	Early	1856-1889 bonds
Barnabas	Jefferson	1810
Gilbert	Fayette	1828-97
Isaac P.	Fayette	1828-97
Joshua	Randolph	1845-94
Martha	Jasper	1820-23
Mathew	Emanuel	1843
Susannah Mrs.	Screven	1810-1929

GEDDES

Ann E. Mrs.	Baldwin	1843

GEE

Peter	Putnam	1823-56
Samuel	Wilkinson	1916

GEGNILLAL

W. Robert	McIntosh	1873-1915

GENTRY

Burgess	Campbell	1825-1900
Elisha	Clarke	1802-22

GENTRY (continued)

J. T.	Polk	1857-1936
John	Campbell	1825-1900
T. J.	Polk	1857-1936
William	Talbot	--

GEORGE

Daniel	Walton	1827-31
David	Henry	1834-9
James	Jasper	1820-23
James R.	DeKalb	1840-69
Tunstel B.	DeKalb	1840-69
William	Oglethorpe	1793-1807

GERALD

Isaac	Coweta	1849-92

GERMAIN

Michael	Colonial	1753

GERMANY

Mary A.	Pike	1844-76

GEVIN

Lucy	Greene	1817-42

GHEESLING

Benjamin	Warren	1838

GHOLSON

Dabney	Madison	1812-41
Eggleston	Baldwin	1823

GIBBS

William	Elbert	1829

GIBBONS

Ann	Laurens	1809-40
John	Colonial	1770
Joseph	Colonial	1769
Samuel	Floyd	1861-71
William	Colonial	1769
William	Colonial	1771

GIBSON

Abel	Troup	1832-48
Annie	Cobb	1864i
Cornelia	Polk	1857-1936
George W.	Upson	1826-1910
Glory	Campbell	1825-1900
H. A.	Paulding	1850-77
Springer, admr		
Henry B.	Taliaferro	1826-66
Hugh	Coweta	1828-48
Jacobus	Coweta	1849-92
James	Upson	1826-1910
James Jr.	Upson	1826-1910
Jane	Wayne	1822-70
John	Taliaferro	1826-66
John	Wayne	1822-70i
John	Wilkes	1819-36
Luke	Coweta	1849-92
Ruth B.	Coweta	1849-92
S. R.	Cobb	1898
Silvanus	Upson	1826-1910
Springer	Polk	1857-1936
Taylor F.	Crawford	1852-94
Walter	Wilkes	1779-92
William	Polk	1857-1936
William T.	Polk	1857-1936

GICHAM

Joseph	Marion	1846-1915

GICKIE

James H.	Glynn	1844-53

GIDEON

Francis	DeKalb	1840-69

GIDEON (continued)		
James	Jackson	1802-60
Katherine	Irwin	1821-64

GIEGEL		
David	Effingham	1829-59

GIGNILLIAT		
James	Glynn	1844-53
Joseph	Cobb	1896 minors
N. P.	Cobb	1871
William R.	Cobb	1882

GILBERT		
Benjamin	Greene	1786-1795
Drewry	Upson	1826-1910
Drury	Washington	1829-71 divs
Edmund	Bibb	1851-71
Felix	Wilkes	1792-1801
Felix H.	Wilkes	1810-16
Frances	Putnam	1823-56
Isaac	Bartow	1836-85
Jaber	Upson	1826-1910
Jane U. Mrs.	Camden	1868-1916
John	Early	1856-1927
John	Franklin	1786-1813
John	Jackson	1802-60
John Henry	Clayton	1859-1921
Louisa	Clayton	1859-1921
M. R.	Houston	1855-96
Mary	Franklin	1786-1813
Samuel B.	Wilkinson	1888
Thomas	Houston	1855-96
William	Colonial	1768
William P.	Houston	1855-96

GILDER		
Mary	Pike	1844-76

GILES		
John	Elbert	1794
Thomas	Putnam	1808-22

GILHAM		
Ezekiel M.	Oglethorpe	1833-66
Thomas	Oglethorpe	1833-66

GILL		
Days	Baldwin	1819-64
Edward W.	Early	1834-1902
Jackson M.	Marion	1846-1915
John	Morgan	1830-60
Martin	Richmond	1840-53
William	Meriwether	1831-59

GILLAM		
Ann	Morgan	1814-30
Charles	Morgan	1814-30
William	Wilkes	1792-1801

GILLESPIE		
Robert	Oglethorpe	1833-66
Robert Jr.	Oglethorpe	1833-66
Sarah	Oglethorpe	1833-66
W. G.	Union	1877-1942

GILLEY		
Matilda	Carroll	1852-96

GILLHAM		
Ezekiel	Oglethorpe	1793-1807

GILLIAM		
Robert	Greene	1817-42

GILLILAND		
H. M.	Upson	1826-1910

GILLIS		
Angus	Montgomery	1806-63
August	Emanuel	1868i
John	Emanuel	1868 L/A
Murdock	Emanuel	1868i
Norman	Montgomery	1806-63
Roderick	Montgomery	1806-63

GILLISON		
W. D.	Chattooga	1856-1924

GILLY		
Jane	Early	1834-1902
Nathan S.	Early	1834-1902
William T.	Early	1834-1902

GILMER		
George R.	Oglethorpe	1833-66
M. Thomas	Oglethorpe	1807-26
Thomas	Oglethorpe	1807-26

GILMORE		
James Sr.	Hall	1837-67
John	Washington	1829-71 divs
John	Washington	1852-1903
John H.	Pike	1823-29
L. C. Mrs.	Washington	1852-1903
Mary Mildred	Washington	1852-1903
Thomas	Washington	1827-71 divs
W. C	Appling	1877-1925

GILREATH		
C. A.	Bartow	1836-85
E. O.	Chattooga	1856-1924

GILSON		
David	Morgan	1814-30

GILSTRAP		
Benjamin	Burke	1853-70
Jeremiah	Pulaski	1816-50

GILSUM		
Francis	Jones	1826-50

GINLEY		
G. E.	Polk	1857-1936

GINN		
Isaac	Elbert	1829-60
Jesse C.	Bartow	1836-85

GINNINGS		
Susanna	Chattooga	1856-1924

GIOVANOLI		
John	Colonial	1770

GLADEN		
James	Baldwin	1845

GLADIN		
Jonathan	Washington	1852-1903
Solomon	Washington	1852-1903

GLADNEY		
Thomas M.	Floyd	1852-61i

GLASCOCK		
Amelia	Bibb	1851-71

GLASGO		
Miles	Cobb	1867i

GLASS		
James	Sumter	1838-55 bonds
John	Wilkes	1806-08
Richard	Fayette	1828-97
William	Harris	1850-75

GLAZE		
Martha	Lumpkin	1845-1923
Mary	Lincoln	1831-69
Mary A.	Marion	1846-1915
Reuben	Oglethorpe	1833-66
Susannah	Lincoln	1831-69
Thomas	Lincoln	1796-1805
Thomas G.	Lincoln	1831-69
William	Harris	1850-75
GLENN		
Duke	Greene	1786-95
James	Early	1856-1927
James	Jackson	1802-60
John A.	Oglethorpe	1833-66
John Walker	Floyd	1861-71
Joseph	Stewart	1850-90
Joseph	Franklin	1786-1813
Mary	Oglethorpe	1833-66
Nancy	Oglethorpe	1833-66
O.	Washington	1829-71 divs
Simeon	Elbert	1814
Susan I.	Washington	1852-1903
Thomas	Henry	1822-34
Thomas	Oglethorpe	1833-66
Thomas M.	Oglethorpe	1833-66
Thornton T.	Jasper	1831-9
William	Oglethorpe	1833-66
William Sr.	Oglethorpe	1833-66
GLORE		
George W.	Cobb	1865
GLOVER		
Annie	Cobb	1862i
Edward	Cobb	1862 minor
Edward	Cobb	1872 minor
Henry	Houston	1855-96
J. B. Jr.	Cobb	1897
Jane S.	Cobb	1862i
John J.	Gwinnett	1852-86
Joseph	Cobb	1862 minor
Kelly	Wilkinson	1852
Maria Miss	Cobb	1862 minor
T. W.	Cobb	1903
Thomas W.	Cobb	1862 minor
GOACH		
William	Lumpkin	1845-1923
GOBER		
Eliza V.	Cobb	1867 minor
John E.	Cobb	1865i
Thomas	DeKalb	1840-69
William	Newton	1823-51
William J.	Gwinnett	1852-86
GODARD		
Simon	Jones	1826-50
GODBEE		
Francis G.	Burke	1853-70
Homer	Burke	1853-70
Mulkey	Burke	1853-70
Newton	Burke	1853-70
Robert	Burke	1853-70
Simon S.	Burke	1853-70
GODDARD		
Jane	Polk	1857-1936
GODFREY		
Francis H.	Bibb	1823-55
George	Meriwether	1831-59
J. E.	Stewart	1850-90
GODWIN		
Arnold	Sumter	1838-55
John L.	Dooly	1847-1901

GOFF		
Council W.	Sumter	1838-55
Lou Ella	Randolph	1845-94
GOGGINS		
Elizabeth	Paulding	1850-77 retn
H.	Paulding	1850-77 retn
GOLDEN		
Allison W. C.	Carroll	1871
Caleb	Carroll	1850
Henrietta	Early	1886-1927
GOLDMAN		
Francis	Lincoln	1831-69
GOLDSBERRY		
Robert	Marion	1846-1915
GOLDSMITH		
Thomas Sr.	Colonial	1772
GOLDSON		
John	Hancock	1803
GOLDWIRE		
Benjamin	Colonial	1766
John Sr.	Colonial	1774
GOLIGHTLY		
James Sr.	Washington	1829-71 divs
Nancy Mrs.	Polk	1857-1936
GOLLMAN		
John C.	Henry	1822-34
GOMER		
Sarah	Houston	1827-55
GONEKE		
Willie Batts Mrs.	Lee	1854-1955
GOOBER		
Milton M.	Early	1856-1927
GOOCH		
Nathan	Greene	1817-42
GOOCHEN		
Milton M.	Early	1856-1929 L/A
GOOD		
Theophilus	Jasper	1822-26
GOODALL		
James	Colonial	1768
GOODBROE		
Ernest	Lee	1854-1955
Sallie Mrs.	Lee	1854-1955
GOODE		
Jesse	Jasper	1831-9
John	Upson	1820 1910
John C.	Putnam	1823-56
Starling	Jasper	1820-23
Thomas W.	Upson	1826-1910
William	Jasper	1813-19
GOODEN		
Robert A.	Crawford	1852-94
GOODGES		
Jordan	Hancock	1822
GOODING		
Wilkinson	Wilkes	1779-92

GOODMAN
Elizabeth	Harris	1850-75
Henry	Laurens	1809-40
John T.	Jackson	1802-60
Susie E. Mrs.	Lee	1854-1955

GOODSON
| Arthur | Putnam | 1808-22 |
| Mary Mrs. | Carroll | 1852-96 |

GOODWIN
Charles J.	Macon	1856-1909
D. F.	Lowndes	1871-1915
George	Wilkes	1819-36
J. B.	Macon	1856-1909
James	Wilkes	1819-36
Jerry	Bibb	1851-71
Nancy Mrs.	Burke	1853-70
Reuben B.	Baldwin	1826
Ruffin J.	Talbot	--
Shadrack	Jones	1826-50
Solomon	DeKalb	1840-69

GOOLSBE
Aaron	Early	1834-1902
Henry T.	Early	1834-1902
Lazarus	Early	1834-1902

GOOLSBY
Andrew J.	Oglethorpe	1833-66
Anne	Oglethorpe	1833-66
Isaac	Oglethorpe	1833-66
John	Jasper	1825-31
L. M.	Oglethorpe	1833-66
Peter	Wilkes	1779-92
Peter Richard	Oglethorpe	1833-66

GORDON
Alexander	Jefferson	--
(of Burke Co.)		
Alexander	Oglethorpe	1807-26
C. F.	Putnam	1823-56
Gaven	Jones	1812-23
George Clinton	Richmond	1840-53
John	Morgan	1830-60
Joseph	Franklin	1786-1813
Kenneth	Putnam	1808-22
Marcus L.	Gwinnett	1852-86
Moses	Wilkes	1792-1801
Nancy	Jones	1826-50
R. C.	Franklin	1848-67
Richard	Washington	1829-71 divs
Richard	Washington	1852-1903
Samuel	Burke	1853-70
Samuel	Jefferson	1805
Thomas	Franklin	1786-1813
William	Bartow	1836-85

GORHAM
Ann	Camden	1795-1829
John	Franklin	1786-1813
William	Camden	1795-1829

GORMAN
Claiborn	Campbell	1825-1900
John B.	Talbot	1869
Thomas B.	Bibb	1851-71

GORTZINGER
| Peter | Screven | 1810-1929 |

GOSS
Benjamin	Lumpkin	1833-55
Charles	Greene	1806-16
Elizabeth	Elbert	1815
Ezekiel F.	Meriwether	1831-59
Horatio J.	Elbert	1829-60
I. J. M. Dr.	Cobb	1897
John C.	Meriwether	1831-59

GOSSER
| John | Meriwether | 1831-59 |

GOULDING
| Thomas | Muscogee | 1847 |

GOVELY (Gavely)
| James | Wilkes | 1779-92 |

GOWDER
| Olivia | Hall | 1837-67 |

GOWEN
| James | Wilkes | 1779-92 |

GOWDER
| Olivia | Hall | 1837-67 |

GOWEN
| James M. | Jackson | 1802-60 |

GOWER
| Robert M. | Gwinnett | 1852-86 |

GOYNNE
| Sarah M. | Gwinnett | 1852-86 |
| William | Warren | 1816 |

GOZA
| Aaron | DeKalb | 1840-69 |
| Robert J. | Gwinnett | 1852-86 |

GRACE
Elizabeth	Houston	1855-96
James	Houston	1827-55
John	Tattnall	1839
Sally	Coweta	1828-48i
Samuel	Houston	1855-96
Thomas	Hancock	1806
Thomas J.	Houston	1827-55

GRADY
Arthur	Houston	1827-55
James	Wilkes	1810-16
Nettie Cobb	Clayton	1859-1921

GRAGG
| John | Cobb | 1891 |

GRAHAM
Alexander	Camden	1795-1820
Anderson	Lumpkin	1845-1923 gdn
D.	Telfair	1869-1921
Ezekiel	Bartow	1836-85
Greene G.	Pulaski	1816-50
James	Madison	1812-41
John	Effingham	1829-59
Josiah	DeKalb	1840-69
Mungo	Colonial	1766
Patrick	Colonial	1755
Selete	Effingham	1829-59
Thompson	Upson	1826-1910
W. W.	Appling	1877-1925
William	Madison	1812-41
Willis	Harris	1850-75

GRAINS see Gains

GRAMLING
| R. M. | Cobb | 1903i |

GRAMMAGE
| Eveline | Macon | 1856-1909 |

GRAMMER
| Peter | Hancock | 1824 |

GRANADE
| Benjamin | Oglethorpe | 1793-1807 |

GRANADE (continued)

Stephen	Oglethorpe	1807-26

GRANBERRY

George	Harris	1850-75
George	Jefferson	1804
Sarah	Jefferson	1817

GRANBURY

Moses	Warren	1808

GRANT

Arthur	Glynn	1844-53
Daniel	Wilkes	1792-1801
Harry	Glynn	1844-53
Thomas J.	Habersham	1847-1900
William	Wilkes	1819-36
William A.	Wilkes	1819-36

GRANTHAM

John	Wilkes	1779-92

GRANTLAND

Samuel	Upson	1826-1910
Seaton	Baldwin	1819-64

GRAVES

Catharine	Wilkes	1837-77
Charles	Fayette	1828-97
Humphrey	Wilkes	1792-1801
James	Lincoln	1796-1805
Joanna	Walton	1834-9
John	Putnam	1823-56
John H.	Floyd	1861-71
Sarah	Wilkes	1819-36
Solomon	Newton	1823-51
Susan	Fayette	1828-97
William	Franklin	1786-1813

GRAY

Abraham	Coweta	1849-92
Ambrose	Fayette	1828-97
Anna	Clarke	1802-22
B. H.	Coweta	1842-94
Baldwin	Houston	1855-96
Curtis G.	Houston	1855-96
Daniel W.	Glynn	1844-53
Eliza A.	Cobb	1878
Elvira Mrs.	Coweta	1828-48
Enoch	Washington	1829-71 divs
F. M. Adams	Lumpkin	1833-55
George	Colonial	1766
Harriett	Tattnall	1836-40i
Isaac	Lincoln	1831-69
James	Wilkes	1779-92
James T.	Richmond	1840-53
John	Henry	1834-69
John W.	Camden	1829-68
Joseph Sr.	Elbert	1822
M. M.	Burke	1853-90
Minchi	Burke	1853-90
Priscilla	Baldwin	1822
Richard	Burke	1853-70
Richard	Muscogee	1848
Robert	Murray	1840-72
Sarah	Fayette	1828-97
Sarah	Lee	1854-1955
Thomas	Putnam	1823-56
Thomas M.	Chattooga	1856-1924
William	Bartow	1836-85
William	Bibb	1851-71
Zachariah	Baldwin	1815

GRAYBILL

Henry	Hancock	1820
John N.	Washington	1829-71 divs
Michael	Baldwin	1839
Midas	Bibb	1851-71

GREEN

Abraham	Cobb	1870i
Allen	Jones	1826-50
Burrill	Jasper	1826-31
Burwell Sr.	Pike	1844-77
Clara J.	Cobb	1892
Clotilda	Cobb	1886
David	Washington	1829-71 divs
Delilah	Screven	1810-1929
Ellen A.	Lee	1854-1955
Frederick	Sumter	1838-55
George	Greene	1796-1806
John	Jackson	1802-60
John	Polk	1857-1936
Joseph	Cobb	1870i
Martha	Washington	1852-1903
Martha Ann	Emanuel	1848
orph of Daniel		
Mary	Putnam	1823-56
Mary A.	Lee	1854-1955
Napoleon B.	Cobb	1874i
Piety	Cobb	1906
Rachel	Jefferson	1816
Renie J.	Polk	1857-1936
Rossie	Screven	1810-1929
Ruthy	Greene	1817-42
Samuel	Fayette	1828-97
Sarah	Bibb	1851-71
Thomas G.	Upson	1826-1910
William	Greene	1817-42
William	Henry	1834-69

GREENE

Elizabeth	Baldwin	1842
Isabelle	Talbot	--
James	Wilkes	1818-19
Jesse	Bibb	1851-71
Jesse P.	Burke	1853-70
Joel A.	Harris	1850-75
Martha R.	Upson	1826-1910
Robert W.	Upson	1826-1910
W. C.	Cobb	1870
William	Wilkes	1806-08

GREENLEE

Airy	Habersham	1847-1900
wife of Joseph		
Samuel	Baldwin	1822

GREENWAY

Alfred G.	Washington	1852-1903

GREENWOOD

B. L.	Richmond	1840-53
George A.	Rabun	1863-88
Georgianna T.	Richmond	1840-53
Hugh B.	Franklin	1786-1813
John	Oglethorpe	1793-1807
John P.	Polk	1857-1936
Robert A.	Richmond	1840-53

GREER

A. E.	Chattooga	1856-1924
Allin H.	Macon	1856-1009
Aquila	Greene	1786-95
Gilbert	Coweta	1849-92
James	Clarke	1822-42
John	Troup	1832-48
Robert	Greene	1796-1806
Robert	Greene	1817-42
Thomas	Greene	1817-42

GREGG

E. A.	Cobb	1874i
George C.	Pike	1844-76

GREGOR

Ezell	Early	1834-1902
Thomas G. M.	Early	1834-1902

GREGOR (continued)
William H.	Early	1834-1902

GREGORY
Hardy	Putnam	1823-56
Ivey W.	Stewart	1850-90
Lewis	Jasper	1823-33
Rosannah	Colonial	1774

GREINER
Elizabeth	Screven	1810-1929

GRESHAM
Amanda	Cobb	1871 minors
Archibald	Greene	1817-42
Archibald	Taliaferro	1826-66
E. B.	Burke	1853-70
Eliza L.	Meriwether	1831-59
Elizabeth (Betty)	Oglethorpe	1807-26
George	Wilkes	1837-77
George W.	Cobb	1868i
James	Wilkes	1806-08
James D.	Taliaferro	1826-66
Jeremiah	Lincoln	1831-69
John	Upson	1826-1910
Kaufman	Wilkes	1837-77
Margaret	Cobb	1903
Marmaduke	Stewart	1837-49
Martha Williams	Oglethorpe	1833-66
Mary	Oglethorpe	1793-1807
Mary W.	Wilkes	1837-77
S. M. Mrs.	Burke	1853-70
T. R.	Cobb	1868 minors
Watson	Cobb	1867
William	Cobb	1867i
Young	Clarke	1802-22

GREY
James	Butts	1826-41
Rachel	Butts	1826-41

GRICE
Ann Martin	Henry	1822-34
Garry	Henry	1822-34
Gary	Henry	1822-34
Larry	Carroll	1852-96
Stephen	Henry	1822-34

GRIER (Greer)
A. W.	Taliaferro	1826-66
Aaron	Warren	1827
(Rev. Soldier)		
Elijah F.	Wilkinson	1867
Elizabeth	Effingham	1829-59
Moses	Early	1856-1927
Phebe	Bibb	1851-71
Robert Sr.	Wilkes	1819-36
Samuel A.	Randolph	1845-94
Thomas	Morgan	1814-30
Thomas M.	Early	--

GRIFFIN
Andrew	Greene	1786-95
Ann	Oglethorpe	1807-26
Charles W.	Carroll	1852-96
David	Oglethorpe	1793-1807
David C.	Polk	1857-1936
E. B.	Meriwether	1831-59
Ezekiel	Henry	1822-34
Flora	Lee	1854-1955
Francis	DeKalb	1840-69
G. W.	Meriwether	1831-59
Isham	Lee	1854-1955
J.	Polk	1857-1936
J. V.	Carroll	1852-96
James	Stewart	1837-49
James W.	Bibb	1851-71
Jane	Polk	1857-1936
John	Oglethorpe	1807-26

GRIFFIN (continued)
John	Paulding	1850-77 appr
John	Wilkes	1810-16
John W.	Marion	1846-1915
John W.	Stewart	1837-49
Joseph	Oglethorpe	1807-26
Joseph B.	Lee	1854-1955
Larkin	Bibb	1851-71
Martha	Taliaferro	1826-66
Mary	Stewart	1837-49
Mary A. C.	Houston	1855-96
Owen	Wilkes	1779-92
Owen	Wilkes	1819-36
Peter G.	Lee	1854-1955
R., orph of	Coweta	1828-48
R. P.	Lee	1854-1955
Rebecca	Crawford	1835-52
Reubin	Early	1856-1927
Richard	Lincoln	1796-1805
Silas	Oglethorpe	1833-66
Thomas H.	Carroll	1852-96
William	Early	1856-1927
William	Henry	1834-69
William	Ware	1879-1915

GRIFFIS
Dempsey	Hancock	1823

GRIFFITH
G. W.	Fayette	1828-97
James	Madison	1842-96
John	Oglethorpe	1807-26
L. H.	Campbell	1825-1900
R. P.	Madison	1842-96
Robert	Madison	1812-41
William S.	Emanuel	1867i

GRIGGS
Catharine	Marion	1846-1915
Charles D.	Lumpkin	1845-1923
G. Jesse	Hancock	1810
John	Hancock	1825
John	Putnam	1823-56
Lee	Hancock	1807
Peggy B.	Hancock	1817
Rhodom	Hancock	1822
Robert	Putnam	1823-56
William	Hancock	1817
William W.	Fayette	1828-97

GRIGSBY
Bathsheba	Jones	1812-23
William	Greene	1806-16

GRIMAGE
Joshua	Lincoln	1808-32

GRIMES
David	Stewart	1850-90
George G.	Decatur	1824-52 Mts
Hiram	Montgomery	1806-63
John	Baldwin	1841
John	Stewart	1850-90
Josiah	Muscogee	1847
Thomas	Greene	1817-42
Thomas M.	Madison	1811-40
William	Elbert	1794

GRIMMET
William	Jasper	1826-31

GRIMSLEY
J.	Early	1856-1927
Joseph	Early	1856-1927
Lewis	Early	1856-1927
Sarah	Early	1856-1927

GRINER
James	Screven	1810-1929

GRINES		
Amy	Henry	1834-69

GRISHAM		
Jeptha J.	Pike	1844-76
L.	Pike	1844-76

GRIST		
Martha R.	Early	1856-1927

GRISWELL		
Louvina	Gwinnett	1852-86

GRIZZLE		
Grigsby	Jones	1810-28

GROCE		
Ann	Bibb	1823-55
Hannah	Meriwether	1831-59
Margaret	Bibb	1851-71
Shepherd	Lincoln	1808-32

GROGAN		
F. W.	Paulding	1850-77 admr
(est J. C. Adams)		
F. W.	Paulding	1850-77 gdn
(for Easterlings orphs)		
Thomas	DeKalb	1840-69
Thomas W.	Cobb	1877i
Thomas W.	Paulding	1850-77

GROOVER		
J. N.	Cobb	1876

GROSS		
John J.	Screven	1810-1929

GROVE		
Jared	Lincoln	1796-1805

GROVENSTEINE		
Henry L.	Effingham	1829-59

GROVER		
John	Colonial	1772
L. H.	Lincoln	1831-69

GROVES		
Joseph L.	Cobb	1874 minors
Samuel	Madison	1842-96
William F.	Cobb	1893

GUANN		
Christena	Effingham	1829-59
Christopher	Effingham	1829-59
Jonathan	Effingham	1829-59
Solomon	Effingham	1829-59

GUDGER		
Anna	Gilmer	1836-53 bond

GUERRY		
James	Houston	1855-96
James	Sumter	1838-55

GUESS		
Henry	Cobb	1867i

GUEST		
David	Franklin	1848-67
Thomas	Wilkes	1810-16

GUICE		
Emily	Muscogee	1838-62
John	Clayton	1859-1921
Jonas	Marion	1846-1915
Peter	Lincoln	1831-69
Samuel	Meriwether	1831-59

GUINN		
Franklin	Jasper	1831-9

GULLATT		
Nancy	Wilkes	1837-77
Peter	Wilkes	1837-77

GUNBY		
Sevin	Camden	1795-1829
William	Lincoln	1831-69

GUNN		
Gabril	Jasper	1812-17
George	Wilkes	1810-16
George W.	Taliaferro	1826-66
T. B.	Montgomery	1806-67
William	Taliaferro	1826-66

GUNNELL		
W. B.	Cobb	1885
Willis	Madison	1842-96

GUNTER		
David	Cobb	1889
Isham	Clayton	1859-1921
Jessie	Elbert	1829

GURLEY		
David Jr.	Coweta	1849-92
J. C.	Coweta	1849-92

GURTHER		
William J.	Coweta	1828-48 retn

GUSSWALD		
Sarah A. L. Mrs.	Coweta	1849-92

GUTHREE		
Robert	Elbert	1797

GUTHRIE		
Jane Mrs.	Marion	1846-1915

GUYTON		
John	Bartow	1836-85
Philip J.	Bartow	1836-85

GWYN		
James	Upson	1826-1910

HAAS		
John	Baldwin	1819-64

HABERSHAM		
James Sr.	Colonial	1775

HACKETT		
Drucilla	Habersham	1847-1900

HACKNEY		
J. H.	Polk	1857-1936
Nathan	Morgan	1814-30

HADDEN		
Elizabeth	Jefferson	1830
Gordon	Stewart	1850-90
William	Jefferson	1813

HADDOCK		
William Sr.	Habersham	1847-1900

HADLEY		
Lewis	Thomas	1826-36 minor

HAGAN		
Edward	Clarke	1802-22
Edward	Paulding	1890
J. W.	Screven	1810-1929
William	Putnam	1823-56
HAGENIN		
Edward D.	Bibb	1851-71
Julia E.	Bibb	1851-71
HAGGARD		
Samuel	Jackson	1802-60
HAGIN		
John	Camden	1795-1829
HAGOOD		
Gideon	Hancock	1824
James	Hall	1819-37
HAIL		
F. M.	Henry	1834-69
James	Crawford	1835-52
James	Morgan	1814-30
Thomas	Clarke	1822-42
HAILE		
Hosea	Clarke	1822-42
HAINES		
M. Jane	Washington	1852-1903
Nathan	Washington	1829-71 divs
Nathan	Washington	1852-1903
HAIRBACK		
Lawrence	Sumter	1838-55
HAIRSTON		
Thomas J.	Cobb	1866i
HAISTEN		
John	Fayette	1828-97
HALAWAY		
Solomon	Carroll	1852-96
HALDOX		
Rachel	Upson	1826-1910
HALE		
Andrew	Troup	1832-48
Christopher	Oglethorpe	1807-26
Hugh H.	Lee	1854-1955
John	Paulding	1850-77
Jonas	Walton	1870-74
Joseph	Pike	1844-76
Josey	Jasper	1820-23
Mary	Screven	1810-1929
Obed	Walton	1870-74
Samuel	Richmond	1840-53
Thomas	Fayette	1828-97
Thompson	Gwinnett	1852-86
HALEY		
John W.	Franklin	1848-67
Josiah	Franklin	1786-1813
William	Elbert	1830
HALL		
Absalom	Glynn	1844-53
Addie B. Mrs.	Screven	1810-1929
Alexander	Meriwether	1831-59
Annie Mrs.	Washington	1852-1903
Benjamin	Baldwin	1843
Christina	Pike	1844-76
Daniel M.	Marion	1846-1915
David	Glynn	1844-53
Drury R.	Murray	1840-72
Elisha	Greene	1806-16

HALL (continued)		
Elizabeth	Elbert	1832
Enoch J.	Randolph	1845-94
Gemper	Emanuel	1828
Hansford A.	Wilkinson	1908
Hugh	Greene	1798
Ignatius	Thomas	1837-45
Instance	Appling	1877-1925
Isaac	Wilkinson	1868
J. W.	Chattooga	1856-1924
James	Hancock	1840
James	Montgomery	1806-63
James	Thomas	1837-45i
Jeremiah	Madison	1811-40
Jeremiah	Madison	1812-41
Jeremiah	Sumter	1838-55
John	Hancock	1833
John	Jasper	1823-33
John	Wilkinson	1850
John W.	Lumpkin	1845-1923
Josiah A.	Stewart	1850-90
Josie	Wilkinson	1910
Kindred	Thomas	1837-45
Lucy	Taliaferro	1826-66
M. O. Mrs.	Cobb	1874i
Mary Louise	Washington	1852-1903
Matthew	Franklin	1786-1813
Pool	Jefferson	1800
Rabun W.	Washington	1852-1903
Raleigh	Bartow	1836-85
Richard A.	Randolph	1845-94
Robert P.	Crawford	1835-52
Samuel	Hancock	1814
Seaborn	Appling	1877-1925
Selina P.	Bibb	1823-55
Simeon	Elbert	1829-60
Thomas	Tattnall	1836-40
Thomas F.	DeKalb	1840-69
Thomas Lent	Warren	1799
W. F.	Polk	1857-1936
William Bennett	Washington	1852-1903
William H.	Franklin	1786-1813
William R.	Washington	1852-1903
HALLEY		
B. J.	Marion	1846-1915
J. M.	Marion	1846-1915
Samuel	Hancock	1802
HALLOWAY		
William	Jasper	1825-31
HALLUMS		
William	Lumpkin	1845-1923
HALSON		
Joakin et al	Franklin	1786-1813
HALSTEAD		
Jonathan	Jones	1810-28
HAM		
Benjamin	Troup	1832-48
John	Elbert	1821
HAMAN		
Susanna	Madison	1842-96
HAMBLETON		
Barton	Clarke	1822-42
Robert	Morgan	1808-13
HAMBRICK		
Charles	Lincoln	1796-1808
James M.	Coweta	1828-48 retn
John	Lincoln	1796-1808
Joseph	Greene	1786-95
M. C.	Pike	1823-29

HAMBY
D. C.	Cobb	1864i
John	Lumpkin	1845-1923
P. T. (minors of)	Cobb	1866i

HAMER
Z. A. E. Mrs.	Marion	1845-1915

HAMES
Cysander	McIntosh	1873-1915
J. B.	Chattooga	1856-1924

HAMIE
Clarissa	Pike	1844-76

HAMIL
Clark	Pike	1844-76

HAMILTON
A. N.	Habersham	1847-1900
Adin	Houston	1855-96
Ann	Wilkes	1819-36
Clarissa	Montgomery	1806-63
Duke	Hancock	1813
F.	Glynn	1844-53
George	Oglethorpe	1793-1807
Henry	Colonial	1760
James	Elbert	1816
John	Hancock	1811
John	Harris	1850-75
John	Newton	1823-51
John	Warren	1826
Josiah	Montgomery	1806-63
Matthew T.	Gwinnett	1852-86
Moses	Meriwether	1831-59
Nancy	Newton	1823-51
S. J.	Chattooga	1854-1924
Stewart	Montgomery	1806-63
Rebecca	Newton	1823-51
William	Hancock	1809
William	Pulaski	1812-17
Winny	Jasper	1812-17

HAMLIN
John Sr.	Jones	1812-23
John E.	Houston	1827-55
Richard Sr.	Jones	1812-23

HAMM
Elizabeth	Early	1834-1902

HAMMETT
James	Baldwin	1807

HAMMOCK
Benedict	Wilkes	1792-1801
Benjamin	Walton	1827-39 admr
Gracie E. Mrs.	Marion	1846-1915
Jeremiah	Butts	1826-41
Mary	Crawford	1835-52
Rebecca D.	Crawford	1852-94
Robert Sr.	Wilkes	1792-1801
Samuel	Lincoln	1796-1805
Susan Mrs.	Carroll	1852-96
Talbot D.	Crawford	1852-1894
Travis Sr.	Walton	1834-9
Willoby	Franklin	1786-1813

HAMMOND
Abner	Baldwin	1819
Abner H.	Bibb	1851-71
John	Dooly	1847-1901
Mary	Richmond	1840-53
Samuel	Henry	1834-69
Thomas	Morgan	1830-60

HAMMONS
Jacob	Lincoln	1796-1805
Jacob	Wilkes	1819-36

HAMON
Henry	Crawford	1835-52

HAMPTON
A. A.	Polk	1857-1936
Andrew	Laurens	1809-40
George	Madison	1842-96
Jacob	Houston	1855-96
James	Burke	1853-70
Joseph P.	Upson	1826-1910
Sarah L.	Stewart	1850-90
Thomas	Wilkes	1779-92

HAMRICK
E. Mrs.	Polk	1857-1936
J. D. Sr.	Carroll	1852-96
James M. Sr.	Carroll	1852-96
John M.	Polk	1857-1936

HANCOCK
Andrew	Randolph	1845-94
Anthony	Jefferson	1806
Charner T.	Clayton	1859-1921
James	Wilkes	1819-36
John Sr.	Lincoln	1808-32
Joseph	Houston	1829-55
Joseph	Wilkinson	1840
Major	Hall	1837-67
Margarett	Houston	1829-55
Richardson	Madison	1842-96
William	Crawford	1852-94

HAND
B. E.	Floyd	1852-61
Joseph	Henry	1834-69
Joseph	Marion	1846-1915
Sherod	Carroll	1852-96
William R. L.	Appling	1877-1925

HANDBREAK
Tarpley	Macon	1856-1909

HANDS
Richard	Pulaski	1816-50

HANDY
Jacob	McIntosh	1873-1915

HANES
A. R.	Clayton	1859-1921
Alsey	Early	1856-1927
H. C.	Houston	1855-96
Thomas	Early	1856-1927
W. A.	Clayton	1859-1921

HANEY
A. J.	Cobb	1869i
Daniel J.	Cobb	1877i
M. H.	Floyd	1861-71
Martha	Cobb	1874 minors
William	Cobb	1866i

HANGEL
Sarah	Tattnall	1836-40i

HANNAH
G. W. T.	Upson	1826-1910
Sanford	Gwinnett	1852-86
Thomas	Clarke	1802-22
Thomas	Jefferson	1817

HANNAN
Samuel B.	Cobb	1877
W. W.	Bartow	1836-85

HANNICK
Mary D.	Clayton	1859-1921

HANSARD

Jane	Elbert	1826
John	Elbert	1829–60
William	Elbert	1798

HANSELL

A. J.	Lumpkin	1833–52
Caroline Mrs.	Cobb	1866i

HANSFORD

Benoni	Jones	1812–23
Charles P.	Upson	1826–1910

HANSON

Edward	Morgan	1808–13
Fielding T.	Sumter	1838–55 bonds
James	Morgan	1830–60
John	Wilkes	1810–16
Mary	Wilkes	1819–36
Phillip H.	Oglethorpe	1833–66
Samuel	Morgan	1814–30
Thomas	Jackson	1802–60
Thomas	Newton	1823–51
William	Morgan	1830–40

HAPP

P.	Washington	1852–1903

HARALSON

Bradley	Morgan	1830–60
Clara Mrs.	Troup	1832–48
David C.	Troup	1832–48
Hiram	Randolph	1845–94
Jonathan	Greene	1817–42
Jonathan	Troup	1832–48
Vincent	Walton	1834–9

HARBER

John	Bartow	1836–85
Seaborn J.	Coweta	1849–92

HARBICT

Thomas	Hancock	1799

HARBIN

B. T.	Cobb	1866 minors
John N.	Telfair	1869–1921
Richard G.	Cobb	1866i
Richard M. et al	Cobb	1866 minors
William	Elbert	1820

HARBUCK

Nicholas	Warren	1822

HARDAGE

George W.	Cobb	1889

HARDAMAN

Parkin G.	Madison	1842–96

HARDAWAY

Francis	Meriwether	1831–59
Levi	Morgan	1830–60

HARDEE

John	Camden	1829–68
Sarah	Camden	1829–68

HARDEGREE

Thomas C.	Gwinnett	1852–86

HARDEMAN

John	Oglethorpe	1793–1807

HARDEN

Effie	Talbot	--
Hattie Mrs.	Cobb	1903
James	Pike	1844–76
Mark	Warren	1813

HARDEN (continued)

Martin	Franklin	1786–1813
Moses J.	Harris	1850–75
R. R.	Cobb	1879
Sally	Oglethorpe	1807–26
William	Franklin	1786–1813

HARDIE

John	Wilkinson	1851
Lorenzo	Wilkinson	1890
William	Stewart	1837–49
William M.	Stewart	1850–90 nunc

HARDIMAN

Thomas	Pike	1823–29

HARDIN

Jacob M.	Lumpkin	1845–1923
John	Oglethorpe	1807–26
John	Stewart	1850–90
John Sr.	Bartow	1836–85
Martin L.	Bibb	1823–55
William	Bartow	1836–85

HARDISON

James W.	Houston	1855–96
John M.	Early	1834–1902
Seth	Early	1834–1902
W. J.	Houston	1855–96
William B.	Marion	1846–1915

HARDMAN

Hariett M.	Cobb	1864 minor
James	Cobb	1863 minor
John	Oglethorpe	1793–1807
John J.	Cobb	1864 minor
Naaman	Oglethorpe	1793–1807
Robert S.	Oglethorpe	1833–66
Uriah	Cobb	1871i
William	Oglethorpe	1807–26

HARDWICK

Charles W.	Stewart	1850–90
William	Greene	1796–1806
William	Hancock	1825
William P.	Washington	1852–1903
Z. S.	Washington	1852–1903

HARDY

Carrie E.	Henry	1834–69
Edward	Putnam	1808–22
Jesse Sr.	Lincoln	1808–32
John	Bibb	1851–71
Sarah	Lincoln	1808–32
Whitmell	Bibb	1823–55

HARFORD

Thomas	Oglethorpe	1793–1807

HARGIS

Milton	Bartow	1836–85

HARGRAVES

Abraham J.	Ware	1879–1915
George Sr.	Muscogee	1847

HARGROVE

Asbury	Cobb	1879
Dewitt O.	Floyd	1852–61
Henry	Burke	1853–70
James	Franklin	1786–1813
James	Jackson	1802–60
Pleasant Wall	Jefferson	--
Z. B.	Bartow	1836–85

HARKNESS

Amanda H.	Cobb	1902

HARLOW		
Cinthia	Cobb	1897
T. B.	Cobb	1874i
HARMAN		
Charles	Oglethorpe	1807-26
Michael	Stewart	1850-90
William M.	Macon	1856-1909
HARN		
Martha	Greene	1806-16
HARNESBERGER		
Mary	Lincoln	1808-32
HAROLD		
Susan E. Mrs.	Houston	1855-96
HARP		
Dixon	Upson	1826-1910
Henry	Warren	1805
Warren J.	Lowndes	1871-1915
William	Bartow	1836-85
William	Henry	1822-34
William	Pike	1844-76
HARPE		
Falby	Chattooga	1856-1924
HARPER		
Armsted R.	Floyd	1861-71
B. F.	Fayette	1828-97
Bannister	Wilkes	1792-1801
Benjamin	Hancock	1827
Catharine	Sumter	1838-55 bonds
Edmond	Elbert	1829-60
Elijah	Chattooga	1856-1924
Elizabeth	Harris	1850-75
Fannie	Clayton	1859-1921
G. H.	Clayton	1859-1921
George	Clarke	1802-22
George	Jones	1826-50
H. S.	Lee	1854-1955
Henry A.	Newton	1823-51
James	Wayne	1822-70
John	Richmond	1840-53
John	Troup	1832-48
John P.	Elbert	1801
John W. Sr.	Clarke	1822-42
Martha	Lincoln	1808-32
Mary	Hancock	1836
Mildredge	Upson	1826-1910
Miles	Chattooga	1856-1924
Nancy	Lincoln	1831-69
Pleasant	Wilkes	1792-1801
Rhoda	Henry	1834-69
Robert	Greene	1806-16
Sally	Elbert	1802
William	Lincoln	1808-32
HARRAL		
James	Jasper	1822-26
HARRELL		
Amarah	Chattooga	1856-1924
Barbara	Upson	1826-1910
H.	Dooly	1847-1901
Hardy	Bibb	1823-55
James L.	Lumpkin	1845-1923
Jane	Early	1856-1927
Jesse	Stewart	1837-49
Miles	Pulaski	1816-50
Reuben	Wilkinson	1838
Samuel	Crawford	1852-94
Thomas	Muscogee	1838-62
HARRELSON		
William	Montgomery	1806-63

HARRINGTON		
Alfred	Lumpkin	1845-1923
Druryr of Amanda	Lincoln	1808-32
Jackson	Cobb	1879
Wiley A.	Hall	1837-67
HARRIS		
A.	Forsyth	1833-44i
Absolom	Hancock	1818
Agnes	Morgan	1814-30
Alexander Robert	Lee	1854-1955
Bennett Dr.	Jefferson	1843
Brittain	Jasper	1822-26
C.	Forsyth	1833-44i
Charles	Forsyth	1833-44i
Churchwell	Washington	1852-1903
David	Newton	1823-51
David	Wilkes	1779-92
E. G.	Clayton	1859-1921
Edwin	Jones	1812-23
Eli	Putnam	1823-56
Elisha	Hancock	1811
Francis	Colonial	1771
G. J.	Macon	1856-1909
George	Greene	1796-1806
George	Warren	1817
Gilford	Clayton	1859-1921
Graves	Morgan	1814-30
H. W.	Paulding	1850-77 appr
Henry	Meriwether	1831-59
Henry P.	Lincoln	1831-69
Hope	Polk	1857-1936
Isaac	Jefferson	1812
Isham	Jasper	1825-31
J. A.	Polk	1857-1936
J. Wiley	Warren	1834
James	Lincoln	1796-1805
James	Sumter	1838-55 bonds
James D.	Chattooga	1856-1924
James L.	Polk	1857-1936
James M.	Crawford	1835-52
James M.	Lumpkin	1845-1923
James Taylor	Houston	1855-96
Jerry (Col)	Gwinnett	1852-86
Jesse	Jackson	1802-60
Joel	Wilkes	1779-92
John	Glynn	1844-53
John	Harris	1850-75
John	Morgan	1830-60
John	Oglethorpe	1807-26
John	Pike	1844-76
Jordan	Greene	1817-42
Joseph	Jackson	1802-60
Joshua	Early	1856-1927
Joshua	Jones	1812-23
Lewis	Richmond	1840-53
M. H.	Bartow	1836-85
Margaret L.	Cobb	1877i
Mary	Wilkes	1837-77
Mary S.	Washington	1852-1903
Matthew	Coweta	1849-92
Matthew	Greene	1806-16
Morris	Fayette	1828-97
Nelson	Hancock	1820
O. F.	Clayton	1859-1921
Ralph	Morgan	1814-30
Rebecca	Clarke	1802-22
Richard	Jones	1826-50
Richard	Washington	1852-1903
Robert	Fayette	1828-97
Robert	Wilkes	1819-36
S. Y.	Cobb	1869i
Samuel	Greene	1786-95
Samuel	Hancock	1829
Samuel H.	Wayne	1822-70i
Sarah R.	Walton	1827-39
Simon	Houston	1855-96
Stephen W.	Putnam	1823-56
T. A.	Bibb	1851-71

HARRIS (continued)

Thomas	Baldwin	1816
Thomas	Greene	1806-16
Thomas E. K.	Bartow	1836-85
Thomas W.	Pike	1844-76
Thomas W.	Walton	1827-39
(in right of his wife, est of C. Hobson)		
Tyre	Coweta	1849-92
Walton	Greene	1806-16
William	Greene	1817-42
William	Houston	1855-96
William	Morgan	1814-30
William	Pike	1844-76
William	Richmond	1840-53
William T.	Crawford	1852-94
William Thomas Sr.	Liberty	1772-1887

HARRISON

B. T.	Bartow	1836-85
Benjamin	Warren	1833
Benjamin F.	Oglethorpe	1833-66
Charity	Randolph	1845-94
Coleman	Jackson	1802-60
D. M.	Clayton	1859-1921
Eli	Glynn	1844-53
Elizabeth	Newton	1823-51
F. E.	Cobb	1909
G. B.	Washington	1852-1903
Henry	Pulaski	1816-50
Jacob	Newton	1823-51
James	Butts	1826-41
James	Hancock	1816
James L.	Gwinnett	1852-86
James M.	Macon	1856-1909
James P.	Lumpkin	1845-1923
John	Jackson	1802-60
John B.	Sumter	1838-55 bonds
John E.	Washington	1852-1903
Joseph	Jackson	1802-60
Joseph	Jones	1826-50
Joseph	Taliaferro	1826-66
Joseph	Washington	1852-1903
Maria	Cobb	1873
Mary	Taliaferro	1826-66
Mary Ann	Muscogee	1838-62
Nathan	Murray	1840-72
Nathaniel	Campbell	1825-1900
Nathaniel	Putnam	1823-56
Oliver	Franklin	1848-67
Polly	Fayette	1828-97
Sarah	Tattnall	1836-40i
Thomas F.	Glynn	1844-53
Tillmann	Jackson	1802-60
W. H. Jr.	Macon	1856-1909
William	Pulaski	1816-50
William	Stewart	1850-90
William D.	Washington	1852-1903

HARSHAW

Aaron W.	Floyd	1852-61
Sidney S.	Union	1877-1942

HART

Archibald	Madison	1842-96
Barnabas	Marion	1846-1915
Eli	Taliaferro	1826-66
Fannie W.	Marion	1846-1915
Harris J.	Madison	1842-96
John	Liberty	1772-1887
Robert	Jones	1826-50
S. W.	Washington	1852-1903
Samuel	Carroll	1852-96
Samuel	Hancock	1807
Susannah	Taliaferro	1826-66
Warren	Jones	1826-50

HARTLEY

Arthur	Lee	1855-1955

HARTLEY (continued)

Isaac	Fayette	1828-97
James D.	Crawford	1852-94
Jonas B.	Washington	1852-1903
Mary A. J.	Washington	1852-1903
Mary T.	Bibb	1851-71

HARTSFIELD

Berry	Oglethorpe	1833-66
D. T.	Clayton	1859-1921
Godfrey	Henry	1834-69
Godfrey	Wilkes	1818-19
James M.	Cobb	1863 minor
Moses A.	Cobb	1864i

HARTWELL

James	Hall	1819-37

HARTY

Edward	Warren	1842
Mary	Wilkes	1837-77

HARVARD

Jordan F.	Dooly	1847-1901

HARVELL

James	Greene	1806-16
L. S. L.	Clayton	1859-1921

HARVES

Bennett	Lincoln	1808-32
Isaac	Lincoln	1808-32
Spencer	Lincoln	1808-32

HARVEY

Blassingame Sr.	Jefferson	1799
Charles	Jefferson	1800
E. W.	Macon	1856-1909
Evan	Putnam	1808-22
Hamilton	Macon	1856-1909
J. M.	Marion	1846-1915
James	Baldwin	1808
James	Hancock	1807
Jeremiah C.	Houston	1813
John	Clarke	1822-42
John C.	Hancock	1813
John H.	Pulaski	1816-50
John P.	Jefferson	1812
Judith	Clarke	1822-42
M. M.	Marion	1846-1915
M. P.	Campbell	1825-1900
Mary	Lee	1854-1955
Michael	Baldwin	1810
Mollie M. Mrs.	Marion	1846-1915
Moses	Marion	1846-1915
Rebecca L.	Randolph	1845-94
Richard	Crawford	1852-94
Sarah	Sumter	1838-55
Sarah Savannah	Randolph	1845-94
T. W.	Marion	1846-1915
William	Clarke	1802-22
William	Colonial	1744
Zephemiah	Jasper	1831-9

HARVIE

Frederick	Jackson	1802-60
Martha	Oglethorpe	1793-1807
Richard	Oglethorpe	1793-1807

HARVILL

Ellis	Wilkinson	1873

HARVILLE

Mason	Jasper	1820-23

HARWELL

Isham	Hancock	1816
James R.	Putnam	1823-56
John	Colonial	1755

HARWELL (continued)		
Littleton T. P.	Morgan	1830-60
Mark	Oglethorpe	1833-66
Mason	Jasper	1820-23

HARY

Allen	Lumpkin	1845-1923

HASELDEN

S. M. B.	Pike	1844-76

HASLAM

Frank	Houston	1855-96

HASSELL

William	Jones	1812-23

HATAWAY

Baton	Washington	1852-1903

HATHAWAY

Henry B.	Pulaski	1816-50

HATCH

HATCHER

James	Camden	1829-68
James	Wilkinson	1842
Jesse	Jefferson	1815
Priss Mrs.	Jefferson	1833
Samuel J.	Muscogee	1838-62
Valentine	Jefferson	1812

HATCHETT

Edward	Wilkes	1837-77
John	Bartow	1836-85

HATFIELD

George W.	Wilkinson	1909
Lucy S.	Wilkinson	1876
Richard	Wilkinson	1848
Samuel W.	Wilkinson	1873

HATILY

John	Carroll	1852-96

HATTAWAY

Walter L.	Campbell	1825-1900

HATTON

Robert	Meriwether	1831-59

HAUGHTON

William M.	Harris	1850-75

HAVER

Timothy	Putnam	1808-22

HAVIGAL

Sarah	Tattnall	1800-35 deeds

HAWES

John	Lincoln	1831-69
Laton	Lincoln	1831-69
N.	Lincoln	1808-32

HAWK (or Hawks)		
Catherine	Randolph	1845-94
Chester	Bartow	1836-85

HAWKINS

Alexander	Oglethorpe	1793-1807
Alexander	Oglethorpe	1807-26
Benjamin P.	Jones	1812-23
Hardress	Hancock	1817
Henry	Washington	1852-1903
J. M.	Chattooga	1856-1924
Jasper N.	Chattooga	1856-1924
Jesse	Pike	1844-76

HAWKINS (continued)		
John	Oglethorpe	1833-66
John W.	Walton	1827-39
Julia E.	Chattooga	1856-1924
Mary	Oglethorpe	1807-26
Nicholas	Putnam	1823-56
Samuel	Jones	1812-23
Thomas D.	Camden	1868-1916

HAWS

C.	Jones	1826-50
Clayborn	Baldwin	1826
J. H.	Murray	1840-72
L. B.	Bartow	1836-85
Littleton	DeKalb	1840-69

HAWSON

Samuel	Henry	1834-69

HAWTHORNE

James	Gwinnett	1852-86
Mahalia	Wilkinson	1885

HAY

Catherine	Wilkes	1819-36
David P.	Randolph	1845-94
Gilbert	Franklin	1786-1813
Gilbert	Wilkes	1819-36
James	Sumter	1838-55
William	Oglethorpe	1793-1807

HAYDEN

George	Jackson	1802-60
William	Jackson	1802-60

HAYES

Calvin	Camden	1868-1916
George N.	Polk	1857-1936
J. O.	Cobb	1878i
James	Franklin	1786-1813
Martha A.	Washington	1852-1903

HAYLES

Margaret J.	Pulaski	1816-50

HAYMAND

Elisha	Burke	1853-70

HAYNES

D.	Oglethorpe	1807-26
Elizabeth	Oglethorpe	1807-26
Henry	Greene	1806-16
Henry	Lee	1854-1955
John	Early	1856-89
		admrs bonds
John B.	Lee	1854-1955
Letty	Elbert	1829-60
Lunna M.	Stewart	1850-90
Mamye	Lee	1854-1955
Milly A. C.	Forsyth	1833-44
Moses	Elbert	1829
Robert	Oglethorpe	1833-66
Thomas	Warren	1822
William P.	Washington	1852-1903

HAYNIE

Charles	Oglethorpe	1833-66

HAYS

Alexander	Early	1834-1902
Archibald	Wilkes	1819-36
G.	Thomas	1837-45
George	Jackson	1802-60
Hugh	Greene	1817-42
Josiah	Appling	1877-1925
Richard	Clarke	1802-22
William W.	Upson	1826-1910

HAYSLIP		
Jonas	Lee	1854-1955

HAYSRADT		
Jacob W.	Polk	1857-1936

HAZLEHURST		
Couper	Glynn	1844-53
R. & J. H.	Bibb	1851-71
Robert	Bibb	1851-71

HAZLERIG		
F. A.	Macon	1856-1909

HAZZARD		
John R.	Glynn	1844-53

HEAD		
Amanda	Lumpkin	1845-1923
Baldwin B.	Morgan	1830-60
Benjamin	Campbell	1825-1900
C. A. J.	Lumpkin	1845-1923
Charles	Lumpkin	1845-1923
Harrison	Gwinnett	1852-86
James	Elbert	1795
James Sr.	Morgan	1830-60
James D.	Pike	1844-76
James W.	Fayette	1828-97
John	Upson	1826-1910
Kitty	Lumpkin	1845-1923
Martha Virginia	Morgan	1830-60
Thomas	Putnam	1823-56
W. K. P.	Lumpkin	1845-1923

HEAKS		
Hillery	Washington	1829-71 divs

HEALD		
William G.	Sumter	1838-55

HEALY		
Michael M.	Jones	1826-50

HEARD		
Abraham	Greene	1817-42
Barnard	Wilkes	1779-92
Charles	Butts	1826-41
Charles	Wilkes	1792-1801
Eliza	Jackson	1802-60
Faulkner	Morgan	1814-30
George	Screven	1810-1929
George	Wilkes	1779-92
Isaac (Col)	Wilkes	1837-77
James	Houston	1827-55
Jesse	Wilkes	1779-92
Jesse	Wilkes	1837-77
John	Jasper	1823-33
John	Troup	1832-48
John	Wilkes	1779-92
John	Wilkes	1792-1801
Joseph	Morgan	1830-60
Richard	Jackson	1802-60
Stephen	Butts	1826-41
Stephen	Morgan	1814-30
Thomas	Greene	1806-16
Thomas	Jasper	1813-19
William	Jackson	1802-60
William	Thomas	1837-45i

HEARN		
Asa	Henry	1822-34
Asa	Putnam	1823-56
Benjamin	Putnam	1823-56
Elizabeth	Henry	1822-34
Jonathan	Putnam	1823-56
Joshua	Coweta	1849-92
Lot	Putnam	1823-56
Nancy J.	Campbell	1825-1900
Phebe	Putnam	1823-56

HEARN (continued)		
Seth	Putnam	1823-56

HEARNE		
Osborne	Henry	1834-69

HEARNSBURGER		
Stephen	Upson	1826-1910

HEATH		
Abraham	Warren	1807
C. F.	Sumter	1838-55
Elizabeth	Meriwether	1831-59
F. M.	Lee	1854-1955
Henry	Washington	1852-1903
Isaac L.	Burke	1853-70
Joel	Warren	1810
John A.	Screven	1810-1929
John B.	Talbot	--
Jordan	Burke	1853-70
Moenetius (?)	Campbell	1825-1900
Richard	Hall	1819-37
Richard	Jasper	1826-31
Richard	Warren	1807
Stirling	Putnam	1808-22
William	Newton	1823-51
William	Warren	1813

HEATON		
John R.	Polk	1857-1936

HEEKS		
Grace	Crawford	1852-94

HEETH		
William	Warren	1813
William	Warren	1838

HEFLER		
Wiley	Henry	1834-69

HEISLER		
Daniel	Macon	1856-1909
Elbert	Lee	1854-1955

HELMS		
Uriah	Muscogee	1847

HELTON		
H. J.	Lumpkin	1845-1923
Sarah	Jones	1826-50

HELVESTON		
Joseph Jr.	Effingham	1829-59
McGillis	Camden	1868-1916

HEMBREE		
Cicero	Cobb	1869 minor
Elizabeth J.	Cobb	1867i
S. G.	Cobb	1868
Warren W.	Cobb	1866

HEMPHILL		
C. E. Mrs.	Chattooga	1856-1924
Edmund	Franklin	1786-1813
Elizabeth	Morgan	1830-60
Samuel	Morgan	1814-30
Thomas	Lincoln	1808-32

HENDALL		
Jarred	Early	1856-89 L/A

HENDERSON		
A. H.	Jackson	1802-60
Andrew J.	Fayette	1828-97
Brock	Early	1834-1902 bonds
Cynthia A. Mrs.	Screven	1810-1929
D. B.	Cobb	1873 minor
David	Jackson	1802-60

HENDERSON (continued)		
E. L.	Polk	1857-1936
Greenville	DeKalb	1840-69
Helen B.	Wilkes	1837-77
James	Putnam	1808-22
James D.	Jackson	1802-60
John	Hancock	1824
John	Jasper	1820-23
John	Jasper	1820-23 minor
John G.	Jackson	1802-60
John W.	Cobb	1877 minor
Joseph	Wilkes	1837-77
Josiah	Jackson	1802-60
Mitchell	Fayette	1828-97
Richard	Henry	1822-34
Richard	Henry	1834-69
Robert	Madison	1842-96
Robert J.	Clayton	1859-1921
S. S.	Cobb	1872i
Samuel	Jackson	1802-60
Samuel R.	Jackson	1802-60
Simeon	Elbert	1831
Susan Adaline	Chattooga	1856-1924
T. P.	Chattooga	1856-1924

HENDLEY (Henly, Hendly)		
Abraham	Emanuel	1866 L/A
Edmund	Franklin	1786-1813
Hartford	Chattooga	1856-1924
John	Emanuel	1866 L/A
John	Stewart	1850-90
John Sr.	Wilkes	1806-08
S. B.	Chattooga	1856-1924
William	Pulaski	1816-50

HENDON		
Andrew	Troup	1832-48
Isham	Clarke	1802-22
Robinson	Oglethorpe	1833-66
Robinson	Troup	1832-48
Zurah	Lumpkin	1845-1923 admx

HENDRICK (Hendricks)		
Benjamin	Wilkes	1779-92
G. W.	Lumpkin	1845-1923
Hugh	Henry	1822-2¾34
Humphrey	Oglethorpe	1807-26
Isaac	Franklin	1786-1813
Jack	Franklin	1786-1813
Jacob	Franklin	1786-1813
Jacob P.	Muscogee	1838-62
James	Wilkes	1806-08
John	Floyd	1852-61
Julius	Polk	1857-1936
Kitty	Wilkes	1819-36
Sarah Elizabeth	Randolph	1845-94
Warren D.	Union	1877-1942

HENDRIX		
Barnett	Franklin	1848-67
Edmund	Clarke	1802-22
Elizabeth	Early	1834-1902 bonds
Fennel	Jackson	1802-60
Gilbert	Early	1834-1902 bonds
James	Early	1834-1902 bonds
James	Franklin	1848-67
James	Jasper	1825-31
Mary	Early	1834-1902 bonds
Seaborn	Early	1834-1902 bonds

HENDRY		
Alexander	Randolph	1845-94
Robert	Liberty	1772-1887
Robert Lee	Harris	1850-75

HENRI		
Marguerite Jean	Colonial	1772

HENRY		
Dexter	Wilkes	1837-77
George	Troup	1832-48
James	Henry	1822-34
Lambert H.	Coweta	1849-92
Robert A.	Chattooga	1856-1924
Samuel	Coweta	1828-48
Samuel	Stewart	1850-90

HENSON		
Charles	Greene	1817-42
J. T.	Chattooga	1856-1924
John	Union	1877-1942
W. H.	Union	1877-1942

HEPBURN		
Joseph L.	Baldwin	1822

HERBERT		
R. G.	Polk	1857-1936

HERMUSSY		
John F.	Henry	1834-69

HERNDON		
Benjamin	Elbert	1804
Edward	Meriwether	1831-59
George	Appling	1877-1925
James	Chattooga	1856-1924
John	Marion	1846-1915

HERRIN		
H. L.	Ware	1879-1915

HERRING		
A.	Montgomery	1806-63
David	Walton	1870-74
Jack Ann	Dooly	1847-1901
William	Clarke	1802-22
William Asher	Elbert	1830

HERRINGTON		
Berry	Burke	1853-70
Cinderilla	Sumter	1833-55 admr
Ephraim	Emanuel	1829
Ephraim	Sumter	1838-55 bonds
J. B. Mrs.	Camden	1868-1916
Richard	Screven	1810-1929
Silas	Jefferson	1849

HERRON		
James	Colonial	1771

HERTZ		
Charles	Washington	1829-71 divs

HESLEP		
D. D.	Polk	1857-1936

HESTER		
Edith	Effingham	1829-59
James	Lincoln	1796-1805
Joseph	Effingham	1829-59
Rebecca	Laurens	1809-40
Samuel	Clarke	1822-42
Stephen	Clarke	1822-42
Stephen Sr.	Effingham	1829-59
Zachariah	Jones	1826-50

HEWETT		
Lavina B.	Lowndes	1871-1915

HEWEY		
Henry	DeKalb	1840-69
W. F.	Chattooga	1856-1924

HEWITT		
Caroline A.	Ware	1879-1915

HEWSTON		
James	Morgan	1830-60
HEYD		
George	Colonial	1770
HICKLIN		
R. H.	Washington	1829-71 divs
HICKMAN		
Aaron	Upson	1826-1910
William	Jackson	1802-60
HICKOX		
Johnathan	Ware	1879-1915
HICKS		
D. A.	Polk	1857-1936
Daniel	Clarke	1802-22
David A.	Polk	1857-1936
Green	Carroll	1852-96
John J.	Morgan	1814-30
Jones	Macon	1856-1909
Joseph	Jasper	1820-23
Joseph	Jasper	1822-26
M. T. Mrs.	Polk	1857-1936
Robert	Crawford	1835-52
Samuel	Upson	1826-1910
William	Troup	1832-40
William M.	Polk	1857-1936
HICKSON (Hixon)		
William	Colonial	1770
HIGDON		
C. H.	Dooly	1847-1901
Robert	Emanuel	1839 bill of sale
HIGG		
R. R.	Marion	1846-1915
HIGGINBOTHAM		
Benjamin	Elbert	1791
Benjamin	Elbert	1809
Jacob	Jasper	1823-33
Joseph	Jasper	1822-26
Robert	Jasper	1823-33
Samuel	Glynn	1829-60
Sarah	Elbert	1829-60
HIGGINS		
Cormack	Franklin	1786-1813
J. J.	Upson	1826-1910
Lucinda	Gwinnett	1852-86
Silas	Gwinnett	1852-86
V. O.	Lumpkin	1845-1923
Wiley G.	Macon	1856-1909
HIGH (Highs)		
Fielding	Lincoln	1808-32
John	Morgan	1830-60
HIGHNOTE		
Benjamin	Marion	1846-1915
HIGHSMITH		
H. H.	Wayne	1822-70
James	Elbert	1824
John	Wayne	1822-70
HIGHT		
Howell	Warren	1821
T. G.	Floyd	1861-71
HIGHTOWER		
Annie E.	Lowndes	1871-1915
D. H.	Early	1856-1927 bonds
Daniel	Harris	1850-75
Daniel	Pike	1844-76

HIGHTOWER (continued)		
Elias D.	Sumter	1838-55
Henry A.	Early	1856-1889
James	Upson	1826-1910
James M.	Pike	1844-76
Joel	Early	1856-1927
John	Stewart	1850-90
John J.	Upson	1826-1910
Kate Mrs.	Polk	1857-1936
Martha	Pike	1844-76
Thomas	Greene	1796-1806
HILBURN		
J. H.	Telfair	1869-1921
HILEY		
John	Macon	1856-1909
HILL		
A. R.	Stewart	1837-49
Abner	Wilkes	1779-92
Abraham Sr.	Wilkes	1792-1801
Adam	Bartow	1836-85
Adam	Ware	1879-1915
B. D.	Screven	1810-1929
Dennis	Floyd	1861-71
Elisha	Fayette	1828-97
Elisha	Macon	1856-1909
Elizabeth	Sumter	1838-55 bond
Frances	Coweta	1849-92
Frances	Greene	1806-16
George	Putnam	1808-22
Green	Houston	1855-96
Green	Troup	1832-40
Guilliam	Burke	1853-70
Henry	Warren	1801
Henry K.	Muscogee	1838-62
Isaac	Clarke	1822-42
Isaac	Jasper	1825-31
Isabell	Oglethorpe	1793-1807
J. E.	Glynn	1844-53
James	Early	1856-1927 bonds
James	Jasper	1823-33
James	Wilkes	1779-92
John	Cobb	1875i
(Sylvester, wid)		
John	Greene	1817-42
John	Putnam	1823-56
John	Troup	1832-48
John	Walton	1834-9
John W.	Cobb	1834
Mary E.	Cobb	1910
Miles	Oglethorpe	1833-66
Noah	Oglethorpe	1793-1807
Reuben J.	Lumpkin	1845-1923
Richard	Murray	1840-72
Richard A.	Camden	1829-68
Robert	Henry	1822-34
Robert J.	Sumter	1838-55 bonds
Samuel R.	DeKalb	1840-69
Sarah	Wilkes	1819-36
Silvester	Habersham	1847-1900
Slaughter	Macon	1856-1909
Theophilus	Jasper	1813-19
Theophilus	Walton	1827-31
Theophilus	Walton	1834-9
V. A.	Harris	1850-75
Wiley	Wilkes	1837-77
Wiley P.	Wilkes	1837-77
William	Jasper	1812-17
William	Jasper	1813-19
William N.	Fayette	1828-97
HILLHOUSE		
David P.	Wilkes	1837-77
Sarah	Wilkes	1819-36
HILLMAN		
Frances	Warren	1832

HILLMAN (continued)		
Winder Rev.	Warren	1822
HILSABECK		
Henry	Morgan	1830-60
HILSON		
John	Warren	1800
HILTON		
John C.	Randolph	1845-94
N. C.	Screven	1810-1929
Thomas	McIntosh	1873-1915
HILYARD		
Richard	Wilkes	1810-16
HINDEMAN		
John	Coweta	1849-92
HINDLEY		
Jacob	Wilkes	1818-19
HINDMON		
M. A.	Madison	1842-96
HINDSMEN		
Michael	Wilkes	1819-36
HINER		
Lewis	Jackson	1802-60
HINES		
Churchill	Washington	1852-1903
Elias	Jasper	1820-23
Elias D.	Harris	1850-75
George F.	Burke	1853-70
H. Augusta	Washington	1852-1903
James	Greene	1806-16
John	Jones	1810-28
John B.	Baldwin	1822
Joseph	Washington	1829-71 divs
Leonidas W.	Washington	1852-1903
Martha	Screven	1810-1929
Rachel	Burke	1853-70
Robert	Jasper	1820-23
Samuel	Harris	1850-75
Sterling	Decatur	1828-38
Thomas J. Sr.	Stewart	1850-90
W. H.	Polk	1857-1936
HINNARD		
John	Fayette	1828-97
HINSLEY		
Solomon	Effingham	1829-59
HINSON		
William	Telfair	1869-1921
HINTON		
Catherine J.	Chattooga	1856-1924
Demsy	Wilkes	1777-78
Demsy	Wilkes	1779-92
Hardey & L.	Henry	1822-34
Jacob	Campbell	1825-1900
James	Wilkes	1837-77
Micajah	Wilkes	1779-92
Robert	Warren	1798
Walter B.	Chattooga	1856-1924
Wiley P.	Chattooga	1856-1924
HIPPS		
Joseph Sr.	Bartow	1836-85
HIRSH		
Raphral	Cobb	1896
Sarah	Cobb	1874 minor

HITCHCOCK		
David	Hancock	1834
Jesse	Jasper	1826-31
Jesse	Walton	1827-39
Meshack	Hancock	1834
R. E.	Madison	1842-96
Turner R.	Washington	1829-71 divs
HIX		
John	Lincoln	1796-1808
Nathaniel	Madison	1842-96
William	Chattooga	1856-1924
HOADLEY		
Thomas	Jasper	1831-19
HOBBS		
Daniel	Crawford	1835-52
Jacob C.	Stewart	1850-90
HOBBY		
Eliza Miss	Screven	1810-1929
Elizabeth A.	Richmond	1840-53
Sarah A.	Screven	1810-1929
HOBGOOD		
Louis	Campbell	1825-1900
HOBSON		
C. (Thomas W. Harris, admr, in right of his wife)		
see below		
Christopher	Walton	1827-31
Christopher Dr.	Jasper	1822-26 inv
John	Colonial	1767
John	Jasper	1825-31
John	Jones	1821-23
N.	Jackson	1802-60
HODGE		
Ann	Madison	1812-41
D. H.	Bartow	1836-85
James	Jackson	1802-60
John	Clarke	1802-22
John	Elbert	1795
John	Greene	1817-42
William	Elbert	1794
William	Madison	1812-41
HODGES		
Ann	Greene	1806-16
Archibald	Tattnall	1836-40i
(gdn for Cornelia C., Elliott & Mary Duke)		
E. E. Mrs.	Houston	1855-96
Edmund E.	Sumter	1838-55 bond
Elbert	Dooly	1847-1901
Elias	Jefferson	1821
Elizabeth	Sumter	1838-55
Elton	Burke	1853-70
James	Newton	1823-51
Jesse	Houston	1855-96
John	Early	1856-1927
John	Meriwether	1831-59
John J.	Sumter	1838-55
Jordan	Stewart	1837-49
Joseph S.	Camden	1795-1829
Lawrence	Screven	1810-1929
Lydia	Randolph	1845-94
Mary	Tattnall	1800-34 deeds
Mary C.	Muscogee	1846
Richard	Jefferson	1824
Robert J.	Sumter	1838-55
Samuel R.	Muscogee	1840
Stephen L.	Early	--
Susannah	Jones	1826-50
HODGSON		
Margaret T.	Burke	1853-70

HODNETT		
Benjamin Sr.	Jasper	1820-23
HODO		
Peter	Warren	--
HOFF		
Charles	Oglethorpe	1833-66
HOGAN		
Isham T.	Walton	1834-9
James	Lincoln	1831-69
James	Paulding	1850-77 bond
John G. R.	Wilkinson	1858
Shadrack	Lincoln	1796-1808
William	Lincoln	1796-1808
HOGANS		
James Sr.	Coweta	1849-92
HOGE		
Martha T.	Carroll	1852-96
R. W. A.	Polk	1857-1936
HOGG		
Henry F.	Polk	1857-1936
James	Hancock	1803
John	Screven	1810-1929
William	Greene	1786-95
William	Polk	1857-1936
HOGUE		
Jacob	Clarke	1802-22
S. K. Sr.	Polk	1857-1936
HOKE		
Michael	Lee	1854-1955
HOLBROOK		
John	Franklin	1786-1813
HOLCOMB		
Robert W.	DeKalb	1840-69
Sherwood	Habersham	1847-1900
HOLCOMBE		
James	Richmond	1840-53
John	Lumpkin	1845-1923
HOLDER		
Jeremiah	Greene	1806-16
John	Clarke	1822-42
John D.	Jefferson	1852
Uriah B.	Stewart	1850-90
HOLDSTOCK		
James	Coweta	1828-48 retn
HOLEMAN		
David	Wilkes	1779-92
HOLIFIELD		
Wiley	Jasper	1831-9
HOLLADAY		
John	Jones	1826-50
Margaret	Warren	1803
Robert M.	Jackson	1802-60
HOLLAN		
John	Franklin	1786-1813
HOLLAND		
C. T.	Chattooga	1905
Elizabeth	Putnam	1823-56
Henry I.	Jasper	1823-33
J. J.	Polk	1857-1936
Jacob	Stewart	1837-49
James	Glynn	1844-53

HOLLAND (continued)		
Jerusha	Carroll	1852-96
John	Houston	1855-96
John	Tattnall	1839- inv
John Jr.	Tattnall	1836-40i
Lavinia	Jasper	1831-9
Martha	Baldwin	1853
Middleton	Hancock	1795
Wiley	Wilkinson	1883
HOLLEMAN		
Henry T.	Campbell	1825-1900
Richard S.	Campbell	1825-1900
HOLLENSWORTH		
George	Laurens	1809-40
HOLLEY		
Jonathan	Laurens	1809-40
HOLLIDAY		
Allen	Wilkes	1837-77
N. R.	Stewart	1850-90
William	Wilkes	1779-92
HOLLIFIELD		
H. N.	Washington	1852-1903
HOLLIMAN		
Barnett	Houston	1855-96
C. W.	Houston	1855-96
David	Wilkes	1777-78
David	Wilkinson	1858
Eaton	Stewart	1850-90
Harriett	Houston	1855-96
Lewis	Upson	1826-1910
Richard	Hancock	1798
Thomas J.	Wilkinson	1874
William	Upson	1826-1910
HOLLINGSHEAD		
S. A.	Bartow	1836-85
HOLLINGSWORTH		
Boyd	Franklin	1786-1813
Isaac	Screven	1810-1929
J.	Camden	1795-1829
Jacob	Franklin	1786-1813
Joseph	Newton	1823-51
Samuel	Franklin	1786-1813
Thomas	Franklin	1786-1813
HOLLIS		
Henry	Marion	1846-1915
Howell T.	Marion	1846-1915
Richard	Talbot	--
HOLLOMON		
Zachariah	Crawford	1835-52
HOLLON		
James A.	Dooly	1842-1901
HOLLOWAY		
A. P.	Polk	1857-1936
David	Jefferson	1825
Edward	Upson	1826-1910
Francis	Upson	1826-1910
Isom	Jasper	1812-17
Jesse	Jasper	1822-26
Jesse	Jasper	1825-31
Patrick G.	Upson	1826-1910
Peter	Upson	1826-1910
Reuben	Upson	1826-1910
Robert S.	Upson	1826-1910
Thomas	Greene	1796-1806
William	Jasper	1826-31
--	Troup	1832-48 (page 47 opp. 66)

HORNE (continued)
John E.	Sumter	1838-55 bonds
Mary	Sumter	1838-55 bonds

HORTON
Daniel	Stewart	1850-90
Harrell	Washington	1852-1903
Isaac	Washington	1852-1903
James	Elbert	1834
John	Wilkes	1792-1801
Nicholas	Colonial	1774
Prosser	Jackson	1802-60
R. C. Mrs.	Chattooga	1856-1924
Stephen	Baldwin	1815

HOSCH
J. J.	Chattooga	1856-1924
Mathew	Walton	1834-9

HOSKINS
Harrison D.	Houston	1827-55
John	Jones	1826-50
Paschal	Crawford	1852-94

HOTCHKISS
James T.	Lowndes	1871-1915

HOUDLETT
Warren R.	Lee	1854-1955

HOUGH
A. B. C.	Pulaski	1816-50
James	Talbot	1857

HOUGHTON
Elizabeth	Lincoln	1831-69
James	Greene	1796-1806
James	Oglethorpe	1793-1807
John W.	Richmond	1840-53
Joshua	Greene	1786-95
Joshua	Greene	1817-42
Matthew	Greene	1817-42
Thomas	Greene	1817-42
William	Greene	1806-16

HOUSE
Elizabeth	Stewart	1850-90
F. C.	Cobb	1883
Henry	Cobb	1890
Jacob	Cobb	1882
John	Cobb	1866i
(Elizabeth, wid)		
John G.	Cobb	1868i
Lewis	Lincoln	1831-69
Lott	Lincoln	1831-69
Thomas	Stewart	1850-90
William	Cobb	1876
William	Lincoln	1796-1805
William	Wilkes	1779-92
William T.	Cobb	1867 minor

HOUSER
D. H.	Houston	1855-96
Fred M.	Houston	1855-96
William A.	Houston	1855-96

HOUSTEIN
Rosalie	Ware	1879-1915

HOUSTON
Alexander	Coweta	1849-92
John	Coweta	1849-92
Martha	Coweta	1849-92
Samuel	Coweta	1849-92
Sarah	Coweta	1849-92

HOUSTOUN
Patrick Sir	Colonial	1761
Priscilla	Colonial	1772

HOWARD
Abel	Oglethorpe	1807-26
Abraham	Lumpkin	1845-1923
Amanda	Lumpkin	1845-1923
Anna Mrs.	Houston	1855-96
Benjamin	Baldwin	1808
Christine	Liberty	1772-1887
Elizabeth F.	Oglethorpe	1833-66
Francis	Putnam	1808-22
Hardy	Jackson	1802-60
Henry	Putnam	1823-56
Hezekiah	Screven	1810-1929
Hiram	Clarke	1802-22
J. Frank	Polk	1857-1936
John	Bibb	1823-55
John	Early	1856-1889
John	Franklin	1786-1813
John	Putnam	1823-56
John	Richmond	1791-5
John A.	Houston	1855-96
Joseph	Hancock	1803
Joseph	Morgan	1814-30
Lemuel	Washington	1852-1903
Louisa	Sumter	1838-55
Lucy H.	Oglethorpe	1833-66
M. Woodward	Franklin	1786-1813
Mary	Oglethorpe	1833-66
Michael	Houston	1827-55
Moses	Screven	1810-1929
N. T.	Lumpkin	1845-1923
Nemeah	Elbert	1796
Sarah	Jackson	1802-60
Sarah	Lee	1854-1955
Solomon	Washington	1829-71 divs
Starling	Morgan	1830-60
Stephen	Dooly	1847-1901
Thomas	Lincoln	1808-32
Willis Sr.	Jefferson	1824

HOWE
Robert	Wayne	1822-70
William	Greene	1796-1810
William J.	Pike	1844-76

HOWELL
Andrew	Lumpkin	1833-52
Ann	Greene	1817-42
Augusta	Cobb	1878 minors
Burwell	Upson	1826-1910
Casper	Upson	1826-1910
Catharine	Camden	1795-1829
Clement C.	Cobb	1867i
Daniel	Lumpkin	1845-1923
Daniel	Screven	1810-1929
Evan	Gwinnett	1852-86
Evan D.	Early	1856-1927
G. W.	Lowndes	1871-1915
Isaac	Cobb	1866i
J. Hannah	Chattooga	1856-1924
James	Sumter	1838-55
James	Wilkes	1779-92
Jesse B.	Upson	1826-1910
John	Colonial	1771
John	Houston	1827-55
John	Wilkinson	1850
Joseph	Hancock	1819
Joseph Sr.	Campbell	1825-1900
Lewis	Henry	1834-69
Matthew	Taliaferro	1826-66
Matthew C.	Taliaferro	1826-66
Nathaniel	Greene	1796-1806
William	Oglethorpe	1807-26

HOWSON
Elizabeth	Wilkes	1837-77

HOXLEY
Asa	Wilkes	1819-36

HOY		
William	Campbell	1825-1900

HOYLE		
Eli W.	DeKalb	1840-69

HOYT		
H. F.	Habersham	1847-1900

HUBANKS		
Lane	Dooly	1847-1901

HUBBARD		
Booker W.	Oglethorpe	1833-66
Catharine	Telfair	1869-1921
Claiborne Camp	Paulding	1850-77
Elihu	Camden	1829-68
James	Morgan	1830-60
John	Elbert	1794
John C.	Hall	1837-67
Joseph	Hall	1837-67
Joseph	Oglethorpe	1807-26
Mary Ann	Wilkes	1837-77
Sara	Wilkinson	1837
T. B.	Polk	1857-1936
Thomas	Greene	1817-42
William	Polk	1857-1936
Winnifred	Camden	1829-68
Woodson	Wilkes	1819-36
Woodson, admr of	--	--

HUBERT		
Benjamin	Warren	1793

HUBSON see Hudson

HUCKABA		
Lucrecy	Oglethorpe	1833-66

HUCKABEE		
Josiah	Hancock	1828
Sarah	Hancock	1832

HUCKABY		
Isham	Hancock	1801
James	Oglethorpe	1793-1807
William	Oglethorpe	1833-66

HUDDLESTON		
Selina	Meriwether	1831-59
William	Hancock	1805

HUDESTON		
William	Jefferson	1828

HUDGENS		
S. W.	Dooly	1847-1901

HUDLOW		
William B.	Lumpkin	1845-1923

HUDMAN		
A.	Henry	1834-69
John	Henry	1834-69

HUDNELL		
Patrick	Early	1856-1889

HUDSON		
Ann Mrs.	Clayton	1859-1921
Ann	Franklin	1786-1813
Charles	Putnam	1823-56
Cutherd	Elbert	1799
Eli	Jefferson	1833
Hillary H.	Randolph	1845-94
Irby	Putnam	1823-56
James	Bibb	1823-55
Joakin	Franklin	1786-1813
John	Laurens	1809-40

HUDSON (continued)		
John	Putnam	1823-56
John W.	Polk	1857-1936
Joshua	Franklin	1786-1813
L. W.	Putnam	1823-56
Lucy J.	Oglethorpe	1833-66
Martha	Jefferson	1844
(wid of Richard Sr.)		
Martha E.	Muscogee	1834
Phoebe	Hancock	1821
Richard	Houston	1855-96
Richard Sr.	Jefferson	1834
Robert	Coweta	1828-48
Ward	Meriwether	1831-59

HUDSPETH		
Charles	Jefferson	1811
William	Harris	1850-75
William	Wilkes	1806-08

HUEY		
Alexander B.	Harris	1850-75

HUFF		
Edward	Bibb	1823-55
Franklin	Pike	1844-76
James	Hancock	1825
Peter	Wilkes	1792-1801
Polly	Baldwin	1831
Thomas	Jasper	1813-19
Travis	Bibb	1851-71

HUFLIN (or Hefler)		
William J.	Henry	1834-69

HUGBY		
J. A.	Tattnall	1802-60

HUGENIN		
Edward D.	Bibb	1851-71
Julia	Bibb	1851-71

HUGER		
William	Early	1834-1902 bonds

HUGGINS		
Asa	Oglethorpe	1849-92
James	Oglethorpe	1849-92
William E.	Screven	1810-1929

HUGHES		
Alexander	Elbert	1829-60
Benjamin	Coweta	1849-92
David	Colonial	1764
G.	Lumpkin	1845-1923
Goodman	Lumpkin	1845-1923
James G.	Cobb	1894
Mariah	Ware	1879-1915
Robert	Wilkes	1818-19
Tharpe	Wilkes	1779-92
William	Wilkes	1810-16

HUGHIE		
H. J.	Coweta	1849 92
Thomas M.	Union	1877-1942

HUGHLEY		
Margaret	Pike	1844-76
Martha A.	Pike	1844-76
Susannah Mrs.	Pike	1844-76

HUGHRY		
Joseph	Walton	1827-39

HUGHS		
Francis M.	Bibb	1851-77
James	Lincoln	1796-1808
James	Morgan	1814-30
James T.	Wilkinson	1901

HUGHS (continued)

John P.	Wilkinson	1864
Mary Mrs.	Montgomery	1806-63
Nancy	Stewart	1850-90
Thomas	Lincoln	1796-1808
William	Sumter	1838-55

HUGULEY

Alley	Wilkes	1837-77
George	Lincoln	1808-32
John	Wilkes	1819-36
John J.	Upson	1826-1910
Rebecca	Wilkes	1837-77

HUIE

B. M.	Clayton	1859-1921
John M.	Clayton	1859-1921

HULING

Andrew	Harris	1850-75
James	Wilkes	1818-29

HULL

Sarah	Richmond	1840-53

HULME

John	Elbert	1829-60

HULSEY

Adler	Hall	1837-67
James J.	Hall	1837-67
Micajah	Paulding	1850-77

HUMAN

Bazzle	Elbert	1795
Susannah	Madison	1840-60

HUMLEY

William A.	Harris	1850-75

HUMPHREY

John	Madison	1812-41
Joseph	Jackson	1812-40
Rachel	Cobb	1875

HUMPHREYS

David	Murray	1840-72
James C.	Screven	1810-1929
Joab	Murray	1840-72

HUMPHRIES

J. R.	Cobb	1900
James T.	Screven	1810-1929

HUNLEY

Martha	Marion	1846-1915

HUNNICUTT

Littleton M.	Coweta	1849-92

HUNT

Alexander	Jones	1826-50
Aurora Strong	Lumpkin	1845-1923
Cicero A.	Cobb	1874 minor
Elijah	Elbert	1829-60
Elisha	Cobb	1872
Elizabeth	Bibb	1823-55
Elizabeth H.	Randolph	1845-94
George	Coweta	1828-48
James	Elbert	1818
Joel	Franklin	1786-1813
John	Greene	1817-42
John	Hancock	1799
Judson	Hancock	1817
Majer	Screven	1810-97
Moses	Elbert	1829-60
Nancy M.	Elbert	1829-60
Richardson	Elbert	1818
Silas F.	Washington	1852-1903

HUNT (continued)

Stephen A.	Polk	1857-1936
William	Washington	1852-1903
William W.	Harris	1850-75

HUNTER

A.	Henry	1822-34
Alexander	Henry	1822-34
Ambrose	Harris	1850-75
Beth	Talbot	--
Elisha	Greene	1817-42
Ephraim	Oglethorpe	1793-1807
Ephraim	Screven	1810-1929
George R.	Bibb	1851-71
Hardy	Houston	1855-96
J. L.	Cobb	1908
James	Glynn	1844-53
Job	Lincoln	1796-1805
Margaret Sophia	Habersham	1847-1900
Marvin	Union	1877-1942
Moses	Lowndes	1871-1915
Samuel	Bibb	1851-71
Samuel	Lincoln	1796-1805
Samuel B.	Bibb	1851-71
Thomas	Gwinnett	1852-86
Thomas T.	Wilkes	1837-77

HURLEY

Henry	Wilkes	1810-16
John	Wilkes	1806-08

HURST

Felix	Effingham	1829-59
George W.	Burke	1853-70
Jeremiah	Burke	1853-70
Thomas	Thomas	1837-45

HURT

Charles S.	Putnam	1823-56
Elisha	Warren	1829
Sarah	Putnam	1823-56

HUSK

Martha	Cobb	1891

HUSON

Charles B.	Baldwin	1850
Thomas	Cobb	1868i

HUSSEY

Hiram H.	Meriwether	1831-59

HUST

Henry	Washington	1829-71 divs

HUSTON

James	Colonial	1774
William	Glynn	1844-53

HUTCHESON

John	Madison	1842-96
Samuel	Greene	1794-1810

HUTCHING

Anthony	Early	1834-1902 bonds
Jefferson	Early	1856-1927

HUTCHINGS

Robert	Jones	1826-50
Robert	Polk	1857-1936

HUTCHINS

Andrew J.	Gwinnett	1852-86
David	Harris	1850-75
Elizabeth	Jefferson	1836
Henry	Early	--
J. C.	Chattooga	1856-1924
Mathew L. Sr.	Gwinnett	1852-86

HUTCHINSON		
Aaron	Emanuel	1866i
Arthur	Carroll	1852-96
Charles	Upson	1826-1910
F.	Clayton	1859-1921

HUTSON		
Caty	Clarke	1802-22

HUTTEN		
Elenor	Taliaferro	1826-66

HYDE		
Henry	Coweta	1849-92

HYMAN		
John	Warren	1831

INGERSOLL		
Elizabeth	Lumpkin	1845-1923

INGRAM		
D.	Forsyth	1833-44i
David	Wilkinson	1828
George	Jefferson	1820
Isaac	Lincoln	1796-1808
James Sr.	Jefferson	1827
John	Hancock	1827
John	Jefferson	1817
John	Putnam	1823-56
John L.	Henry	1834-69
John M.	Screven	1810-1929
Margaret	Talbot	--
Margarett	Marion	1846-1915
Mathew J.	Union	1877-1942
Thomas	Putnam	1823-56
Thomas G.	Polk	1857-1936
William	Hancock	1804
William	Harris	1850-75
William	Jefferson	1807
William	Wilkes	1779-92

INMAN		
Allen	Burke	1853-70
Mary A.	Washington	1852-1903
Sophia	Burke	1853-70

INSHEEP		
George	Elbert	1829

INZER		
Mark P.	Cobb	1877

IRBY		
Abraham	Greene	1806-16
Amanda	Cobb	1873i
Martha	Taliaferro	1826-66

IRVINE		
S. E. Mrs.	Cobb	1901

IRWIN		
Alexander	Washington	1829-71 divs
James	Morgan	1814-30
Jane	Bibb	1851-71
Margaret M.	Washington	1829-71 divs
Sally	Putnam	1808-22
Samuel	Clayton	1859-1921
Samuel	Jefferson	1822
Thomas A.	Houston	1827-55
Thomas L.	Marion	1846-1915

ISBELL		
James	Franklin	1848-67

ISLER		
Nathan W.	Wilkinson	1891
William	Pulaski	1816-50

ISOM		
William	Franklin	1786-1813
William	Talbot	1867

ISON		
Christian	Morgan	1814-30
John	Pike	1844-76

IUGH		
Paul	Franklin	1786-1813

IVES		
William A.	Upson	1826-1910

IVESTER		
George	Habersham	1847-1900

IVEY		
Anthony	Greene	1794-1810
Bythan	Jones	1826-50
Lot	Jasper	1812-17
Peoples	Warren	1834
Robert	Baldwin	1843
Sampson	Warren	1814

IVIE		
W. S.	Gwinnett	1852-86

IVY		
Marion	Lincoln	1831-69

JACK		
Samuel	Wilkes	1810-16

JACKSON		
Allen	Washington	1852-1803
Clark	Early	1834-1902
Daniel	Clayton	1858-1921
Daniel	Wilkes	1779-92
Daniel E.	DeKalb	1840-69
David	Greene	1817-42
David	Putnam	1808-22
David H.	Houston	1855-96
David W.	Putnam	1808-22
Drury	Baldwin	1823
Drury	Wilkes	1792-1801
Edmund	Fayette	1878-97
Edward	Houston	1855-96
Elizabeth R.	Houston	1855-96
Ephraim	Carroll	1852-86
Felder	Houston	1855-96
George	Talbot	--
George Thos. Richardson	Campbell	1825-1900
H. C.	Cobb	1873
Hamilton	McIntosh	1873-1915
Harriet Miss	Wilkinson	1888
Henry	Clarke	1822-42
Henry	Lee	1854-1955
Ida Mrs. M.	Upson	1826-1910
Irwin	Washington	1852-1903
Isaac	Upson	1826-1910
J. M.	Pike	1844-76
James	Wilkinson	1873
James H.	Wilkinson	1880
James W.	Bartow	1836-85
Jeremiah	Greene	1817-92
Jesse	Henry	1834-69
Jesse	Jefferson	1812
Jesse C.	Sumter	1838-55 bonds
John	Cobb	1905

JACKSON (continued)

John	Henry	1834–69
John	Jasper	1813–19
John	Wilkes	1819–36
John J.	Sumter	1838–55 bond
John S.	Upson	1826–1910
Jordan	Fayette	1828–97
Joseph	Jefferson	1800
Joseph	Sumter	1838–55 bonds
Lowe	Warren	1813
M. C.	Bartow	1836–85
Mark	Bartow	1836–85
Mark	Hancock	1797
Martha	Cobb	1870i
Martha F.	Lowndes	1871–1915
Martha I.	Wilkinson	1829
Mathew N.	Campbell	1825–1900
Nathan	Henry	1834–69
Nathan	Washington	1852–1903
Nathaniel	Upson	1826–1910
Nimrod	Crawford	1852–94
Peter	Baldwin	1826
Peter	Morgan	1814–30
Rebecca	Campbell	1825–1900
Reuben A.	Fayette	1828–97
Robert	Pike	1844–76
Rowland	Pike	1844–76
Samuel	Walton	1827–39
Sarah	Washington	1852–1903
Sarah	Wilkes	1837–77
Shadrach	Cobb	1873
Squire	Cobb	1909
Thomas	Hall	1819–37
Thomas	Jasper	1820–23
Thomas	Wilkinson	1867
Wellborn	Union	1877–1942
Wilkins	Jones	1826–50
William	Henry	1834–69
William	Wilkes	1779–92
William	Wilkinson	1831
Woody	Oglethorpe	1833–66

JACOBS

Keziah	Wayne	1822–70
William G.	Gwinnett	1852–86

JAGGER

John	Colonial	1760

JAMES

Anderson	Upson	1826–1910
Ben	Jefferson	1800
Berryman	Bartow	1836–85
Charles	Campbell	1825–1900
Charles	Irwin	1821–64
Edmund (Col)	Washington	1852–1903
Elias	Putnam	1823–56
John	Crawford	1835–52
John	Franklin	1786–1813
John	Marion	1846–1915
Robert B.	Oglethorpe	1833–66
Robertson	Walton	1834–9 gdn
S. T.	Cobb	1876i
S. W.	Cobb	1907
Stephen Sr.	Campbell	1825–1900
William	Walton	1834–9 minor

JAMISON

Henry	Baldwin	1822
Peter	Lee	1854–1955

JARRARD

John G.	Lumpkin	1845–1923
John G.	Union	1877–1942

JARRATT

Alexander	Baldwin	1850
Atha	Fayette	1828–97
Blake	Jones	1826–50

JARRATT (continued)

James S.	Clarke	1822–42

JARRELL

Bennett	Screven	1810–1929
J. E.	Telfair	1869–1921
Mattie E.	Screven	1810–1929
R. F. Sr.	Screven	1810–1929
Wiley P.	Screven	1810–1929
William B.	Screven	1810–1929

JARRETT

Archelus	Elbert	1827
Deverix	Wilkes	1779–92
Johnson T.	Taliaferro	1826–66
Martha	Jackson	1802–60
Robert	Wilkes	1779–92

JARVIS

Elizabeth	Jefferson	1818
J. H.	Marion	1846–1915

JAY

Betsy Ann	Lumpkin	1833–52
David Jr.	Lumpkin	1833–52
David Sr.	Lumpkin	1833–52

JAZEE

John	Tattnall	1836–40i

JEFFERS

H. L.	Paulding	1850–77
Thomas	Burke	1853–70

JEFFERSON

H. E. Mrs.	Marion	1846–1915

JEFFORDS

Harmon F.	Ware	1879–1915
Simon P.	Ware	1879–1915
Virginia H.	Camden	1795–1829

JEFFRIES

Swepston C.	Taliaferro	1826–66
William	Wilkes	1779–92

JEFFRY

Thomas B.	Marion	1846–1915

JELKS

William	Pulaski	1816–50

JEMISON

Henry	Bibb	1823–55
Robert	Lincoln	1796–1808
Thomas	Bartow	1836–85

JENKINS

Arthur	Warren	1834
C. D.	Paulding	1850–77 bond
C. E.	Early	1856–1927 L/A
Charles C.	Emanuel	1832
Charles J.	Jefferson	1828
Cyrus R.	Jasper	1820–23
Elefair	Washington	1852–1903
Elias C.	Bibb	1851–71
Elijah	Morgan	1830–60
James	Greene	1817–42
James	Madison	1842–96
James	Polk	1857–1936
James R.	Greene	1806–16
Jesse	Baldwin	1824
John	Burke	1853–70
John	Pike	1844–76
John J.	Burke	1853–70
Kincheon	Gwinnett	1852–86
L. G.	Ware	1879–1915
Lewis	Greene	1796–1806
Lewis	Greene	1817–42

JENKINS (continued)

Mary	Houston	1855-96
Osbert B.	Sumter	1838-55i bond
(Royal, exr)		
Peyton R.	Morgan	1814-30
Polly W.	Baldwin	1828
Samuel	Houston	1827-55
Sterling	Wilkes	1819-36
Thomas G.	Lowndes	1871-1915
Thomas J.	Polk	1857-1937
Uriah	Washington	1829-31 divs
Uriah	Washington	1852-1903
William	Jefferson	1777
(father of Jas. J.)		
William	Talbot	--
William F.	Houston	1827-55
William M.	Polk	1857-1936
Williamson	Fayette	1828-97

JENKS

D.	Glynn	1844-53
Jonathan	Oglethorpe	1793-1807

JENNINGS

John A.	Fayette	1828-97
Joshua	Oglethorpe	1807-1826
Miles	Oglethorpe	1833-36
Nancy	Oglethorpe	1833-36
Solomon	Oglethorpe	1833-36
William	Wilkes	1792-1801

JERNIGAN

Bryant	Sumter	1838-55 bond
Hardy	Early	1856-1927
Hardy	Hancock	1836
Lewis A.	Washington	1852-1903
Needham	Hancock	1804

JETER

Andrew	Bibb	1823-55
Barnett	Elbert	1826
Garland	Lincoln	1796-1808
Oliver	Lincoln	1796-1808

JETT

Daniel	Greene	1817-42

JILES

David	Cobb	1907

JIMERSON

William	Upson	1826-1910

JINKENS

Charles E.	Early	1856-1927 gdns
Francis	Jasper	1831-9
Jane	Butts	1826-41

JINKS

Mathew	Butts	1826-41

JINNING

Priscilla	Morgan	1814-30

JOHN

David	Colonial	1764

JOHNS

Enoch	Lee	1854-1955
Isaac D. N.	Bibb	1851-71
John	Wilkes	1819-36
Ward	Appling	1877-1925

JOHNSON

A. W.	Early	1856-1927 L/A
Aaron	Carroll	1852-96
Able	Bartow	1836-85
Abraham	Warren	--
Adeline	Macon	1856-1909

JOHNSON (continued)

Alexander	Jasper	1825-31
Alexander	Lincoln	1796-1808
Alexander	Montgomery	1806-63
Allen	Polk	1857-1936
Allen	Tattnall	1836-40i
Angus	Paulding	1850-77 retn
Anna	Taliaferro	1826-66
Annis	Jasper	1831-9 minor
Archibald	DeKalb	1840-69
B. F.	Polk	1857-1936
Bartholomew	Morgan	1830-60
Bartholomew	Taliaferro	1826-66
Benjamin	Jasper	1823-33
Burton S.	Macon	1856-1909
Calvin	Marion	1845-1915
Cary	Oglethorpe	1833-66
Charles T.	Wilkinson	1862
Cincinnatus	Taliaferro	1826-66
Cornelius	Putnam	1808-22
D. Thomas	Henry	1822-34
Daniel	Bartow	1836-85
Daniel	Hancock	1800
Daniel	Thomas	1837-45i
Elander	Cobb	1873i
Elijah	Wilkes	1806-08
Elisha	Henry	1834-69
Elizabeth Mrs.	Chattooga	1856-1924
Elizabeth	Coweta	1828-48 retn
Elizabeth	Randolph	1845-94
Elizabeth A.	Coweta	1849-92
Elizabeth C.	Coweta	1849-92
Felix A.	Wilkinson	1902
George	Chattooga	1856-1924
George W.	Paulding	1850-77 bond
Gerkins	Dooly	1847-1901
Green	Putnam	1823-56
H. G.	Pike	1823-29
Henrietta	Newton	1823-51
Henry	Bibb	1851-71
Isaac F.	Wilkinson	1887
J. W. Sr.	Appling	1877-1925
Jacob	Wilkes	1837-77
James	Oglethorpe	1833-66
James	Walton	1870-74
James	Wilkes	1792-1801
James J.	Elbert	1829-60
James M.	Cobb	1867i
Jane	Madison	1842-96
Jason	Murray	1840-72
Joel	Cobb	1864i
John	Chattooga	1856-1924
John	Elbert	--
John	Elbert	1802
John	Elbert	1817
John	Greene	1796-1806
John	Hancock	1814
John	Lincoln	1831-69
John	Morgan	1830-60
John W.	Chattooga	1856-1924
John W.	Screven	1810-1929
Jordan	Clayton	1858-1921
Joseph	Franklin	1786-1813
Joseph	Putnam	1823 56
Joseph A.	Early	1856-1927 bonds
Joshua	Early	1856-1927
Joshua	Wilkes	1779-92
Lachlin	DeKalb	1840-69
Littleberry	Murray	1840-72
Lucy Mrs.	Chattooga	1856-1924
Luke	DeKalb	1840-69
M. Isaac	Henry	1822-34
(or Isaac M.)		
Malcolm	Bartow	1836-85
Marcus	Pike	1844-76
Margaret	Putnam	1823-56
Mark M.	Bartow	1836-85
Martin	Sumter	1838-55 bond
Mary	Morgan	1830-60

JOHNSON (continued)

Mary	Newton	1823–51
Mary	Randolph	1845–94
Mary Hutchinson	Campbell	1825–1900
Mattie Mrs.	Telfair	1869–1921
Moses	Upson	1826–1910
Nancy	Meriwether	1831–59
Nathan	Newton	1823–51
Nathan	Oglethorpe	1793–1807
Nehemiah D.	Hancock	1819
Newton	Gilmer	1836–53i
Nicholas	Troup	1832–48
Peter	Wilkes	1792–1801
Polly Ann	Gwinnett	1852–86
Prudence	Cobb	1910
R. B.	Chattooga	1856–1924
Reese	Warren	1835
Reuben	Oglethorpe	1807–26
Richard	Houston	1855–96
Richard	Wilkes	1779–92
Robert	Coweta	1828–48
Ruby J.	Floyd	1861–7
Russel V.	Emanuel	1866i
S. D.	Henry	1834–69
Sanford	Henry	1822–34
Samuel	Baldwin	1850
Samuel	Jasper	1825–31
Samuel	Taliaferro	1826–66
Sanford W.	Jackson	1802–60
Sankey (?)	Harris	1850–75
Sarah	Taliaferro	1826–66
Smith	Oglethorpe	1793–1807
Solomon	Dooly	1847–1901
Solomon D.	Oglethorpe	1833–66
Steve	Polk	1857–1936
Susan J.	Carroll	1852–96
Thomas	Clayton	1858–1921
Thomas	Fayette	1828–97
Thomas	Greene	1817–42
Thomas	Jackson	1802–60
Thomas	Jones	1826–50
Thomas	Oglethorpe	1793–18807
Thomas	Oglethorpe	1833–66
Thomas	Putnam	1823–56
Thomas	Wilkes	1779–92
Thomas D.	Henry	1822–34
Thomas M.	Oglethorpe	1807–26
Thomas W.	Lee	1854–1955
Thomas Y.	Burke	1853–70
W. F.	Carroll	1852–96
W. M.	Cobb	1880
Walter	Jasper	1820–23
William	Bibb	1823–55
William	Camden	1795–1829
William	Carroll	1852–96
William	DeKalb	1840–69
William	Emanuel	1837
(bill of sale)		
William	Houston	1855–96
William	Jasper	1822–26
William	Jasper	1825–31
William	Jones	1826–50
William	Liberty	1772–1887
William	McIntosh	1873–1915
William	Morgan	1814–30
William	Morgan	1830–60
William	Sumter	1838–55 bond
William	Washington	1852–1903
William Jr.	Wilkes	1819–36
William Sr.	Jasper	1822–26
William Sr.	Wilkes	1819–36
William L.	Crawford	1835–52
William M.	Pike	1844–76
William S.	Bibb	1851–71
William T.	Carroll	1852–96
Woodford A.	Morgan	1830–60

JOHNSTON see Johnson

JOINER

Burrell	Sumter	1838–55 bond
Burwell	Laurens	1809–40
Cynthia	Henry	1822–34
Elizabeth	Sumter	1838–55 bond
Jesse	Laurens	1809–40
John	Marion	1846–1915
Lewis	Sumter	1838–55 bond
William	Washington	1829–71 divs
Woodward	Henry	1822–34

JOLLY

Joseph	Bartow	1836–85

JONES

A. R. Mrs.	Washington	1852–1903
Aaron	Lincoln	1796–1808
Aaron	Pike	1844–76
Abraham	Montgomery	1806–63
Abram	Burke	1853–70
Adam	Laurens	1809–40
Adam	Warren	1826
Adam	Wilkinson	1845
Allen	Lowndes	1871–1915
Allen	Putnam	1808–22
Allen J.	Clayton	18599–1921
Ann	Fayette	1828–97
Ann E.	Meriwether	1831–59
Anna	Early	1834–1902 bonds
Annie U. Mrs.	Polk	1857–1936
Arthur	Elbert	1835
Arthur	Franklin	1786–1813
B. A.	Fayette	1828–97
Barra	Taliaferro	1826–66
Benjamin	Taliaferro	1826–66
C. Jones orphs	Walton	1834–9
C. S.	Fayette	1828–97
Casper W.	Randolph	1845–94
Charles H.	Oglethorpe	1845–1923
Claiborne	Walton	1827–39
Cyrus	Chattooga	1856–1924
D.	Glynn	1844–53
Daniel M.	Muscogee	1838–62
David	Clayton	1859–1921
Deborah	Stewart	1837–49
Donald B.	Dooly	1847–1901
Drewry H.	Sumter	1838–55i
Dudley	Walton	1827–39
Edward	DeKalb	1840–69
Edward	Jasper	1812–17
Edward	Oglethorpe	1833–66
Edward F.	Dooly	1847–1901
Elijah	Newton	1823–51
Elizabeth	Carroll	1852–96
Elizabeth	Jones	1826–50
Elizabeth A.	Burke	1853–70
Elizabeth J.	Polk	1857–1936
Emily	Elbert	1829–60
Eugenia L. Mrs.	Polk	1857–1936
Francis	Colonial	1768
Francis A.	Burke	1853–70
Gabriel	Randolph	1845–94
George W.	Upson	1826–1910
Harrel	Carroll	1852–96
Henry	Hall	1819–37
Henry	Lincoln	1808–32
Henry	Oglethorpe	1845–1927
Henry P.	Burke	1853–70
Henry W.	Lincoln	1796–1808
Hiram	Wilkinson	1844
Hugh	Greene	1794–1810
Hugh	Jasper	1813–19
Isaac	Morgan	1814–30
Isaac W.	Pike	1844–76
J. J.	Bartow	1836–85
J. W.	Union	1877–1942
Jacob R.	Jones	1812–23
James	Campbell	1825–1900
James	Cobb	1876

JONES (continued)

James	Gilmer	1836-53i
James	Glynn	1844-53
James S.	Clayton	1859-1921
James W.	Burke	1853-70
Jane	Jackson	1802-60
Jeamie W. Mrs.	Polk	1857-1936
Jincy J.	Floyd	1852-61 minor
Joel	Newton	1823-51
John	Baldwin	1819-64
John	Camden	1795-1829
John	Early	1856-1927 L/A
John	Hancock	1805
John	Jones	1826-50
John	Morgan	1830-60
John	Newton	1823-51
John	Pulaski	1816-1924
John	Thomas	1837-45
John L.	Wilkinson	1830
Jonathan	Early	1834-1902 bonds
Jonathan	Laurens	1809-40
Joseph	Liberty	1776-1887
Joseph B.	Burke	1853-70
Josiah	Early	1834-1902 bonds
L. D.	Bartow	1836-85
Larkin	Franklin	1786-1813
Lewis	Elbert	1801
Lucy C.	Randolph	1845-94
M. D.	Burke	1853-70
M. L.	Oglethorpe	1845-1923
Malachi	Washington	1852-1903
Malachi Jr.	Washington	1852-1903
Malissa G.	Polk	1857-1936
Margaret A.	Chattooga	1856-1924
Mary	Houston	1855-96
Mary	Liberty	1772-1887
Mary	Pulaski	1816-50
Mary	Wilkes	1837-77
Mary E.	Polk	1857-1936
Mathew	Screven	1810-1929
Matilda	Macon	1856-1909
Mitchell	Lowndes	1871-1915
Nancy (wid)	Paulding	1850-77 admx bond
Orran	Carroll	1852-96
P. E. H.	Burke	1853-70
R. H.	Polk	1857-1936
Randal	Muscogee	1847
Randall	Harris	1850-75
Reuben	Putnam	1808-22
Reuben Sr.	Randolph	1845-94
Robert D.	Chattooga	1856-1924
Russell	Jackson	1802-60
Russell	Taliaferro	1826-66
S. A. H.	Washington	1852-1903
S. M.	Lee	1854-1955
Sallie P. Mrs.	Polk	1857-1936
Sam	Cobb	1876
Samuel	Oglethorpe	1845-1923
Samuel	Wilkes	1792-1801
Samuel	Wilkes	1837-77
Sarah	Fayette	1828-97
Sarah H.	Coweta	1849-92
Seaborn A.	Burke	1853-70
Seaborn H.	Burke	1853-70
Seaborne	Polk	1857-1936
Sharod	Gilmer	1836-53i
Simeon R.	Taliaferro	1826-66
Solomon	Elbert	1829-60
Standley	Elbert	1828
Stephen B.	Morgan	1830-60
Susannah	Warren	1831
T. G.	Paulding	1850-77
Thomas	Elbert	1809
Thomas	Harris	1850-75
Thomas	Lincoln	1831-69
Thomas	Walton	1819-37
Thomas	Walton	1827-39 orphs
Thomas	Wilkes	1777-8

JONES (continued)

Thomas	Wilkes	1837-77
Thomas	Wilkinson	1845
Thomas A.	Oglethorpe	1833-66
Thomas B.	Carroll	1852-96
Thomas B. G.	Coweta	1828-48
Thomas F.	Early	1856-1927
Tignal	Franklin	1786-1813
Uriah	Houston	1855-96
W. A.	Fayette	1828-97
W. J.	Fayette	1828-97
Washington	Burke	1853-70
Wiley	Polk	1857-1936
Wiley W.	Elbert	1827
William	Colonial	1768
William	Emanuel	1845
William	Greene	1806-16
William	Hall	1837-67
William	Lincoln	1796-1808
William	Oglethorpe	1845-1923
William	Paulding	1850-77 exrs
(& Susan Baker)		
William	Screven	1810-1929
William	Taliaferro	1826-66
William	Union	1877-1942
William	Wilkes	1792-1801
William A.	Talbot	--
William P.	Sumter	1838-55 bond
Willis	Meriwether	1831-59

JORDAN

Abraham	Marion	1846-1915
Absalom	Bibb	1851-71
Absalom	Elbert	1798
Ann	Early	1856-1927
Benjamin	Wilkes	1779-92
Cornelius	Washington	1852-1903
David A.	Ware	1879-1915
E. T.	Baldwin	1819-64
Edmond	Oglethorpe	1833-66
Ephraim D.	Washington	1852-1903
Green H.	Baldwin	1819-64
H. A.	Marion	1846-1915
Harty A. D.	Washington	1852-1903
Henry	Oglethorpe	1833-66
Hezekiah	Morgan	1814-30
Jesse	DeKalb	1840-69
John	Wilkes	1837-77
John M.	Crawford	1835-52
John M.	Harris	1850-75
John T.	Pike	1844-76
Joseph	Lee	1854-1955
M. V.	Carroll	1852-96
Mabry	Stewart	1850-90
Mollie J.	Randolph	1845-94
Rachel Mrs.	Polk	1857-1936
Reuben	Oglethorpe	1807-26
Robert	Jones	1826-50
(of Sumter d. S. C.)		
Sarah	Houston	1855-96
Thomas	Madison	1842-96
William D.	Washington	1852-1903
William M.	Cobb	1895
William P.	Dooly	1047-1901
Williamson	Putnam	1823-56

JORDIN

Britton	Washington	1829-71 divs
Charles	Wilkes	1779-92
Jesse	Washington	1829-71 divs
John	Washington	1829-71 divs
Thomas Sr.	Washington	1829-71 divs

JOSEY

Henry	Marion	1846-1915
Henry	Meriwether	1831-59
John W.	Washington	1829-71 divs
Malachi	Marion	1846-1915
Mary E.	Washington	1852-1903

JOURDAN		
Charles	Walton	1834-9
Elbert	Cobb	1871i
Henry	Lincoln	1796-1808
N. C. et al	Cobb	1870 minors
JOYCE		
James	Tattnall	1800-35 deeds
James	Tattnall	1836-40i
Robert	DeKalb	1840-69
Telitha	Marion	1846-1915
JOYNER		
Hurt A.	Washington	1829-71 divs
Moses	Washington	1829-71 divs
Sarah	Screven	1810-1929
JUDKINS		
J. W.	Polk	1857-1936
JUDSON		
Henry C.	Muscogee	1838-62
Joseph	Camden	1795-1829
JUHAN		
D. B.	Carroll	1852-96
Jessie	Carroll	1852-96
JULIAN		
-- Mrs.	Cobb	1866i
S. J.	Gwinnett	1852-86
Samuel	Cobb	1870 retn
JUNKIN		
Samuel	Murray	1840-72
JUSTINCE		
David	Jackson	1802-60
Dempsey	Baldwin	1826
Eliza H.	Jones	1826-50
John	Jackson	1802-60
Mary	Dooly	1847-1901
KAPPELL		
Diana M.	Wilkes	1837-77
KARR		
John	Coweta	1849-92
KAY		
Baley	Bartow	1836-85
John W.	Habersham	1847-1900
KAYLOR		
Jacob	Lee	1854-1955
KEA		
Mary	Screven	1810-1929
Spencer	Emanuel	1855
William C.	Emanuel	1866i
KEABRIDGE		
Richard C.	Camden	1795-1829
KEATON		
Benjamin M.	Early	1856-1927
KEE		
Joseph	Henry	1822-34
KEEBLES		
James	Effingham	1829-59
KEEGAN		
Allen	Camden	1795-1829

KEEL		
Noah	Wilkinson	1842
KEEN		
Gilbert	Oglethorpe	1807-26
KEENUM		
Alexander	Taliaferro	1826-66
KEESE		
J. H.	Carroll	1852-96
KEETON		
Jesse	Putnam	1823-56
KEIBEN		
B. W.	Early	1856-1927
KEIFFER		
Ephraim	Effingham	1829-59
KEITH		
David	Meriwether	1831-59
George	Hall	1837-67
Henery Clay	Ware	1879-1915
John	Early	1856-1927 L/A
KELBY		
John	Wayne	1822-70
KELLER		
Godfrey	Jefferson	1838
KELLEY		
Barney	Elbert	1829-60
Bryan	Colonial	1766
Jane	Wilkes	1779-92
John	Colonial	1741
John	Wilkes	1779-92
Margarett A.	Clayton	1859-1921
Sanford	Clayton	1859-1921
Seaborn R.	Washington	1852-1903
William	Upson	1826-1910
William	Wilkes	1779-92
KELLOGG		
Daniel	Wilkes	1779-92
George	Lumpkin	1845-1923
KELLON		
George	Lumpkin	1845-1923
KELLUM		
Samuel	Madison	1842-96
KELLY		
Amey	Houston	1827-55
Daniel	Jasper	1823-33
Francis	Bibb	1851-71
James	Lumpkin	1845-1923
James	Wilkes	1792-1801
James M.	Houston	1827-55
John	Early	1856-1927 L/A
John	Hancock	1813
John	Putnam	1808-22
John A.	Stewart	1850-90
Julia	Bibb	1851-71
Loyd	Hancock	1835
Martha	Ware	1879-1915
Marvell	Meriwether	1831-59
Michael	Muscogee	1838-62
William	Early	1834-1902 bonds
William	Lincoln	1796-1808
William J.	Taliaferro	1826-66
KELPIN		
W. M.	Cobb	1897

KILLEBREW

Robert	Putnam	1823–56

KILLEN

James H.	Houston	1827–55
Jane	Houston	1827–55
John	Houston	1855–96
William E.	Houston	1855–96

KILLGORE

James	Wilkes	1810–16
Mary T.	Wilkes	1837–77
Ralph	Wilkes	1777–78
William	Wilkes	1837–77

KILLIAN

William	Union	1877–1942

KILLINGSWORTH

Elizabeth	Early	1856–1889 L/A
F. R.	Murray	1840–72
James A.	Early	1834–1902
Jane	Washington	1852–1903

KILLOUGH

Isaac	Oglethorpe	1793–1807

KILPATRICK

Richard	Meriwether	1831–59
William	Bibb	1851–71
William J.	DeKalb	1840–69

KIMBALL

Elbert	Upson	1826–1910
Walter	Early	1856–1927 L/A

KIMBELL

Benjamin	Henry	1834–69
Christopher	Henry	1834–69

KIMBROUGH

Fleming	Lee	1854–1955
Jesse F.	Harris	1850–75
Jesse J.	Harris	1850–75
John	Greene	1808–16
Josiah	Greene	1817–42
Mary Mrs.	Lee	1854–1955
Thomas	Muscogee	1847
Thomas	Putnam	1823–56
William	Greene	1796–1806

KINARD

Martin	Floyd	1852–61

KINCHEN

William	Houston	1855–96

KINDA

David	Lincoln	1831–69

KINEBREW

Henry	Fayette	1828–97

KING

A. J.	Upson	1826–1910
Angus	Sumter	1838–55 bond
B.	Cobb	1875i
Barrington	Cobb	1866i
Benjamin	Early	1856–1927
Butler B.	Upson	1826–1910
C.	Wayne	1822–70i
Carson	Madison	1842–96
Charles	Jefferson	1811
Dolly	Camden	1868–1916
Drury	Greene	1817–42
Elias	Murray	1840–72
Elijah	Baldwin	1819–64
Eliza	Houston	1855–96
Elizabeth	Talbot	1861

KING (continued)

F. P. Mrs.	Cobb	1874i
Frances P. Mrs.	Cobb	1882
George	Franklin	1786–1813 gdn
George C.	Fayette	1828–97
Harris M.	Cobb	1871 minors
Henry	Fayette	1828–97
Henry	Muscogee	1849
Howell	Wilkinson	1871
Hugh M. D.	Sumter	1838–55 bond
Jacob	Upson	1826–1910
James	Wilkinson	1842
James S.	Polk	1857–1936
John	Baldwin	1824
John	Bibb	1823–55
John	Crawford	1835–52
John	Gwinnett	1852–86
John	Houston	1855–96
John	Jackson	1802–60
John	Washington	1852–1903
John L.	Clayton	1858–1921
John M.	Jasper	1813–19
Joshua	Glynn	1844–53
Littleberry	Jones	1810–28
Louisa C. Mrs.	Houston	1855–96
Maderson	Fayette	1828–97
Margaret	Baldwin	1819–64
Margaret	Putnam	1823–56
Mary	Camden	1868–1916
Mary	Wilkes	1837–77
Mary Ann	Bibb	1851–71
Mary E.	Camden	1795–1829
Nehemiah	Dooly	1847–1901
Nehemiah	Houston	1827–55
Noah	Bartow	1836–85
R. Mrs.	Taliaferro	1826–66
R. V. or R. N.	Camden	1868–1916
Samuel	Houston	1827–55
Sarah E.	Chattooga	1856–1924
Search	Carroll	1852–96
Stephen	Polk	1857–1936
Thomas	Bibb	1823–55
Thomas	Greene	1794–1810
Thomas	Harris	1850–75
Thomas III	Camden	1795–1829
Thomas A.	Camden	1795–1829
Thomas D.	Houston	1855–96
Thomas E.	Cobb	1867i
Thomas H.	Early	1834–1902 bonds
Thomas Reed et al	Cobb	1869 minors
William P.	Franklin	1848–67
Willie M.	Polk	1857–1936
Y. S. Jr.	Polk	1857–1936

KINGSBERRY

Sanford	Carroll	1852–96

KINLEY

George M.	Early	1856–1927 L/A

KINNEBREW

William	Lincoln	1796–1808

KINNEY

E. J.	Wilkinson	1914
Elizabeth	Carroll	1852–96
James W.	Wilkinson	1891
Lucy Miss	Habersham	1847–1900
U. S.	Polk	1857–1936
Z. T.	Polk	1857–1936

KINNON

William	Lincoln	1796–1808

KINS

B. C. A.	Union	1877–1942

KINSEY

Joseph W.	Harris	1850–75

LAFAVER
Abraham   Jefferson   1814

LAFOY
John G.   Houston   1827-55

LAFURGUE
John   Camden   1795-1829

LAIDLER
C. B.   Houston   1855-96
Elizabeth   Houston   1855-96
John   Houston   1855-96
John Sr.   Houston   1855-96
Sarah   Houston   1855-96
Watkins   Houston   1855-96

LAKE
James   Floyd   1861-71
Richard   Greene   1796-1806

LAMAR
Basil   Lincoln   1796-1808
Benjamin B.   Bibb   1823-55
Eliza   Bibb   1851-71
Jacob   Lincoln   1796-1808
Jefferson J.   Stewart   1837-49
John   Bibb   1851-71
John   Early   1834-1902 bonds
John   Macon   1856-1909
John B.   Bibb   1851-71
LaFayette   Lincoln   1831-69
Thomas   Baldwin   1810
Zachariah   Baldwin   1832
Zachariah   Clarke   1822-42

LAMB
B. B.   Glynn   1844-53
Frederick   Glynn   1844-53
Isaac   Jefferson   1827
Luke   Macon   1856-1909

LAMBERT
James   Wilkinson   1819
John   Jackson   1802-60
John   Liberty   1772-1887
Thomas   Clarke   1822-42
William   Morgan   1830-60

LAMPKIN
Annis   Polk   1857-1936

LAMPTON
J. T.   Polk   1857-1936

LANCASTER
Leir   Hancock   1803
Samuel   Greene   1817-47
Sarah   Lincoln   1808-32
William   Lincoln   1796-1808

LANCE
David   Lumpkin   1845-1923
J. V.   Union   1877-1942
Martin   Lumpkin   1845-1923

LANCHESTER
Thomas   Liberty   1772-1887

LAND
Nathan   Bartow   1836-85

LANDERS
Elizabeth   Lincoln   1808-32
John   Lincoln   1831-69

LANDING
Harriet   Burke   1853-70
John   Burke   1853-70

LANDING (continued)
Mark   Burke   1853-70

LANDRUM
George T.   Oglethorpe   1833-66
Jeptha   Fayette   1828-97
John   Wilkes   1837-77
Joseph   Jackson   1830-60
Joseph   Oglethorpe   1833-66
Larkin   Fayette   1828-97
Nancy   Wilkes   1819-36
Thomas   Jasper   1812-17
Thomas   Oglethorpe   1833-66
Thomas   Wilkes   1810-16
William W.   Fayette   1828-97

LANE
A. H.   Lowndes   1871-1915
Alexander   Troup   1832-48
Benjamin A.   Lowndes   1871-1915
Benjamin A.   Walton   1870-74
Benjamin S.   Emanuel   1827
  to Benjamin & John   deeds of gift
Bryant   Sumter   1838-55 bond
  admr of James
C. W.   Cobb   1873i
Caroline T.   Cobb   1867
Charles M. et al Cobb   1866 minors
Edward   Emanuel   1853
George W.   Newton   1823-51
Joseph   Newton   1823-51
Lavenia   Burke   1853-70
Lee O.   Lee   1854-1955
M. P.   Polk   1857-1936
Mack T.   Cobb   1868i
R. A.   Cobb   1874
  Matilda, admx
Richard   Oglethorpe   1793-1807
Richard T.   Troup   1832-48
Sampson   Franklin   1786-1813 admr
Sarah   Walton   1827-39
Thomas   Burke   1853-70
Thomas   Elbert   1824
William   Morgan   1830-60
William D.   Newton   1823-51
William T.   Morgan   1830-60

LANEY
David   Harris   1850-75

LANG
Caroline   Camden   1866-1915
Cornelia T.   Camden   1866-1916
Daniel J.   Camden   1868-1916
George Sr.   Camden   1866-1915
Isaac Sr.   Camden   1866-1915
L. G.   Coweta   1849-92
Nancy   Camden   1868-1916
Nancy H. Mrs.   Washington   1852-1903

LANGBRIDGE
Robert   Franklin   1786-1813

LANGFORD
Edmund   Upson   1826-1910
Elizabeth A.   Upson   1826-1910
Euchia   Hancock   1810
James   Marion   1846-1915
Louisa J.   Upson   1826-1910

LANGLEY
David   Gwinnett   1852-86
Osey   Marion   1846-1915

LANGSTON
David   Oglethorpe   1833-66
Moses   Morgan   1814-30
P. C.   Franklin   1848-67
Samuel   Jackson   1802-60

LANIER		
Benjamin	Screven	1810-1929
Davis	Screven	1810-1929
Henry	Greene	1817-42
James	Gwinnett	1856-86
John	Morgan	1830-60
John I.	Bibb	1823-55
N. W.	Screven	1810-1929
Noel	Screven	1810-1929
Sara A.	Ware	1879-1915
William	Emanuel	1867 bond
William	Jasper	1812-17
William M.	Screven	1810-1929
William P.	Polk	1857-1936
LANKFORD		
Amelia	Lincoln	1796-1808
C. Caldwell	Paulding	1850-77
Curtis C.	Gwinnett	1852-86
John	Lincoln	1796-1808
Milly	Lincoln	1796-1808
Curtis C., exr est of		
LANNEAU		
Eliza G.	Cobb	1867 minors
John F.	Cobb	1867
LANSDALE		
Luke	Lincoln	1831-69
LANSFORD		
Henry	Oglethorpe	1807-26
LANTRIP		
Susanna	Richmond	1840-53
LANY		
S. M.	Carroll	1852-96
LARAMORE		
H. H.	Lee	1854-1955
James	Lee	1854-1955
M. E. Mrs.	Lee	1854-1955
W. M.	Lee	1854-1955
LARD		
J. M.	Paulding	1850-77 gdn retn
LARDE		
Samuel	Morgan	1814-30
LARKING		
Edward	Colonial	1777
LARVING		
James	Rabun	1863-88
LASETER		
Lemuel	Pike	1844-76
LASSATER		
Elizabeth	Coweta	1849-92
Reuben M.	Clayton	1859-1921
l ASSETER		
Abraham	Wilkinson	1842
Charles A.	Screven	1810-1929
Jesse	Fayette	1828-97
Shemurl N.	Dooly	1847-1901
William	Burke	1853-70
LASSETTER		
Elisha	Jasper	1812-17
Tobia	Greene	1796-1806
LASSITER		
Elizabeth	Sumter	1838-55 minors
		of David
Elizabeth A.	Sumter	1838-55 bond

LASSITER (continued)		
John H.	Sumter	1838-55i
minor of David		
Willis	Hancock	1814
LATHAM		
George	Hall	1837-67
LATHERS		
Nancy	Madison	1842-96
LATHRAP		
Asa	Camden	1795-1829
LATIMER		
George	Chattooga	1856-1924
George	Oglethorpe	1833-66
Hezekiah R.	Cobb	1866i
Joel N.	Oglethorpe	1833-66
John	Hancock	1824
Rebekah	Warren	1825
Robert	Hancock	1826
Sauel M.	Stewart	1850-90
LATNER		
John V.	Franklin	1848-67
LATTERSTEDT		
Susan H.	Burke	1853-70
LAUD		
Robert	Clarke	1822-42
LAUDERMILK		
Daniel	Union	1877-1942
LAUGHTER		
Jane	Wilkes	1837-77
LAURENCE		
Stephen	Greene	1806-16
LAVENDER		
William	Henry	1834-69
LAVERY		
William	Colonial	1733
LAW		
Charles	Houston	1855-96
James	Hall	1837-67
LAWGINS		
Lewis	Crawford	1835-52
LAWHORN		
Simeon	Marion	1846-1915
LAWLESS		
James	Madison	1842-96
LAWRENCE		
A. D.	Glynn	1844-53
A. I.	Chattooga	1856-1924
Amanda M.	Cobb	1866i
Bennett	Floyd	1861-71
Claborn	Morgan	1841-30
Garrett	Richmond	1840-53
George	Wilkes	1810-16
J. P.	Chattooga	1856-1924
Joseph	Pike	1823-29
Martin A.	Chattooga	1856-1924
Mildred W.	Chattooga	1856-1924
Peyton	Pike	1844-76
Sarah J. Mrs.	Chattooga	1856-1924
Sidney M.	Chattooga	1856-19924
T. J.	Chattooga	1856-1924
Thomas	Muscogee	1838-62
William	Oglethorpe	1807-26

LAWRIMORE

Sarah	Elbert	1833

LAWSON

Adam	Butts	1826-41
Alexander E.	Washington	1852-1903
Davenport	Stewart	1837-49
David	Joseph	1826-31
Hugh	Houston	1855-96
Jennie	Wilkinson	1828
John Sr.	Wilkes	1819-36
John T.	Muscogee	1844
Leatha	Putnam	1823-56
Roger	Jefferson	1803
Roger	Washington	1829-71
Tompson	Washington	1829-71 divs

LAWTON

Buster	Screven	1810-1929
Gilbert	Screven	1810-1929

LAY

Eliza	Jackson	1802-60
Emanuel	Lincoln	1796-1808
Vincent	Lincoln	1796-1808
William N.	Jackson	1802-60

LAYTON

James M.	Early	1856-1927
Lucinda E. Mrs.	Washington	1852-1903

LAZENBY

Alford	Coweta	1849-92
Sauel	Newton	1823-51

LEA

William	Wilkes	1792-1801

LEACH

Louisa	Wayne	1822-70
Robert	Glynn	1844-53

LEAK

Sallie	Bartow	1836-85

LEATH

William	Early	1856-1927

LEATHERS

John	Wilkinson	1827

LEAVEL

A. J.	Cobb	1878 minor
Charles F.	Cobb	1869 minor
Richard	Coweta	1849-92

LEDBETTER

Benjamin	Jones	1812-23
D. M.	Chattooga	1856-1924
Henry	Jasper	1831-9
James R.	Lumpkin	1845-1923
John	Franklin	1848-67
Joseph	Pike	1823-29
Lewis J.	Lumpkin	1845-1923
M.	Forsyth	1833-44i
Patience	Sumter	1838-55 bond
Samuel	Jones	1812-23
Sarah	Putnam	1823-56

LEDFORD

Amos	Union	1877-1942
Silas	Union	1877-1942

LEE

B. C.	Screven	1810-1929
Carrie S.	Wilkinson	1894
D. J.	Screven	1810-1929
David B.	Screven	1810-1929
David M.	Screven	1810-1929

LEE (continued)

Elias	Early	1834-1902
Elizabeth	Greene	1817-42
Elizabeth Mrs.	Liberty	1772-1887
G. C.	Screven	1810-1929
General J.	Screven	1810-1929
J. Elen	Early	1856-1927
J. L. Mrs.	Screven	1810-1929
J. W.	Chattooga	1856-1924
Jacob	Montgomery	1806-63
James B.	Campbell	1825-1900
James W.	Screven	1810-1929
Jane	Stewart	1850-90
John	Clarke	1822-42
John	Putnam	1808-22
John Thomas	Screven	1810-1929
Josiah	Screven	1810-1929
L. A.	Screven	1810-1929
Margarette	Wilkes	1819-36
Peter	Early	1834-1902
R. W.	Early	1856-1927 L/A
Reuben	Screven	1810-1929
S. C. Mrs.	Screven	1810-1929
Saymer	Oglethorpe	1833-66
Solomon	Henry	1834-69
Thomas	Colonial	1778
Thomas	Gwinnett	1852-86
Thomas E.	Screven	1810-1929
W. D.	Screven	1810-1929
W. T.	Polk	1857-1936
Walter W.	Wilkinson	1887
William	Butts	1826-41
William	Greene	1817-42
William F.	Muscogee	1838-62
William Y.	Paulding	1850-77 gdn retn
Z. L.	Gwinnett	1852-86
Zadoc W.	Early	--

LEEK

George W.	Newton	1823-51
Robert	Newton	1823-51

LEEVES

George	Baldwin	1819-64

LEFERIN

Maria Louisa	Camden	1795-1829

LEGG

Nathaniel	Jackson	1802-60

LEGGETT

Elizabeth	Macon	1856-1909
Elizabeth J.	Houston	1855-96
John	Oglethorpe	1807-26
M. H.	Macon	1856-1909

LeGRAND

William C.	Early	1834-1902 bond

LeGREE

June M.	Macon	1856-1909

LEIGH

Angeline B.	Coweta	1849-92
James J.	Camden	1795-1829

LEL

Alzada	Ware	1879-1915
Lavenia	Ware	1879-1915

LELAND

Samuel W.	Bartow	1836-85

LELY

Edward	Laurens	1809-40

LEMON

Alexander P.	Henry	1834-69

LIGHTFOOT (continued)
William J.	Bibb	1851-71

LIGHTS
Joseph	Henry	1834-69

LIGON
Alexander	Muscogee	1845
Branch	Harris	1850-75
James	Clarke	1802-22
John C.	Polk	1857-1936
Mary	Clarke	1822-42
Thomas	Bartow	1836-85

LIGUEUX
Peter	Bibb	1823-55

LILES
A. H.	Wayne	1822-70
Benjamin	Wayne	1824-55
Mary	Wayne	1824-55
Stephen	Fayette	1828-97

LINDLEY
John B.	Cobb	1872
Jonathan	Cobb	1868

LINDSAY
Clarissa	Greene	1817-42
Jeremiah	Greene	1796-1806
Jeremiah	Greene	1817-42
Reuben	Elbert	1809
Samuel	Jasper	1823-33

LINDSEY
Francis D.	Lee	1854-1955
James	Wilkes	1837-77
John	Upson	1826-1910
John	Wilkes	1779-92
John	Wilkes	1810-16
Letitia	Wilkes	1837-77
N. C. Mrs.	Polk	1857-1936
Samuel	Butts	1826-41
Vashti	Lee	1854-1955

LINES
Isaac	Colonial	1766
Samuel	Liberty	1772-1887
Samuel C.	Screven	1810-1929

LINGEFELT
David	Lumpkin	1845-1923
John	Lumpkin	1845-1923

LINGO
E. W.	Wilkinson	1914
Elizabeth	Wilkinson	1896
Joseph F.	Wilkinson	1913
Sara F.	Wilkinson	1908

LINN
Alfred M.	Bartow	1836-85

LINNEY
William	Henry	1822-34

LINTON
Alexander B.	Clarke	1822-42

LINUS
Moses	Colonial	1767

LINVILL
Mary	Lincoln	1831-69

LIPHAM
Aaron	Wilkes	1819-36

LIPSEY
Barbara	Burke	1853-70
Lincy	Screven	1810-1929

LIRKSY
John	Thomas	1826-36 minor
James	Thomas	1826-36 gdn

LITCHFIELD
L. A.	Cobb	1891

LITTLE
Cage	Taliaferro	1826-66
Dorothy	Henry	1834-69
F. M. exor of F.	Paulding	1850-77
F. M. adm of J. W. Malone	Paulding	1850-77
Francis	Paulding	1850-77
Jacob	Harris	1850-75
Jacob	Sumter	1838-55 bond
James	Franklin	1786-1813
James H.	Franklin	1786-1813
Jesse	Putnam	1823-56
John	Campbell	1825-1900
John	Oglethorpe	1833-66
John	Randolph	1845-94
John H.	Lincoln	1831-69
Robert	Putnam	1823-56
T. Dunlap	Lee	1854-1955
William	Franklin	1848-67
William	Putnam	1823-56
Zabud	Henry	1822-34
Zabud	Henry	1834-69

LITTLETON
Houston	Talbot	1863

LIVELY
Mark	Burke	1853-70

LIVINCSTON
Aron	Greene	1806-16
John	Harris	1850-75
John	Laurens	1809-40
Joseph	Laurens	1809-40
Joseph	Newton	1823-51
Thomas	Muscogee	1838-62

LIVSEY
C. H.	Gwinnett	1852-86

LLOYD
Edmund	Jasper	1823-33
Edward	Oglethorpe	1807-26
Thomas	Colonial	1765

LOCK
Elizabeth	Morgan	1830-60
Jesse	Jefferson	1802
Joseph	Dooly	1847-1901

LOCKETT
David	Franklin	1796
Solomon	Warren	1836
William	Bibb	1851-71

LOCKHART
Britain	Lincoln	1808-32
Henry	Muscogee	1838-62
James	Richmond	1840-53
Jane	Clayton	1859-1921
Lemuel	Sumter	1838-55i
Rhoda	Burke	1853-70

LOCKHEART
James	Franklin	1786-1813

LOCKRIDGE
Daniel	Gwinnett	1852-86

LOWERY (continued)

James L.	Franklin	1786–1813
John	Franklin	1786–1813
John D.	Pike	1844–76
Martha	Jackson	1802–60
Vevi	Jackson	1802–60

LOWMAN

Berry	Lumpkin	1833–52
Elizabeth	Lumpkin	1845–1923
Martin	Lumpkin	1833–52

LOWREY

David	Wilkes	1779–92
John W. F.	Stewart	1850–90

LOWRY

Amos	Gwinnett	1852–86
Peter	Henry	1822–34
Robert	Jefferson	1820
William	Jefferson	1815
William	Polk	1857–1936

LOWTHER

B. F. Sr.	Polk	1857–1936
Joseph	Camden	1795–1829
Katie A. Mrs.	Polk	1857–1936
Susan	Screven	1810–1929

LOYALLESS

James	Wilkes	1792–1801

LOYD

Charles	Harris	1850–75
Daniel	Wilkes	1806–08
Edmund	Jasper	1820–23
Edmund	Jasper	1831–9
James	Houston	1855–96
Mary	Cobb	1866i
Thomas Jr.	Jasper	1812–17
Thomas Jr.	Jasper	1813–19

LUCAS

Barbery	Morgan	1814–30
Isaac	Talbot	––
James	Hancock	1803
John	Hancock	1829

LUCK

Belford	Campbell	1825–1900

LUCKETT

David	Taliaferro	1826–66
Elizabeth	Taliaferro	1826–66
Thomas	Taliaferro	1826–66

LUCKEY

John	Greene	1806–16

LUCKIE

Alexander	Oglethorpe	1793–1807
John	Oglethorpe	1807–26
William	Oglethorpe	1793–1807

LUCY

C. E.	Coweta	1828–48 minors
W. E.	Coweta	1828–48 minors

LUDEN

Mary	Early	1856–1927

LUMPKIN

B.	Telfair	1869–1921
George R.	Floyd	1861–71
George W.	Clarke	1822–42
Henry H.	Sumter	1838–55
Joseph N.	Floyd	1852–61i

LUMSDEN

John G.	Putnam	1823–56
Malinda	Putnam	1823–56

LUNDY

Henry	Hancock	1819

LUNSFORD

Enoch	Bibb	1823–55
Leonard L.	Jasper	1822–26
Nancy	Putnam	1823–56
Priscilla	Bibb	1851–71
William	Elbert	1833
William	Taliaferro	1826–66

LUPTON

John	Colonial	1767

LUSK

John S.	Lumpkin	1833–52

LYLE

Charles L.	Coweta	1849–92
David	Coweta	1849–92
Hugh G.	Cobb	1871
James	Paulding	1850–77 retn
(John Lyle, admr)		
James	Taliaferro	1826–66
James P.	Randolph	1845–94
John	Henry	1834–69
Kirby	Carroll	1852–96
Mathew	Troup	1832–48
Nancy L.	Cobb	1879

LYMAN

Arad	Muscogee	1838–62

LYNCH

Berry E.	Pike	1844–76
Drucilla	Baldwin	1819–64
James W.	Fayette	1828–97

LYNER

Adam	Franklin	1786–1813
Henry	Franklin	1786–1813
Thomas	Franklin	1786–1813 gdn

LYON

Benjamin	Richmond	1840–53
Edmund	Lincoln	1808–32
Elizabeth	Wilkes	1819–36
John	Jasper	1826–31
John	Lincoln	1786–1808
John	Wilkes	1819–36
Jordan	Upson	1826–1910
Mary	Wilkes	1810–16
Nathaniel	Bartow	1836–85
Permelia	Polk	1857–1936
Starling	Walton	1834–9
T. A.	Paulding	1850–77 gdn bond
Thomas	Lincoln	1808–32

LYONS

Frederick R.	Liberty	1772–1887

MABRY

Branch M.	Carroll	1852–96
Charles	Carroll	1852–96
D. S.	Macon	1856–1909
Hillyard B.	Upson	1826–1910
Joshua	Franklin	1848–67

MACHINS

Nancy	Crawford	1852–94

MACK		
John	Walton	1870-74
MACKAY		
Donald	Colonial	1768
Hugh	Jones	1826-50
Isabella	Liberty	1772-1887
John	Colonial	1733
Jonathan	Henry	1834-69
Patrick	Colonial	1768
Thomas Sr.	Campbell	1825-1900
William	Colonial	1762
William	Wilkinson	1870
MACKIE		
Thomas	Elbert	1796
MACON		
Martha Williamson	Greene	1806-16
Nathaniel Green	Greene	1806-16
MADDEN		
David	Bartow	1836-85
MADDOCKS		
Nathan	Pulaski	1816-50
MADDOX		
Anderson	Taliaferro	1826-66
Clayborn	Greene	1817-42
Jane	Lincoln	1796-1808
Joseph	Clarke	1822-42
Josiah E.	Greene	1817-42
Mary	Henry	1822-34
Patrick	Pike	1844-76
Samuel	Hancock	1821
William	Putnam	1823-56
William	Taliaferro	1826-66
MADDUX		
Alexander	Laurens	1809-40
MADISON		
John Ripley	Camden	1795-1829
MADOX		
Berry J.	Madison	1811-40
Joseph	Putnam	1823-56
MAGBEE		
Labon	Cobb	1863i
MAGBY		
Rachael	Butts	1826-41
MAGEE		
Davis	Jones	1812-23
Henry	Screven	1810-1929
MAGHEE		
Edward	Jasper	1812-17
MAGILL		
Eliza R.	Camden	1795-1829
MAGRESS		
George	Lumpkin	1845-1923
MAGUIRE		
Thomas	Gwinnett	1852-86
MAHAFFEY		
Adolphus	Paulding	1850-77 retns
Joseph	Paulding	1850-77
MAHAN		
William	Houston	1827-55

MAHANEY		
Charity	Richmond	1840-53
MAHON		
Eliza H.	Talbot	1862
Rowland	Talbot	1860
Zilpha	Baldwin	1819-64
MAHONEY		
George	Lincoln	1796-1808
George	Lincoln	1831-69
MAILLIER		
Pierre	Colonial	1742
MAIN		
Jessie McClure	Lee	1854-1955
MAINYARD		
John	Jones	1826-50
MAIZE		
Abney	Jasper	1831-69
MAJOR		
Asbury Stephen	Union	1877-1942
Richard	Hall	1819-37
Samuel	Coweta	1828-48
MALCOLM		
Gomoney	Morgan	1830-60
James	Morgan	1814-30
James	Morgan	1830-60
MALCOMB		
Daniel	Walton	1834-9
MALDEN		
Caleb Sr.	Bibb	1851-71
MALLARD		
Hiram	Screven	1810-1929
MALLORY		
Maria G.	Effingham	1829-59
William	Wilkes	1819-36
MALONE		
Charles	Baldwin	1819-64
Cherry	Bibb	1851-71
Elizabeth	Clarke	1802-22
F. W.	Paulding	1850-77 appr
Henry W.	Baldwin	1819-64
J. W.	Paulding	1850-77
John	Butts	1826-41
John	Clarke	1802-22
John J.	Screven	1810-1929
L. Dr.	Cobb	1873i
(Lizzie B., wid)		
Sherrard	Jasper	1831-9
William	Clarke	1822-42
William	Greene	1806-16
William	Franklin	1786-1813
William P.	Muscogee	1849
MALOY		
D. H.	Telfair	1869-1921
MANDERSON		
John	Wilkinson	1818
John H.	Baldwin	1825
MANER		
Alfred	Cobb	1887
George	Screven	1810-1929
W. E.	Cobb	1904
MANES		
Martha E.	Talbot	--

MANGHAM		
Solomon	Hancock	1810
MANGUM		
James P.	Pike	1844-76
L. N.	Pike	1844-76
Wiley	Henry	1822-34
William	DeKalb	1840-69
MANKIN		
Labman	Wilkes	1810-16
MANLEY		
Daniel	Franklin	1786-1813
Isaac D.	Franklin	1786-1813
MANLY		
Henry	Colonial	1746
MANN		
Catherine	Morgan	1814-30
James Sr.	Elbert	1816
Joel W.	Houston	1855-96
John	Lincoln	1796-1808
John	Monroe	1824-47
John A.	Clayton	1859-1921
Nancy	Upson	1826-1910
Reuben	Morgan	1830-60
Sarah	Fayette	1828-97
Sarah	Sumter	1838-55
Thomas	Sumter	1838-55
Washington L.	Sumter	1838-55
William B.	Sumter	1838-55
Zachariah	Clayton	1859-1921
MANNEN		
Henry	Madison	1812-41
MANNING		
Adam	Putnam	1823-56
Ambrose	Cobb	1867i
(Mary, wid)		
John A.	Wayne	1822-70
John S.	Laurens	1809-40
Joseph	Wayne	1822-70
Levi	Jones	1826-50
Louisa Ann Mrs.	Houston	1855-96
Marinda	Dooly	1847-1901
Mary A.	Cobb	1867i
Regenia	Cobb	1868 minor
Sarah A.	Chattooga	1856-1924
Shadrack	Wayne	1822-70i
Simpson	Cobb	1866i
Susannah	Upson	1826-1910
Williby	Laurens	1809-40
MANSFIELD		
Elizabeth	Stewart	1850-90
Lucius	Stewart	1850-90
MANSON		
James	Wilkinson	1829
Mary Ann	Wilkinson	1863
William	Jefferson	1823
MANTZ		
Philip H.	Richmond	1840-53
William	Elbert	1829-60
MAPP		
Jeremiah	Jasper	1813-19
William	Hancock	1799
MAQUER		
Louis	Morgan	1814-30
MARABLE		
Francis	Oglethorpe	1833-66

MARAN		
Charles	Colonial	1772
MARBURY		
Mary Deborah	Jefferson	1817
(wife of Horatio)		
MARCHION		
W. T.	Early	1856-1927
MARCHMAN		
R. H. Sr.	Cobb	1892
MARKES		
John	Wilkes	1779-92
MARKS		
Adaline E.	Muscogee	1838-62
Francis	Muscogee	1839
Stephen	Warren	1826
MARLOW		
Paul	Effingham	1829-59
Stephen	Screven	1810-1902
MARONEY		
Sarah A.	Chattooga	1856-1924
MARSH		
Oscar H.	Screven	1810-1929
Reuben	Irwin	1821-64
		ind of gift
MARSHALL		
Daniel	Wilkes	1837-77
J.	Pike	1823-29
John	Richmond	1840-53
Joseph	Jefferson	1839
Julius	Lee	1854-1955
M.	Houston	1855-96
Mary A.	Talbot	--
Matthew	Jefferson	1849
Matthew	Lowndes	1871-1915
Matthew	Wilkes	1792-1801
P. G.	Pike	1844-76
Stephen F.	Harris	1850-75
Stephen F.	Talbot	1868
William	Jefferson	1839
William	Jefferson	1846
William	Jones	1826-50
MARSHBURN		
Nicholas	Houston	1855-96
Samuel	Jefferson	1808
Samuel W.	Fayette	1828-97
MARTAINS		
Absalom	Lumpkin	1833-52
John	Lumpkin	1833-52
MARTIN		
Absalom	Hall	1837-67
Alexander	Richmond	1840-53
Alfred M.	Screven	1810-1929
Angus	Richmond	1840-53
Ann	Henry	1822-34
Annie	Upson	1826-1910
Benjamin F.	Greene	1817-42
Benjamin Y.	Muscogee	1838-62
C. C.	Chattooga	1856-1924
Clement Jr.	Colonial	1775
Clement Sr.	Colonial	1771
Dorcas	Habersham	1847-1900
E. A. Mrs.	Chattooga	1856-1924
E. B.	Carroll	1852-96
E. B.	Lee	1854-1955
Elijah	Jones	1812-23
Elisha	Gwinnett	1852-86
Elizabeth	Crawford	1852-94

MATTHEWS (continued)

Meshack Sr.	Jefferson	1818
Micajah	Crawford	1852-94
Moses	Lincoln	1796-1808
Sarah	Early	1856-1927
Thomas	Gwinnett	1852-86
William	Jackson	1802-60
William	Jefferson	1798
William	Marion	1846-1915

MATTHEWSON

John	Colonial	1734

MATTOX

Aaron	Tattnall	1836-40i
David	Oglethorpe	1833-66
Hardage	Morgan	1830-60
James S.	Taliaferro	1826-66
John	Chattooga	1856-1924
John	Tattnall	1836-40i
John A.	Tattnall	1836-40i
gdn for heirs of Henry McGee		
Michael McKenzie	Tattnall	1800-35 deeds
Nathan	Oglethorpe	1833-66
Sarah	Oglethorpe	1833-66

MAUK

Rachel	Wilkes	1810-16

MAULDIN

James D.	Washington	1852-1903

MAUND

Jim	Talbot	--
John C.	Talbot	--

MAUNDER

Isaac	Glynn	1844-53

MAUNEY

Laura	Union	1877-1942
Mary E.	Union	1877-1942

MAURER

George	Colonial	1775

MAURITZEN

Henry L.	Muscogee	1838-62

MAURNEY

Jacob	Bartow	1836-85

MAURY

John	Madison	1842-96

MAUVE

Matthew	Colonial	1770

MAXCEY

Hail	Oglethorpe	1833-66

MAXEY

John	Clarke	1802-22

MAXWELL

Audley	Colonial	1769
Benson	Wilkes	1810-16
John	Colonial	1767
John	Talbot	--
Mary	Colonial	1770
Robert	Washington	1852-1903
Sara L.	Cobb	1895
Thomas Sr.	Elbert	1829-60

MAY

Benjamin	Bibb	1851-71
Edmund Sr.	Washington	1829-71 divs
James	Crawford	1835-52
James	Wilkes	1779-921

MAY (continued)

John	Pike	1844-76
John	Wilkes	1779-92
Kinchen	Bibb	1851-71
Major W.	Greene	1817-42
Middleton D.	Floyd	1852-61 orph
William	Early	1856-1927
William	Washington	1829-71 divs
William J.	Sumter	1838-55 bonds

MAYES

Elizabeth	Cobb	1891
H. M.	Cobb	1891
John	Warren	1839
Robert H.	Lumpkin	1845-1923

MAYFIELD

Jacob	Campbell	1825-1900
M. B. Mrs.	Clayton	1859-1921

MAYO

D. A.	Clayton	1859-1921
Harmon	Dooly	1847-1901
Howell	Washington	1852-1903
James	Clayton	1859-1921
James	Stewart	1850-90i
John A.	Dooly	1847-1901
Richard G.	Sumter	1838-55 bonds
Samuel	Jefferson	1804
Temperance	Pulaski	1816-50
William	Dooly	1847-1901
William	Pulaski	1816-50

MAYS

A. N.	Franklin	1848-67
Benjamin	Jackson	1802-60
G. M.	Lumpkin	1845-1923
Sarah	Harris	1850-75
Valentine	Wilkes	1792-1801
William	Cobb	1866i
William	Cobb	1871i
William B.	Richmond	1840-53

McADAMS

Thomas	Bartow	1836-85

McAFEE

A. H.	Lee	1854-1955
Abraham J.	Crawford	1852-94
Greene	Jasper	1812-17
Jesse	Washington	1829-71 divs
William M.	Lee	1854-1955

McALESTER

Charles	Jefferson	1808

McALLISTER

--	Carroll	1852-96
James C.	Morgan	1830-60
Katharine	Montgomery	1806-63
Sarah Ann	Washington	1852-1903
Westley	Lumpkin	1845-1923

McALPIN

Alexander	Wilkes	1779-92
Ellis	Morgan	1830-60

McARTHUR

Alexander	Montgomery	1806-63
John	Bibb	1823-55
John	Montgomery	1806-63
John	Tattnall	1836-40i

McBANE

John	Laurens	1809-40

McBEAN

Laughlin	Colonial	1756

McCORMICK (continued)

F. A.	Polk	1857–1936
James	Baldwin	1806–19
James M.	Early	1856–89
John	Early	1856–89
John	Warren	1828
Joseph	Lincoln	1796–1808
Maston	Early	1856–89
Nancy	Early	1856–89
W. T.	Early	1856–89

McCOURN

William	Morgan	1814–30

McCOY

Abner	Upson	1826–1910
Archibald	Putnam	1823–56
Augustus C.	Talbot	--
Augustus C.	Talbot	1857
Daniel	Wilkes	1779–92
Daniel S.	Lumpkin	1833–52
David	Warren	1840
Ewell	Morgan	1830–60
Greer	Butts	1826–41
H. C.	Talbot	--
Henry	Clarke	1802–22
Henry	Upson	1826–1910
James	Campbell	1825–1900
John	Morgan	1830–60
John B.	Talbot	--
John H.	Talbot	--
Lucy A. E.	Talbot	--
Martha	Lumpkin	1833–52
Sara Jane	Talbot	--
Thomas	Campbell	1825–1900

McCRADY

Elizabeth	Richmond	1840–53

McCRARY

Francis M.	Baldwin	1819–64
James	Talbot	--
John B.	Talbot	--
John T.	Sumter	1838–55i
Mahala	Lumpkin	1845–1923
Martha Northingham	Talbot	--
Samuel	Hall	1837–67
Wiley C.	Crawford	1852–94

McCRASKEY

W. H.	Lumpkin	1845–1923

McCREE

Mary	Henry	1834–69

McCRELESS

John	Decatur	1824–52
John	Decatur	1828–38

McCRIDIE

David	Lincoln	1831–69

McCROSKEY

Samuel M.	Habersham	1847–1900

McCULLAR

R. D.	Wilkinson	1915

McCULLEN

John	Washington	1829–71 divs

McCULLER

Hiram	Marion	1846–1915
Mary	Jefferson	1803
Mathew	Stewart	1837–49

McCULLERS

Kit	Washington	1852–1903

McCULLOCK

Hardy D.	Dooly	1847–1901
William	Clarke	1822–42

McCULLOUGH

Anthony	Early	1834–1920
John	DeKalb	1840–69
John R.	Henry	1834–69
Leonard P.	Early	1834–1920

McCUNE

John M.	Elbert	1819
Thomas B.	Jasper	1820–23

McCURDY

Stephen	Murray	1840–72

McCURLEY

John	Gwinnett	1852–86

McCURRY

Amos	Rabun	1863–1888
Angus Sr.	Elbert	1829–60
William L.	Rabun	1863–1888

McCUTCHEON

Anna	Henry	1822–34
William	Henry	1822–34

McDANIEL

Archibald	Bartow	1836–85
Benjamin W.	Jasper	1831–9
Benjamin W.	Jones	1812–23
Christian	Meriwether	1831–59
D. P.	Gwinnett	1852–86
Eli J.	Gwinnett	1852–86
Jacob	Jasper	1831–39
James	Gwinnett	1852–86
James (of Burke Co.)	Jefferson	1811
Joshua	Early	--
Phillip	DeKalb	1840–69
William	Wilkinson	1906

McDONALD

Agnes	Lincoln	1796–1808
Alexander Gilbert	Clayton	1859–1921
Angus	Wayne	1822–1870
Catherine	Baldwin	1819–64
Donald	Upson	1826–1910
Gillis	Camden	1795–1829
James	Jefferson	1800
James	Newton	1823–51
Jennie Pye Mrs.	Lee	1854–1955
Jeremiah	Tattnall	1836–40i
John	DeKalb	1840–59
John	Elbert	1823
John A.	Early	1856–1889 L/A
John A.	Early	1856–1927 L/A
John B.	Sumter	1838–55 bonds
Maria	Baldwin	1819–64
R. H.	Polk	1857–1936
Robert	Colonial	1773
Roderick	Putnam	--
Sarah admx of Angus	Sumter	1838–55 bond
Stephen L.	Hall	1837–67
William	McIntosh	1873–1915
William A. Sr.	Ware	1879–1915

McDORMAN

Charlotte (nunc)	Camden	1868–1916

McDORR

J.	Bartow	1836–85

McDOUGAL

Andrew	Jones	1812–23
Neal	Elbert	1816

McDOWELL

Charles	Pike	1844-76
James	Franklin	1786-1813
Margaret	Jackson	1802-60
Martha	Franklin	1786-1813
Martha	Jasper	1826-31
Martha A.	Talbot	--
Michael	Jackson	1802-60
Thomas	Wilkes	1779-92
William	Houston	1855-96
William	Jasper	1822-26
William	Jasper	1823-33
William	Jefferson	1802
of Killamey, Ire.		
William Sr.	Jasper	1826-31

McDUFFY

Malcolm	Franklin	1848-67

McEACHIN

D. N.	Cobb	1896
Daniel	Appling	1877-1925
John W.	Houston	1855-96

McELHANNON

John	Jackson	1802-60

McELMURRAY

James	Burke	1853-70
John R.	Crawford	1852-94

McELMURRY

Andrew	Richmond	1840-53

McELRATH

Jacob	Madison	1812-41

McELREATH

John M.	Cobb	1894

McELROY

Henry	Elbert	1829-60
Henry	Fayette	1828-97
James	Fayette	1828-97
James	Jasper	1820-23
John	Oglethorpe	1793-1807
Peter E.	Fayette	1828-97

McELVOY

John S.	Gwinnett	1852-86

McELVY

William	Decatur	1824-52

McELWER

David	Bartow	1836-85

McENEROE

William	Jasper	1831-39

McENTIRE

John C.	Murray	1840-72
Robert H.	Franklin	1848-67

McEVER

Andrew	Madison	1842-96
John L.	Cobb	1893

McEVOY

R. P.	Bibb	1851-71

McEWEN

James	Madison	1842-96

McEWINEY

Rufus	Madison	1842-96

McFARLAND

Dugal	Jones	1826-50

McFARLAND (continued)

John	Franklin	1848-67
Thomas G.	Montgomery	1806-63

McFARLANE

John	Colonial	1766
Sarah	Camden	1795-1829

McFARLIN

Peter	Jones	1812-23
Shearwood	Troup	1832-48
William	Upson	1826-1910

McGAMBLE

Margaret S.	Talbot	--
McCormick	Talbot	--
Neal	Talbot	--
Owen	Talbot	--
Thomas J.	Talbot	--
William R.	Talbot	--

McGARRAH

M. H.	Marion	1846-1915
Thomas	Marion	1846-1915

McGEE

Ansel	Elbert	1834
Chiles	Madison	1842-96
Dorcas	Screven	1810-1929
Emily (Col)	Screven	1810-1929
Henry (Col)	Screven	1810-1929
J. E.	Lumpkin	1845-1923
John	Harris	1850-75
Perry	Bibb	1823-55
Reuben	Warren	1818
W. H.	Screven	1810-1929

McGEEHEE

Catherine	Baldwin	1819-64

McGEHEE

E. T. Dr.	Houston	1855-96
James	Putnam	1823-56
John	Putnam	1808-22
Micajah	Oglethorpe	1807-26
Nathan	Jackson	1802-60
Robert	Jones	1826-50
Roby	Houston	1855-96
W. B.	Pulaski	1816-50
William	Baldwin	1806-19

McGHEE

James	Murray	1840-72

McGILVERY

John	Colonial	1748

McGINNIS

Celia	Forsyth	1833-44i
W.	Forsyth	1833-44i
William	Forsyth	1833-44

McGINTY

H. E.	Cobb	1867i
Henry C.	Cobb	1866 minors
Milly	Richmond	1840-53
Thomas	Cobb	1869i

McGLAMERY

John K.	Union	1877-1942

McGOUIRK

Lydia	Campbell	1825-1900

McGOWELL

Maria	Bibb	1851-71

McGOWAN

David	Jefferson	1796

McGOWAN (continued)

Jacob	Decatur	1828-38
John	Jefferson	1828

McGOWEN

Joseph	Liberty	1772-1887
Martin	Muscogee	1838-62

McGRADY

Silas	Polke	1857-1936

McGRAW

Philip	Richmond	1840-53

McGRAY

L. E.	Dooly	1847-1901

McGREGGOR

James	Camden	1795-1829

McGREGOR

A. B.	Polk	1857-1936
Daniel	Montgomery	1806-63
E. S., admx	Paulding	1850-77
James	Early	--
Rheese	Paulding	1850-77 bond
Samuel	Paulding	1850-77

McGRIFF

Patrick	Montgomery	1806-63
Thomas	Pulaski	1816-50

McGUERIN

William	Lumpkin	1845-1923

McGUIRE

Edward	Colonial	1761
James	Taliaferro	1826-66
John	Walton	1827-39
John	Walton	1834-9
Martha	Bibb	1851-71
Mary	Colonial	1773

McHENRY

James	Colonial	1767

McINTOSH

Daniel	Thomas	1837-45
David	Morgan	1814-30
Eliza	Camden	1795-1829
Jannett	Montgomery	1806-63
K. F.	Montgomery	1806-63
Lachland	McIntosh	1873-1915
Nancy	Montgomery	1806-63

McINTYRE

Archibald M.	Thomas	1826-36
Daniel	Montgomery	1806-63
Lucy	Montgomery	1806-63

McINVALE

Adeline	Houston	1855-96
Robert	Houston	1827-55

McKAIMIE

Philip	Troup	1832-48

McKAY

James	Chattooga	1856-1924
Thomas Sr.	Campbell	1825-1900

McKEE

Elizabeth	Franklin	1786-1813
F. A.	Putnam	1823-56
J. H.	Lumpkin	1845-1923
Jacob	Henry	1822-34
John	Franklin	1786-1813
Joseph	Lumpkin	1845-1923
Mary M.	Carroll	1852-96

McKEE (continued)

R. W.	Carroll	1852-96
Samuel	Franklin	1786-1813
William G.	Sumter	1838-55 bond

McKEITHAN

Dougald	Stewart	1837-49

McKELVY

James	Bartow	1836-85

McKEMIE

John	Jasper	1823-33

McKENLEY

John	Pike	1844-76

McKENNEY

John	Talbot	--
John H.	Talbot	--
Joshua	Upson	1826-1910
Martha	Talbot	--
Thomas G.	Talbot	--

McKENNY

John I.	Upson	1826-1910
Travis	Lincoln	1796-1808
William A.	Upson	1826-1910

McKENZIE

C. J.	Macon	1856-1909
Henry	Lee	1854-1955
J. H.	Macon	1856-1909
James	Morgan	1830-60
John	Macon	1856-1909
John	Richmond	1840-53
Joseph H.	Macon	1856-1909
Kenneth	Franklin	1786-1813
Kenneth	Muscogee	1838-62
William	Colonial	1773
William	Houston	1827-55

McKERTNEY

Alexander	Colonial	1741

McKIBBONS

James S.	Paulding	1850-77 admr
Sara L. G.	Henry	1822-34

McKIE

Mary	Henry	1834-69

McKINDLEY

Joseph	Upson	1826-1910
Robert	Upson	1826-1910
Robert A.	Upson	1826-1910

McKINLEY

Archibald Carlisle	Oglethorpe	1833-66
William	Putnam	1823-56
William	Talbot	1857

McKINNEY

Benjamin	Houston	1855-96
Benjamin	Macon	1856-1909
Charles	Jackson	1802-60
George	Wilkes	1837-77
John K.	Talbot	1855
Moses	Warren	1832
Moses Sr.	Warren	1801
Sarah	Crawford	1852-94
Valentine	Sumter	1838-55 bonds

McKINNIE

Hicks	Hancock	1810

McKINNON

Murdock	Thomas	1837-45

McKINNY
Kinchen	Marion	1846-1915

McKINZIE
Aaron Sr.	Hancock	1796
J. P.	Carroll	1852-96
James F.	Upson	1826-1910

McKISSACK
John	Putnam	1802-22

McKNIGHT
James	Coweta	1849-92

McLAIN
Amanda	Cobb	1909
Hugh A.	Dooly	1847-1901
James P.	Cobb	1866 minors
John	Wilkes	1792-1801
Mariney	Wilkes	1792-1801
Mary	Fayette	1828-97

McLAMORE
Charles	Jones	1812-23
Henry	Houston	1827-55

McLAREN
James	Muscogee	1845

McLARIN
Harrison	Campbell	1825-1900
Mariah W.	Campbell	1825-1900

McLARTY
John	Campbell	1825-1900
John	Paulding	1850-77
L. H.	Paulding	1850-77 retn
L. W.	Paulding	1850-77 retn

McLEAN
James	Wilkes	1806-08
John	Colonial	1773
John	Fayette	1828-97
John	Telfair	1869-1921
Oliver	Fayette	1828-97

McLEMORE
Catherine	Jasper	1822-26
John	Jasper	1822-26

McLENDON
Dennis	Houston	1855-96
E.	Thomas	1826-36i
E.	Thomas	1837-45 retn
Elizabeth	Henry	1822-34
Frances	Putnam	1823-56
Jeremiah M.	Troup	1832-48
John Sr.	Lee	1854-1955
Judah	DeKalb	1840-69
Lucinda	Talbot	--
Mason	Wilkinson	1826
Penelope Ann	Randolph	1845-94
Samuel	Henry	1834-69
William F.	Talbot	

McLEOD
Alexander	Tattnall	1800-35 deeds
Anna C.	Cobb	1873i
Archibald	Lowndes	1871-1915
Christian	Thomas	1837-45i
Daniel	Lowndes	1871-1915
E. L.	Lowndes	1871-1915
James	Glynn	1844-53 retn
John	Glynn	1844-53
John W.	Glynn	1844-53
Katharine	Montgomery	1806-63
Mary	Tattnall	1836-40 orph
Mary A.	Cobb	1875
Sumpter	Lowndes	1871-1915

McLEOD (continued)
Turtle	Tattnall	1836-40 orph

McLEROY
Thomas	Harris	1850-75

McLERVY
John	Madison	1842-96

McLESKEY
James R.	Jackson	1802-60

McLESTER
Joseph	Jackson	1802-60
Leonidas	Randolph	1845-94
William	Jackson	1802-60

McLIN
David	Coweta	1849-92

McLINNON
Peter	Thomas	1837-45i

McLOUD
Roderick	Colonial	1775

McMAHAN
Bennett	Walton	1834-9
John	Butts	1826-41
John	Jefferson	1809
Woodward	Walton	1870-74

McMATH
Joseph	Warren	1824
M. H.	Meriwether	1831-59

McMICHAEL
David	Jasper	1831-39
Green L.	Jasper	1822-26
James R.	Marion	1846-1915
John	Marion	1846-1915
John B.	Bibb	1851-71
Seaborn	Marion	1846-1915
Zachariah	Jasper	1820-23

McMICHEL
William	Jasper	1813-19
William	Jasper	1821-27

McMILLAN
Archibald	Montgomery	1806-63
John	Baldwin	1806-19
John	Gwinnett	1852-86
John	Macon	1856-1909
Rhesa	Gwinnett	1852-86
Willis	Cobb	1895

McMINN
Joseph	Hall	1837-67

McMORRILL
James	Burke	1853-70
Lafayette	Burke	1853-70
Sarah E. Mrs.	Burke	1853-70

McMULLEN
Andrew	Carroll	1852-96
J. M.	Clayton	1859-1921
John	Elbert	1819
N. S.	Clayton	1859-1921
W. F.	Clayton	1859-1921

McMURRAN
John	Sumter	1838-55

McMURRAY
Henry	Marion	1846-1915
James	Baldwin	1819-64
M.	Bartow	1836-85

McMURRAY (continued)

William	Morgan	1808-13

McNABB

Andrew	Oglethorpe	1793-1807
Elizabeth	Burke	1853-70

McNAIR

Daniel	Wilkinson	1862
Gilbert	Early	1856-1889 L/A
Samuel	Henry	1834-69

McNAMARA

P. J.	Polk	1857-1936

McNEAL

John T.	Morgan	1830-60
Neal	Randolph	1845-94

McNEELY

Andrew	Jefferson	1809
Hugh	Jefferson	1816
Margaret	Jefferson	1816
Patrick	Jefferson	1801
Samuel	Jefferson	1797

McNEIL

Henry	Warren	1799
John S.	Baldwin	1819-64

McNICH

William	Camden	1795-1829

McNICHOLAS

James	Pike	1823-29

McPHERSON

Alfred	Sumter	1838-55 bond
William	Colonial	1761

McQUAIG

C. J.	Ware	1879-1915
John	Montgomery	1806-63

McQUEEN

Mary	Montgomery	1806-63
Phillip	Montgomery	1806-63

McQUETERS

David	Montgomery	1806-63
Lucy Mrs.	Montgomery	1806-63

McRAE

Duncan	Telfair	1869-1921
Farguhand	Montgomery	1806-63
John	Montgomery	1806-63
John Sr.	Montgomery	1806-63
Nancy	Wilkes	1810-16
Nancy A.	Wilkes	1837-77
Norman C.	Lumpkin	1845-1923
Robert	Glynn	1844-53

McREE

E. J.	Lowndes	1871-1915
F. J.	Lowndes	1871-1915
James	Lumpkin	1833-52

McRENNON

Thomas	Glynn	1844-53

McREYNOLDS

M. F.	Bartow	1836-85

McRIGHT

James	Henry	1834-69

McTHY

Jacob	Henry	1822-34

McTYRE

Holland	Richmond	1840-53

McWHORTER

Benjamin D.	Oglethorpe	1833-66
Jacob G.	Richmond	1840-53
Leroy	Carroll	1852-96
Moses H.	Oglethorpe	1833-66

McWILLIAMS

John	Campbell	1825-1900
John	DeKalb	1840-39
Margaret	Randolph	1845-94
Thomas N.	Randolph	1845-94
William	Campbell	1825-1900

MEACHAM

Angeline	Baldwin	1819-64
Henry	Baldwin	1819-64
James	Meriwether	1831-59

MEAD

Edward	Morgan	1830-60

MEADOR

Joel	Wilkinson	1820

MEADORS

Berry	Madison	1842-96
Edward	Walton	1834-9
Edwin	Walton	1834-9
Jesse	Walton	1834-9
William S.	Walton	1834-9

MEADOWS

C.	Union	1877-1942
Elijah	Taliaferro	1826-66
James R.	Washington	1852-1903
James W.	Oglethorpe	1833-66
Mary	Union	1877-1942
Sarah L.	Union	1877-1942
William	Union	1877-1942

MEALING

Henry	Richmond	1840-53

MEANS

Hugh	Walton	1834-9
William	Elbert	--

MEARA

James	Bibb	1851-71

MEARS

Henry	Jefferson	1812
J. Wilson	Screven	1810-1929
John B.	Sumter	1838-55
William	Elbert	1819

MEATH

George	Bibb	1851-71

MEDLIN

Nicholas	Coweta	1849-92

MEDLOCK

Charles	Warren	1796
George	Hancock	1813
George	Warren	1800

MEEK

J. Mark	Henry	1822-34
L. James	Henry	1822-34

MEEKS

Bennet B.	Washington	1852-1903
James	Oglethorpe	1807-26
Margaret	Macon	1856-1909
Noah	Sumter	1838-55 bonds

MILBORNE		
Jeremiah	Taliaferro	1826-66
MILBURN		
John I.	Morgan	1830-60
MILES		
Isaac	Crawford	1852-94
John	Baldwin	1824
MILLAN		
Angus	Montgomery	1806-63
MILLEN		
George	Irwin	1821-64
Mary H.	Clayton	1859-1921
MILLER		
A.	Bartow	1836-85
Alice	Talbot	--
Alsey	Oglethorpe	1833-66
Altoona	Talbot	--
Annie	Wilkinson	1895
Boul	Colonial	1769
Bright	Stewart	1850-90i
Catherine	Camden	1795-1829
Charles	Cobb	1876i
(Mattie, wid)		
Charles	Hancock	1820
Charles	Henry	1834-69
Charles F.	Washington	1852-1903
Claudia M.	Talbot	--
Cullen P.	Talbot	--
David	Glynn	1844-53
David	Montgomery	1806-63
E. K. Mrs.	Glynn	1844-53
E. W.	Marion	1846-1915
Elias	Colonial	1762
Enoch	Wilkinson	1895
Ester	Stewart	1850-90 bond
George	Jones	1826-50
George	Talbot	--
George A.	Cobb	1869
Goodwin	Gwinnett	1852-86
Grace	Stewart	1850-90i
Henry	Oglethorpe	1833-66
Isaac R.	Talbot	--
Isabella	Montgomery	1806-63
J. P.	Glynn	1844-53
Jacob	Campbell	1825-1900
James	Colonial	1772
James	Hancock	1821
John	Crawford	1852-94
John	Jackson	1802-60
John	Montgomery	1806-63
John Sr.	Montgomery	1806-63
John Boul	Colonial	1772
John C.	Effingham	1829-59
Jonathan	Hancock	--
Joseph	Montgomery	1806-63
Julia	Lee	1854-1955
L. E.	Screven	1810-1929
Lewis	Stewart	1837-49
Lucy	Talbot	--
Mark Sr.	Gwinnett	1852-86
Martha	Harris	1850-75
Martha	Warren	1833
Matthew F.	Talbot	--
Michael	Burke	1853-70
Missoura	Talbot	--
Nathaniel	Fayette	1828-97
Palser	Colonial	1771
Phincas	Camden	1795-1829
Robert	Campbell	1825-1900
Robert	Colonial	1773
Rosanna	McIntosh	1873-1915
S. F.	Wilkinson	1902
S. T.	Union	1877-1942
Sylvanus	Glynn	1844-53

MILLER (continued)		
T.	Glynn	1844-53
Thomas	Camden	1795-1829
Thomas M.	Montgomery	1806-63
W. A.	Bartow	1836-85
W. E.	Wilkinson	1902
Wiley	Randolph	1845-94
William	Glynn	1844-53
William	Hancock	1824
William	Jasper	1831-9
William	Screven	1810-1929
William	Upson	1826-1910
MILLICAN		
Charles	Madison	1812-41
John	Bartow	1836-85
John	Madison	1812-41
William T.	Franklin	1848-67
MILLIGAN		
James	Wilkes	1792-1801
MILLS		
Alexander	Wilkes	1777-8
Anthony	Screven	1810-1929
Candacy	Screven	1810-1929
Daniel	Washington	1852-1903
Elizabeth	Washington	1852-1903
Francis A.	Washington	1852-1903
H. B.	Screven	1810-1929
Jacob	Jones	1826-50
John	Washington	1829-71 divs
John	Wilkes	1810-16
Moses	Fayette	1828-97
Stephen	Washington	1852-1903
MILLSAP		
Thomas	Jackson	1802-60
MILLWEE		
John	Bartow	1836-85
MILNER		
Arnold	Bartow	1836-85
John B.	Wilkes	1819-36
John E.	Clayton	1859-1921
John H.	Pike	1844-76
Thomas J.	Fayette	1828-97
Willis	Wilkes	1779-92
MILPEN		
Lot	Fayette	1828-97
MILSER		
Aquilla	Henry	1834-69
MILTON		
Elizabeth	Jefferson	1836
J. P.	Appling	1877-1925
Jesse	Ware	1879-1915
Jonathan	Clarke	1802-22
MIMMS		
Wright	Sumter	1838-55 bond
MIMS		
E. E.	Appling	1877-1925
Elizabeth	Coweta	1828-48
Martin	Wilkes	1779-92
Mary K.	Screven	1810-1929
Needham	Bibb	1851-71
William	Jasper	1813-19
Williamson	Houston	1855-96
MINCHEW		
A. P.	Ware	1879-1915
Phillip	Bibb	1823-55

MINER		
Rachael	Gwinnett	1852-86
MINHINETTE		
Francis R.	Cobb	1886
MINIS		
Abraham	Colonial	1754
MINNISH		
Elizabeth	Jackson	1802-60
Isaac	Jackson	1802-60
John	Jackson	1802-60
MINOR		
A. Julia	Oglethorpe	1807-26
Andrew J.	Gwinnett	1852-86
William	Hancock	1797
MINSHAW		
Nathan	Houston	1827-55
MINTER		
John S.	Upson	1826-1910
MINTON		
John	Wilkes	1819-36
M. D.	Cobb	1905
M. W.	Cobb	1874
Rosanna	Cobb	1874
Tabitha	Wilkes	1806-08
MINYARD		
Thomas	Hall	1837-67
MITCHELL		
Alexander	Bibb	1851-71
Augustus	Camden	1868-1916
Daniel	Jasper	1812-17
Elizabeth	Clayton	1859-1921
Elizabeth	Harris	1850-75
G. W.	Gwinnett	1852-86
George G. F.	Marion	1846-1915
Hardy	Cobb	1868
Harriett L.	Clayton	1859-1921
Henry	Washington	1852-1903
Isaac	Forsyth	1833-44i
Isaac	Wilkinson	1840
J. J.	Baldwin	1819-64
Jacob	Greene	1817-42
James	Franklin	1786-1813
John	Macon	1856-1909
John D.	Lincoln	1796-1808
John G.	Carroll	1852-96
John V.	Pulaski	1816-50
Larkin W.	DeKalb	1840-69
Levern	Talbot	--
Margaret N.	Talbot	--
Martha C.	Cobb	1871 minors
N.	Carroll	1852-96
Nimrod S.	Franklin	1848-67
Robert M. I.	Jones	1826-50
Samuel	Hancock	1807
Samuel	Pike	1823-29
Samuel	Pike	1844-76
Serand	Talbot	--
Stephen	Pulaski	1816-50
Thomas	Clayton	1859-1921
Thomas	Thomas	1826-36
Thomas	Wilkes	1779-92
Thomas A.	Taliaferro	1826-66
Wiley	Franklin	1848-67
William	DeKalb	1840-69
William	Franklin	1848-67
William	Henry	1834-69
William	Jasper	1825-31
William	Morgan	1808-13
William	Talbot	--
William Sr.	Clarke	1802-22
MITCHELL (continued)		
William S.	Baldwin	1819-64
MITCHENER		
John	Screven	1810-1929
MIXON		
James D.	Burke	1853-70
Michael	Burke	1853-70
MIZE		
James C.	Polk	1857-1936
John J.	Franklin	1848-67
W. B.	Franklin	1848-67
MIZELL		
Luke	Screven	1810-1929
MOAKS		
Eli	Campbell	1825-1900
MOBLEY		
Esther	Coweta	1849-92
Jethro	Coweta	1849-92
Lewis	Crawford	1835-52
Resin	Coweta	1849-92
MOCK		
A. W.	Screven	1810-1929
Andrew	Screven	1810-1929
John Peavy	Screven	1810-1929
L. G.	Screven	1810-1929
MOFFAT		
Jane	Meriwether	1831-59
MOGAR		
Edward	Emanuel	1851
MOIR see Mori		
MOLDER		
Catherine	Franklin	1786-1813
Daniel	Franklin	1786-1813
Samuel W.	Stewart	1850-90i
MOLLEY		
Benjamin	Muscogee	1838-62
Joseph M.	Oglethorpe	1807-26
MONCRIEF (see Muncrief)		
Austin	Lincoln	1808-32
Wiley	Lincoln	1831-69
MONDEVILLE		
Mary	Richmond	1840-53
MONEY		
Joseph	Colonial	1774
MONFORD (or Montford)		
Ann	Colonial	1762
James	Wilkes	1810-16
Margaret H. Miss	Polk	1857-1936
MONGHAM		
Thomas	Jones	1826-50
William	Jones	1826-50
MONK		
James G.	Cobb	1887
R. B. S.	Dooly	1847-1907
Silas	Decatur	1824-52 Mts
MONROE (see Munroe)		
James D.	Randolph	1845-94
Lorenzo D.	Randolph	1845-94

MONS

Elmira	Lee	1854–1955

MONTFORD

Thomas	Laurens	1809–40

MONTGOMERY

Anne	Jefferson	1835
Benjamin	Jasper	1831–9
Benjamin	Troup	1832–48
David	Jasper	1831–9
David	Wilkes	1779–92
Elizabeth Mrs.	Madison	1842–96
Elizabeth	Troup	1832–48
H. T.	Cobb	1866 minor
James M.	DeKalb	1840–69
John	Madison	1811–40
John N.	Madison	1842–96
Mary	Wilkes	1837–77
Middleton B.	Gwinnett	1852–86
P. Smith	Coweta	1828–48
W. R.	Cobb	1906
William R.	Cobb	1867 minor

MOODY

Elizabeth	Richmond	1840–53
James Sr.	Liberty	1772–1887
Joel	Upson	1826–1910
John	Appling	1877–1925
John W.	Oglethorpe	1833–66
Lelah	Oglethorpe	1833–66
Mary J.	Wayne	1822–70
Robert	Glynn	1844–53
Thomas	Oglethorpe	1833–66

MOON

Alexander	Colonial	1747
Archelaus	Madison	1842–96
C. C.	Cobb	1876 minors
Elizabeth	Cobb	1881i
Francis	Clarke	1822–42
Francis C.	Oglethorpe	1833–66
Gabriel T.	Bartow	1836–85
H. B.	Cobb	1909
H. J.	Clayton	1859–1921
H. P.	Madison	1842–96
J. L.	Cobb	1876 minors
John W.	Cobb	1876i
Jonathan	Hancock	--
Pleasant	Elbert	1818
Pleasant	Madison	1842–96
Richard	Hancock	1795
Robert	Jackson	1802–60
Samuel	Warren	--
Susannah	Hancock	1819
Wells	Henry	1834–69
William	Cobb	1876i
William	Elbert	1810
William	Troup	1832–48

MOONEY

Betsy	Morgan	1814–30

MOONEYHAN

Kincheon	Gwinnett	1852–86

MOOR

Cason	Washington	1852–1903
George	Upson	1826–1910
Mathew	Washington	1852–1903

MOORE

Alexander	Henry	1822–34
Allen	Lowndes	1871–1915
Amanda	Habersham	1847–1900
Benjamin	Morgan	1814–30
Bishop	Jones	1826–50
Calvin J.	Elbert	1829–60
Charles	Hancock	1799

MOORE (continued)

Charles H.	Screven	1810–1929
Curtis T.	Upson	1826–1910
E. A.	Marion	1846–1915
Ebenezer H.	Jones	1826–50
Eliza	Muscogee	1838–62
Elizabeth B.	Cobb	1870i
Ephraim	Hancock	1801
Francis	Greene	1794–1810
Francis	Muscogee	1839
Francis	Richmond	1840–53
Francis B.	Houston	1855–96
George	Paulding	1850–77
George H.	Lowndes	1871–1915
George S. A.	Cobb	1909
George W.	Bibb	1823–55
Green B.	Jones	1826–50
Henry E.	Lowndes	1871–1915
Hopton	Lowndes	1871–1915
Irene	Talbot	--
Isaac	Henry	1834–69
Jacob A.	Gwinnett	1852–86
James	Emanuel	1868i
James	Glynn	1844–53
James S.	Troup	1832–48
Jane	Talbot	--
Jeffrey	Richmond	1840–53
(free man of color)		
Jeremiah	Greene	1817–42
Jeremiah	Upson	1826–1910
Jeremiah A.	Cobb	1871i
John	Cobb	1871i
John	Henry	1834–69
John	Jefferson	1815
John	Jones	1826–50
John	Oglethorpe	1833–66 (1859)
John	Richmond	1840–53
John	Screven	1810–1929
John	Wilkes	1779–92
John C.	Cobb	1897
Jonas	Wilkes	1792–1801
Joseph	Wilkes	1779–92
Joseph	Wilkes	1792–1801
Joseph Sr.	Oglethorpe	1793–1807
Joshua	Greene	1817–42
Luke A.	Baldwin	1819
M. E. Mrs.	Screven	1810–1929
Martha	Taliaferro	1826–66
Mary	Baldwin	1819–64
Mary	Jones	1826–50
Mary J.	Talbot	--
Matthew	Jones	1826–50
Mattie Mrs.	Cobb	1909
Nancy	Troup	1832–48
Priscilla J. M.	Baldwin	1819–64
Ransom	Greene	1817–42
Richard	Campbell	1825–1900
Richard	Walton	1819–37
Robert H.	Lumpkin	1845–1923
Samuel	Henry	1834–69
Seaborn	Talbot	--
Seth	Wilkes	1792–1801
Sinthey	Laurens	1809–40
Thomas	Emanuel	1868 L/A
Thomas	Hancock	1796
W. W.	Carroll	1852–96
Whittington	Baldwin	1819–64
William	Burke	1853–70
William	Clarke	1822–42
William	Colonial	1762
William	Jackson	1802–60
William	Sumter	1838–55 bond
William Walker	Houston	1855–96
Willis	Henry	1834–69

MOORMAN

Andrew	Colonial	1761

MORAN

A. B.	Crawford	1852-94
Elisha	Hancock	1807
J.	Crawford	1835-52
John	Baldwin	1819-64
Kincy	Clayton	1859-1921

MORE

Edward	Jefferson	1805

MOREFIELD

C. H.	Floyd	1861-71

MOREL

John	Colonial	1774
John J. B.	Screven	1810-1929
Peter	Colonial	1752

MORELAND

Colsen	Pike	1844-76
D. A. Mrs.	Dooly	1847-1901
Elsie Coleman	Ware	1879-1915
Francis	Greene	1794-1810
Francis	Jasper	1831-9
John	Wilkinson	1825
John Sr.	Putnam	1823-56
Penelope	Coweta	1849-92
Rebecca	Gilmer	1836-53
Robert O.	Coweta	1849-92
Tuttle H.	Houston	1827-55

MOREMAN

John	Meriwether	1831-59
Thomas	Wilkes	1819-36

MORGAN

B. J.	Screven	1810-1929
Caroline	Polk	1847-1931
Charles C.	Sumter	1838-55 bond
Charles W.	Sumter	1838-55 bond
adm of Charlotte		
Christopher C.	Emanuel	1866i
David	Cobb	1868
David	Jones	1812-23
Elizabeth	Franklin	1786-1813
Ellington	Hancock	1813
G. F.	Polk	1857-1931
G. W.	Paulding	1850-77
G. W.	Polk	1857-1931
George F.	Polk	1857-1931
Hardy	Jefferson	1840
Henry	Coweta	1849-92
Hobson	Meriwether	1831-59
Isham	Elbert	1822
J. A.	Polk	1857-1931
James	Polk	1857-19931
Jesse F.	Dooly	1847-1901
John	Franklin	1786-1813
John	Glynn	1844-53
John	Jefferson	1845
John Sr.	Morgan	1814-30
John B.	Coweta	1849-92
Joseph U.	Sumter	1838-55
Joshua	Taliaferro	1826-66
Lorenzo	Fayette	1828-97
Manerva Mrs.	Polk	1857-1931
Mary Ann	Lowndes	1871-1915
Stephen	Ware	1879-1915
Stephen Sr.	Jefferson	1825
Stokeley	Jasper	1831-9
Susan	Dooly	1847-1901
Susan	Glynn	1844-53
Thomas M.	Coweta	1849-92
Thomas W.	Polk	1857-1931
W. H.	Carroll	1852-96
W. H.	Polk	1847-1931
William	Jackson	1802-60
William	Jasper	1831-9
William	Marion	1846-1915

MORGAN (continued)

William	Meriwether	1831-59
William A.	Washington	1852-1903
William C.	Coweta	1849-92

MORI

Zynthia Elizabeth Mrs.	Screven	1810-1929

MORING

John	Sumter	1838-55 bond

MORLAND

Martin, Capt.	Colonial	1751

MORLEY

Lewis	Greene	1817-42

MORRELL

Jordan	Muscogee	1838-62

MORRIS

A. E.	Madison	1842-96
Alonzo	Henry	1822-34
B. G.	Houston	1855-96
Charles	Taliaferro	1826-66
Delila	Stewart	1850-90i
Elizabeth	Jones	1812-23
Esther	Paulding	1850-77
Frederick	Jefferson	1835
Gideon	DeKalb	1840-69
Henry	Jasper	1826-31
Henry C.	Jackson	1802-60
J. L.	Carroll	1852-96
James	DeKalb	1840-69
James	Randolph	1845-94
John	DeKalb	1840-69
John	Franklin	1848-67
John	Jackson	1802-60
John	Jasper	1812-17
John	Jasper	1822-26
M. S.	Polk	1857-1936
Nathan	Hancock	--
Nathaniel	Jones	1826-50
Obediah	Baldwin	1820
Pauline Mrs.	Appling	1877-1925
Richard A.	Clayton	1859-1921
Richardson L.	McIntosh	1873-1915
Robert E.	Sumter	1838-55 bond
Sarah	Hancock	1841
Simon Sr.	Taliaferro	1826-66
Stephen	Madison	1842-96
T. J.	Appling	1877-1925
T. J.	Polk	1857-1936
Thomas	Bartow	1836-85
Thomas	Jones	1826-50
Thomas	Muscogee	1838-62
Thomas L.	Taliaferro	1826-66
Thompson	Cobb	1895
William	Burke	1853-70
William	Wilkes	1819-36

MORRISON

Alexander	Jackson	1802-60
Charlotte E.	Camden	1795-1829
D. O.	Montgomery	1806-63
Daniel	Montgomery	1806-63
Daniel	Putnam	1808-22
David	Polk	1857-1936
Elizabeth	Montgomery	1806-63
George	Camden	1795-1829
George	Camden	1868-1916
George S.	McIntosh	1873-1915
John	Montgomery	1806-63
Peter	Montgomery	1806-63
Thomas	Wilkes	1779-92

MORROW

E.	Forsyth	1833-44i

MORROW (continued)
Isaac	Bartow	1836-85
J. H.	Clayton	1859-1921
J. W.	Clayton	1859-1921
John	Gwinnett	1852-86
Margaret	Greene	1786-95
Radford E.	Clayton	1859-1921
W. N.	Clayton	1859-1921

MORTON
A. P.	Paulding	1850-77
		gdn bond
John F.	Chattooga	1856-1924
John W.	Chattooga	1856-1924
Joseph	Oglethorpe	1807-26
Silas	Screven	1810-1929

MOSELEY
Benjamin	Henry	1834-69
Benjamin Sr.	Wilkes	1792-1801
Benjamin L. G.	Henry	1822-34
Benjamin T.	Polk	1857-1936
C. D. Mrs.	Chattooga	1856-1924
Henry H.	Henry	1822-34
John H.	Franklin	1848-67
Joseph Sr.	Wilkes	1819-36
Joseph Baker	Coweta	1849-92
Mark	Coweta	1828-48 orph
Osburn	Coweta	1828-48
S. W.	Habersham	1847-1900
Samuel	Chattooga	1856-1924
William	Henry	1822-34 bond
William	Lincoln	1808-32

MOSES
Davis	Talbot	1855
Jacob J.	Muscogee	1838-62
John	Jasper	1812-17
John	Jasper	1813-19
Orien	Montgomery	1806-63
Ralph	Thomas	1837-45i
Samuel	Jasper	1812-17

MOSLEY
Howell	Fayette	1828-97

MOSS
A. Y.	Cobb	1908
Alfred	Cobb	1863i
Charity	Lincoln	1808-32
David M.	Lincoln	1831-69
E. N. Mrs.	Wilkes	1837-77
Gabriel	Harris	1850-75
Gabriel	Troup	1832-48
Henry	Baldwin	1808
John	Newton	1823-51
Lewis	Hancock	1808
Lydia	Lincoln	1831-69
Richard	Habersham	1847-1900
William	Elbert	1829-60
William B.	Richmond	1840-53

MOSTELLER
Jonathan	Carroll	1852-96

MOTLEY
Thomas	Muscogee	1838-62

MOULDER
John	Cobb	1901

MOULTRAY
John	Warren	1795

MOULTRIE
William	Gwinnett	1852-86

MOUND
William	Early	1834-1920

MOUNTAINS
Jane	Jefferson	1830
John	Jefferson	1821

MOUNTCASTLE
Ludwell	Wilkes	1810-16

MOYE
Benjamin	Early	1834-1920 bonds
E. C.	Talbot	--
George	Washington	1829-71 divs
John	Early	1834-1920
John	Early	1856-89
Martha	Early	1834-1920
Mary Jane	Early	1834-1920
Sarah	Jefferson	1845
Sarah	Washington	1852-1903
Thomas E.	Washington	1852-1903
William	Early	1834-1920 bonds
William	Early	1856-89 L/A

MOYER
Enos C.	Talbot	--
William	Chattooga	1856-1924

MUCH
Evan E.	Camden	1795-1829

MUCKLEROY
John	Oglethorpe	1793-1807

MULIEDAY
Thomas	Wilkes	1819-36

MULKEY
Eliza	Morgan	1830-60
James	Jasper	1826-31
James	Morgan	1814-30
John	Wilkes	1779-92
Mary	Taliaferro	1826-66
Ruth	Jefferson	1816
(wid of Philip M.)		(of Burke Co.)
Sarah A.	Randolph	1845-94

MULLALLY
Thomas	Taliaferro	1826-66

MULLIKEN
Syrius	Taliaferro	1826-66

MULLINS
Bud	Paulding	1850-77
Duncan	Montgomery	1806-63
George W.	Randolph	1845-94
James	Randolph	1845-94
Jeremiah	Jones	1826-50
Malone	Hancock	1840
R. D.	Forsyth	1833-44
Robert	Lumpkin	1833-52

MULLIS
James	Randolph	1845-94
John J.	Appling	1877-1925

MUMFORD
Robert	Lincoln	1831-69

MUNCRIEF (see Moncrief)
Anne	Warren	1840

MUNDEN
William	Wayne	1822-70

MUNDY
R. W.	Clayton	1859-1921
Reuben L.	Clayton	1859-1921

MUNROE (see Monroe)
Nathan	Bibb	1851-71

NEAL (continued)

Moses	Coweta	1828–48 retn
R. A. R.	Franklin	1848–67
R. M.	Chattooga	1856–1924
Rhoda C.	Chattooga	1856–1924
Robert	Franklin	1786–1813
Sarah	Greene	1817–42
Sarah	Warren	1814
Scott (Col)	Pike	1844–76
Stephen H.	Carroll	1852–96
William	Morgan	1814–30
William	Paulding	1850–77

NEALY

J. S.	Thomas	1837–45 div
Joseph	Thomas	1837–45

NEAN

Godleib	Effingham	1829–59

NEAVES

James	Baldwin	1818
John	Baldwin	1828

NEEL

Julia	Emanuel	1825
		deed of gift

NEELEY

Eveline Mrs.	Clayton	1859–1921

NEELY

Nancy	Oglethorpe	1833–66
Thomas	Oglethorpe	1833–66
Thomas W.	Burke	1853–70

NEIDLINGER

Ulrich (Tanner)	Jefferson	1781

NEIGHBORS

Jane	Paulding	1850–77 retn
William	Paulding	1850–77
p/a to Samuel		

NEIL

Thomas	Jackson	1802–60

NEILL

James G.	Coweta	1849–92
Robert	Murray	1840–72
William	Coweta	1849–92

NEISLER

David	Lumpkin	1845–1923

NEITHERLIN

James	Richmond	1840–53

NELLY

Jackson	Coweta	1849–92

NELMS

Alice	Elbert	1829–60
Jordan	Elbert	1829–60
Oliver A.	Taliaferro	1826–66
Thomas	Greene	1796–1806
Thomas	Oglethorpe	1793–1807
William	Henry	1822–34

NELSON

Christian	Greene	1817–42
Elizabeth	Richmond	1840–53
John	Taliaferro	1826–66
John	Wilkes	1779–92
Malcolm	Colonial	1778
Matthew	Richmond	1840–53
S. A.	Appling	1877–1925
Taylor	Morgan	1814–30
Thomas J.	Upson	1826–1910

NELSON (continued)

W. D.	Union	1877–1942
Wade S.	Wilkinson	1863
William	Troup	1832–48
Woodford M. D.	Union	1877–1942

NESBIT

Alexander	Wilkinson	1865
James R.	Wilkinson	1883
Sarah	Warren	1839

NESBITT

Mary Ann	Cobb	1865

NESMITH

Isaac	Burke	1853–70

NETTS or Nettles

Mary Mrs.	Cobb	1875i

NEWBERRY

John	Decatur	1824–52 Mts
William	Jones	1812–23

NEWBORN

Archibald	Elbert	1829–60

NEWBY

Jesse	Wilkes	1779–92

NEWCOMB

John	Liberty	1772–1887

NEWELL

Betsy Ann	Coweta	1849–92
D. J.	Cobb	1869
George F.	Cobb	1904
R. J.	Paulding	1850–77 appr
Samuel	Coweta	1849–92

NEWMAN

Allison	Jones	1810–28
Robert L.	Coweta	1849–92
Samuel	Warren	1795
William	Randolph	1845–94

NEWSOM

Ann Maria	Early	1834–1920 bonds
Ella Mrs.	Lee	1854–1955
Henry	Bibb	1851–71
John	Putnam	1823–56
Jorday	Washington	1829–71 divs
Kinchen	Washington	1829–71 divs
Lorenzo D.	Washington	1829–71 divs
Peter	Warren	1805
W. H.	Lee	1854–1955
William Augustus	Lee	1854–1955

NEWSOME

H. K.	Washington	1852–1903
Jorday	Washington	1852–1903
Lucy	Wilkinson	1827
Solomon	Washington	1852–1903
Solomon	Wilkes	1779–92

NEWSON

Elender	Houston	1827–55

NEWTON

Clary	Clarke	1822–42
David B.	Screven	1810–1929
George	Screven	1810–1929
George M.	Screven	1810–1929
George W.	Screven	1810–1929
James	Jasper	1823–33
James	Screven	1810–1929
James H.	Lowndes	1871–1915
John	Oglethorpe	1793–1807
Mary Ann	Screven	1810–1929

NEWTON (continued)		
Moses	Screven	1810-1929
Phillip	Emanuel	1851
Reuben	Screven	1810-1929
William	Jackson	1802-60

NIBLACK		
Thomas	Jackson	1802-60
William	Camden	1795-1829

NIBLET		
Nancy	Meriwether	1831-59

NICHOLS		
Benjamin	Wilkes	1779-92
Fannie	Cobb	1890
Robert	Colonial	1768
Vincent	Crawford	1852-92
W. T.	Cobb	1874

NICHOLSON		
Ann	Jackson	1802-60
J. W.	Stewart	1850-75
John	Screven	1810-1929
Nathaniel	Stewart	1850-90

NICKELSON		
George	Oglethorpe	1833-66

NICKOLS		
Francis	Camden	1795-1829

NICOLSON		
John	Oglethorpe	1807-26

NIGHINGALE		
John Clark	Camden	1795-1829

NILSON		
Abel	Harris	1850-75

NIMMONS		
William	Coweta	1849-92

NIMS		
Joe	Upson	1826-1910

NISBET		
Eugenia A.	Bibb	1851-71
James	Morgan	1830-60
James A.	Bibb	1851-71
James S.	Clarke	1822-42

NIX		
Chesley M.	Habersham	1847-1900
David	Coweta	1849-92
Harrison	Gwinnett	1852-86
Mary J.	Campbell	1825-1900

NIXON		
John	Clarke	1802-22
Mary	Wilkinson	1842
Travis	Jackson	1802-60
William	Bibb	1823-55

NOBLE		
E. S.	Early	1856-1927 L/A
Lewis	Wilkinson	1831
William	Morgan	1814-30

NOCHOLSON		
James	Lincoln	1831-69

NOE (or Noah)		
Bennett	Cobb	1869i

NOEL		
Azariah	Gwinnett	1852-86

NOELL		
Robert	Oglethorpe	1807-26

NOLAN		
James	Clayton	1859-1921
James	Wilkes	1837-77
Thomas	Morgan	1830-60
William Sr.	Lincoln	1808-32

NOLEN		
William	Newton	1823-53

NORMAN		
Argyle	Wilkes	1837-77
Barak	Colonial	1765
Elizabeth	Wilkes	1819-36
Elizabeth	Wilkes	1837-77
G. G.	Wilkes	1837-77
Harman J.	Wilkes	1837-77
Jesse	Wilkes	1837-77
P. W.	Lincoln	1831-69
Sarah	Bibb	1851-71
W. J.	Carroll	1852-96
William	Colonial	1773

NORRIS		
A.	Taliaferro	1826-66
Archibald	Madison	1840-60
Cornelius A.	Upson	1826-1910
James	Elbert	1804
James	Warren	1832
Joel	Warren	1833
Thomas	Camden	1795-1829

NORSWORTHY		
George	Hancock	1802

NORTEN		
A. J.	Paulding	1850-77
M. A. Mrs.	Clayton	1859-1921
W. E.	Clayton	1859-1921

NORTH		
Abraham V.	Coweta	1849-92

NORTHCUTT		
Alfred M.	Cobb	1897
J. J.	Cobb	1888

NORTHEN		
Basset	Clayton	1859-1921

NORTHERN		
Emma	Coweta	1849-92

NORTHINGTON		
James	Morgan	1830-60
James	Oglethorpe	1833-66
Samuel	Greene	1806-18

NORTHRUP		
Immanuel	Oglethorpe	1807-26

NORTON		
Charles B.	Floyd	1852-61
James	Floyd	1852-61
John Wesley	Lee	1854-1955
Patrick	Taliaferro	1826-66
Thomas	Oglethorpe	1793-1807

NORWOOD		
Croxton	Franklin	1848-67

NOYES		
Alice H.	Polk	1857-1936
Annie S.	Polk	1857-1936

NUITE		
Charles H.	Union	1877-1942

NUNES

Daniel	Camden	1795-1829

NUNN

Elis	Emanuel	1867 gdns bond
(Lugenia, Rodolphus, Jackson, Philip R., minors)		
Joshua	Emanuel	1867i
Phillip H.	Emanuel	1866i

NUNNALLY

A. B.	Screven	1810-1929
John	Clarke	1822-42
R. W.	Screven	1810-1929

NUNNELLE

James	Elbert	1829-60
William	Elbert	1804

NUNNELLY

Q. E.	Pike	1823-9

NUTE

Jeremiah	Richmond	1840-53

NUTH

Jane Mrs.	Madison	1842-96
William	Clarke	1802-22

NUTT

Andrew	Morgan	1814-30
Samuel	Marion	1846-1915
W. B.	Marion	1846-1915

OAKS

S. E. Mrs.	Clayton	1859-1921

O'BANNON

John	Wilkinson	1853

OBAU

Malisha	Lumpkin	1833-52

O'CALLAHAN

Michael	Screven	1810-1929

ODAM

Elizabeth	Washington	1852-1903

ODEL

S. F.	Cobb	1878 minor

ODELL

Frances J.	Chattooga	1856-1924

ODOM

Charity	Early	1856-1927
D. W.	Macon	1856-1909
Ezekiel	Muscogee	1838-62
L. A. Mrs.	Lee	1854-1955
Sabra	Bibb	1823-55

O'DRISCAL

Dennis	Lee	1854-1955

ODUM

Green W.	Early	1856-1927 L/A
Mary A.	Randolph	1845-94
Zadock	Early	1834-1920 bonds

OGBURN

Ethelred	Wilkinson	1880
L. B.	Macon	1856-1909

OGDEN

Alexander	Camden	--

OGILBY

Anne	Oglethorpe	1807-26
Francis	Oglethorpe	1807-26
John	Oglethorpe	1807-26
John T.	Walton	1834-9
Martha	DeKalb	1840-69

O'GILVIE

A. W.	Coweta	1849-92

OGILVIE

John	Oglethorpe	1833-66

OGLESBY

Garrott	Wilkes	1837-77
John	Emanuel	1867 insane gdns bond
Lindsay	Bartow	1836-85
William	Elbert	1829-60
Zachariah	Elbert	1829-60

OGLETREE

John	Wilkes	1819-36
Rebecca	Wilkes	1819-36

O'HAGAN

E.	Ware	1879-1915

O'KELLEY

F. D.	Gwinnett	1852-86
James	Walton	1870-74

O'KELLY

Thomas	Madison	1811-40
Thomas	Madison	1812-41
Thomas J.	Hall	1837-67
William J.	Taliaferro	1826-66

OLIFF

Joseph	Emanuel	1868 gdn bond

OLIVE

Anthony	Oglethorpe	1793-1807
Franklin H.	Talbot	1858

OLIVER

Alick	Houston	1855-96
Benjamin	Screven	1810-1929
Benjamin	Warren	1809
Caleb	Elbert	1826
Caleb	Jones	1812-23
Eldridge G.	Crawford	1852-92
Eldridge G.	Macon	1856-1909
Elizabeth	Jackson	1802-60
Henry	Dooly	1847-1901
Howard	Screven	1810-1929
Irena	Sumter	1838-55 bond
(minor of Wm.)		
James	Elbert	1829-60 (1824)
John	Elbert	1816
John	Elbert	1817
John	Screven	1810-1929
John	Wilkes	1792-1801
John S.	Macon	1856-1909
Joseph	Clarke	1808-22
L. L.	Cobb	1906
M. E.	Lumpkin	1845-1923
Peter M.	Cobb	1865
T. W.	Screven	1810-1929
William H.	Macon	1856-1909
Zilpha	Burke	1853-70

OLLIFF

Benjamin	Dooly	1847-1901

OMARY

George W.	Carroll	1852-96

O'NEAL
Edmund	Putnam	1823-56
Irby	Glynn	1844-53
Nathaniel	Wilkes	1792-1801
Sarah	Putnam	1808-22
Warren	Morgan	1814-30
William	Carroll	1852-96
William	Laurens	1809-40
William	Lincoln	1808-32

O'NEIL
John	Wayne	1822-70
Mary	Wayne	1822-70
Sibbiah	Wayne	1822-70

ONEYLAND
David	Sumter	1838-55 bond

OPIE
William T.	Screven	1810-1929

OPPERT
V. H.	Polk	1857-1936

O'PRY
Amos	Houston	1855-96

O'REILLY
Christopher C.	Washington	1852-1903

ORMSBY
Theodore et al	Cobb	1867 minor

ORR
Burrell	Randolph	1845-94
David	Cobb	1907
James	Jackson	1802-60
John	Jackson	1802-60
Jonathan L.	Coweta	1849-92
M.	Pike	1823-29
Nancy M. Mrs.	Washington	1852-1903
Niah W.	Coweta	1849-92
Phillip	Coweta	1828-48
W. D.	Coweta	1849-92
William E.	Cobb	1888

ORTON
Christopher	Colonial	1742

OSBORN
Jesse	Gwinnett	1852-86
John	Paulding	1850-77 appr
Newman	Gilmer	1836-53
Reuben	Washington	1829-71 divs
Sallie	Washington	1852-1903
William	Fayette	1828-97
William	Troup	1832-48

OSBORNE
Isaac	Paulding	1850-77 bond
Robert	Burke	1853-70

OSBURN
John	Clarke	1822-42
John M.	Clayton	1859-1921

OSLIN
Isaac	Greene	1817-42
Jesse L. G.	Henry	1822-34
Sarah A. Mrs.	Clayton	1859-1921

OSTEEN
Samuel	Oglethorpe	1807-26

OSWALD
Joseph	Liberty	1772-1881

OTWELL
William W.	Forsyth	1833-44

OURSBY
Ann Catherine	Warren	1840

OUSLEY
R. A.	Lowndes	1871-1915

OUTLAW
Bentley	Wilkinson	1874

OVERLY
Thomas	Coweta	1849-92
William	Coweta	1849-92

OVERSTREET
Causey	Screven	1810-1929
George M.	Screven	1810-1929
Louis	Screven	1810-1929

OVERTON
Gilchest	Taliaferro	1826-66

OWEN
Davis	Coweta	1849-92
Donald Sr.	Talbot	1860
George	Meriwether	1831-59
Glen	Oglethorpe	1833-66
Hiram	Cobb	1839
J. R.	Paulding	1850-77 bond
Jennie	Cobb	1868 minor
John D.	Talbot	1863
Mary	Upson	1826-1910
Mary A. Mrs.	Randolph	1845-94
Mildred	Wilkes	1806-08
Sarah	Wilkes	1819-36
Uriah	Wilkes	1819-36
William	Polk	1857-1936

OWENS
Benjamin F.	Bibb	1823-55
Elijah	Baldwin	1814
J.	Forsyth	1833-44i
Jacob	Jasper	1826-31
John	Burke	1853-70
John	Colonial	1775
John	Henry	1834-69
John Sr.	Wilkes	1792-1801
John U.	Henry	1834-69
Mary	Crawford	1852-94
Mary	Wilkes	1837-77
Nathaniel L.	Screven	1810-1929
Spencer	Jones	1812-23
Thomas	Lincoln	1796-1808

OWENSBY
S. J. F.	Carroll	1852-96
Thomas	Henry	1834-69

OWINGS
Mathew	Chattooga	1856-1924
W. H.	Chattooga	1856-1924

OWNLY
John P.	Lumpkin	1845-1923

OWSLEY
Newdsy (?)	Hancock	1791

OXFORD
Anna	Henry	1822-34
David	Lumpkin	1833-52
Edward	Henry	1822-34
Edward	Wilkes	1792-1801
Jonathan	Jones	1810-28

OZLEY
Jesse	Elbert	1829-60
Larkin	Elbert	1829-60

PARKER (continued)		
John P.	Campbell	1825-1900
Joseph	Colonial	1766
Lucinda E.	Polk	1857-1936
Mary A.	Bibb	1851-71
Mathew	Dooly	1847-1901
Michael	Screven	1810-1929
Rebecca	Sumter	1838-55
Rebecca	Sumter	1838-55 bond
(admr of James)		
Richard	Taliaferro	1826-66
Sarah	Washington	1829-71
Solomon	Liberty	1772-1881
Stephen	Putnam	1808-22
Thomas	Colonial	1759
Thomas	Screven	1810-1929
W. H.	Screven	1810-1929
William	Polk	1857-1936
William	Talbot	1827
William H.	Washington	1829-71

PARKERSON

Levin	Wilkes	1837-77

PARKINSON

John	Colonial	1769

PARKS

Abraham	Elbert	1829-60
Barton	Walton	1827-39
Bird Jr.	Coweta	1849-92
Bird Sr.	Coweta	1849-92
Charles	Elbert	1805
Charlott	Marion	1846-1915
Effiah J.	Walton	1827-39 orph
Franklin R.	Coweta	1849-92
Henry	Franklin	1786-1813
J. D.	Lumpkin	1845-1923
James	Cobb	1864i
James	Cobb	1871i
James	Walton	1827-39 orph
Joel L.	Early	1834-1920 bonds
John B.	Jasper	1822-26
John G.	Franklin	1848-67
Lewis	Lincoln	1831-69
Lewis G.	Lincoln	1831-69
R. B.	Polk	1857-1936
Samuel	Pike	1844-76
Thomas H.	Coweta	1849-92
Virgil	Lumpkin	1845-1923
Welcome	Coweta	1849-92
William	Clayton	1859-1921
William	Lincoln	1831-69
Wyatt	Muscogee	1847

PARLAND

John	Glynn	1844-53

PARMELA

Thomas J.	Richmond	1840-53

PARNELL

Elizabeth	Sumter	1838-55
John	Elbert	1797

PARR

Charles	Murray	1840-72
William	Harris	1850-75

PARRAMORE

Jeremiah	Early	1856-1927

PARRIS

Sarah L., admx	Paulding	1850-77

PARRISH

Joel	Greene	1817-42
Shadrach	Wilkes	1779-92

PARROT

Henry	Jasper	1820-23
John	Fayette	1828-97

PARROTT

Benjamin	Greene	1817-42
J. R.	Bartow	1836-85

PARSONS

Ann	Jefferson	1826
John	Jefferson	1800
Sarah A.	Burke	1853-70
Thomas	Jefferson	1800
William	Jefferson	1813

PARTAIN

Peter	Jones	1810-28

PARTRIDGE

Sarah	Wilkes	1819-36
William	Wilkes	1818-19

PASCHAL

Samuel	Jasper	1813-19
Samuel	Wilkes	1837-77
William	Lincoln	1831-69

PASLEY

William D.	Upson	1826-1910

PASSMORE

John	Harris	1850-75
Josephus Sr.	Marion	1846-1915

PATE

Amsey D.	Wilkinson	1902
James	Fayette	1828-97
James M.	Clayton	1859-1921
Mary P.	Harris	1850-75
Redding	Washington	1829-71 divs
Redding	Washington	1852-1903
Zelph E. Mrs.	Dooly	1847-1901

PATERSON

John T.	Bibb	1851-71

PATMAN

Elijah W.	Floyd	1861-71
Susannah	Oglethorpe	1833-66
W.	Coweta	1828-48i
William Sr.	Oglethorpe	1807-26

PATRICK

Abram P.	Bibb	1823-55
John	Butts	1826-41
John A.	Chattooga	1856-1924
John H. Sr.	Franklin	1848-67
Joshua	Burke	1853-70
Josiah D.	Oglethorpe	1823-51
N.	Dooly	1842-1901
William	Newton	1823-51

PATTERSON

Francis M.	Fayette	1828-97
G. D.	Wilkes	1877-94
George R. D.	Washington	1829-71 divs
Henry	Madison	1842-96
Isabella	Wilkes	1818-19
James	Elbert	1829-60
James	McIntosh	1873-1915
John	Bartow	1836-85
John	Elbert	1818
John	Muscogee	1842
John Sr.	Elbert	1808
Robert	Jefferson	1822
Robert C.	Murray	1840-72
S. J. Sr.	Camden	1795-1829
Thomas M.	Jefferson	1840
William	Burke	1853-70

PATTERSON (continued)

William	Crawford	1835-52
William	Elbert	1829-60
William	Walton	1834-9
Willie	Jones	1826-50

PATTILLO

Charles F.	Houston	1855-96
David	Morgan	1808-13
James	Henry	1834-69
James (Major)	Jefferson	1804
John	Harris	1850-75
John O.	Greene	1817-42

PATTISHALL

Joshua	Houston	1827-55

PATTISON

Reuben B.	Randolph	1845-94

PATTON

J. P.	Madison	1842-96
Jane	Clarke	1802-22
Matthew	Wilkes	1806-08
Robert H.	Bartow	1836-85
Samuel	Elbert	1810
Samuel	Oglethorpe	1807-26
Samuel Y.	Jackson	1802-60
William	Union	1877-1942

PAUL

Andrew	Early	1834-1920 bonds
Benjamin	Taliaferro	1826-66

PAULETT

David	Jefferson	1810
Elizabeth	Jefferson	1799
Mary	Jefferson	1800
Richard	Campbell	1825-1900

PAULK

John	Wilkinson	1823
Micajah	Wilkinson	1858

PAVERY

Catharine	Effingham	1829-59

PAYN

W. P.	Clayton	1859-1921

PAYNE

Ann	Franklin	1786-1813
Chambliss	Franklin	1786-1813
Cleveland	Franklin	1786-1813
Daniel	Tattnall	1800-35 deeds
Daniel	Wilkes	1779-92
David	Franklin	1786-1813
George	Laurens	1809-40
John	Franklin	1786-1813
John	Greene	1817-42
John	Jasper	1831-9
John A.	Randolph	1845-94
John B.	Union	1877-1942
(to Victor)		
Lotty	Newton	1823-51
Mary	Franklin	1786-1813
Mary	Troup	1832-48
Nancy	Franklin	1848-67
Pollard	Marion	1846-1915
Reuben	Franklin	1786-1813
Robert A.	Upson	1826-1910
Sarah	Franklin	1786-1813
Thomas	Baldwin	1822
Thomas	Franklin	1786-1813
Thomas J.	Franklin	1786-1813
William	Glynn	1844-53
William	Oglethorpe	1807-26
Zebediah	Franklin	1786-1813

PEACOCK

A. P.	Washington	1829-71 divs
Anna	Washington	1852-1903
D. W.	Clayton	1859-1921
Daniel	Jasper	1826-31
Edgar Stiles	Upson	1826-1910
John	Jasper	1826-31
Levi	Wilkinson	1822
Louis	Cobb	1864 minors
Thomas	Colonial	1769

PEAK

Thomas	Randolph	1845-94

PEALMAN

Elizabeth	Lincoln	1831-69

PEARCE

Joel B.	Upson	1826-1910
John	Fayette	1828-97
Joshua	Screven	1810-1929
Kelly	Bartow	1836-85
Leroy L.	Harris	1850-75
Stephen	Screven	1810-1929
Thomas	Harris	1850-75

PEARMAN

William	Wilkes	1818-19

PEARS

T. P.	McIntosh	1873-1915

PEARSON

Christopher	Marion	1846-1915
Enoch	Butts	1826-41
Henry	Wilkes	1810-16
J. W.	Wayne	1822-70
John	Upson	1826-1910
Oliver M.	Fayette	1828-97
Peter	Marion	1846-1915
S. M.	Wayne	1822-70
William	Forsyth	1833-44 minor

PEAVEY

Joseph	Warren	1810

PECK

David	Morgan	1830-60

PEDERO

S. S.	Gwinnett	1852-86

PEEBLES

Henry	Warren	1829

PEEK

E. W.	Lumpkin	1845-1923
Eliza	Lumpkin	1845-1923
Henry	Hancock	1824
Foster	Polk	1857-1936
James	Lumpkin	1845-1923
Margaret	Taliaferro	1826-66
William	Polk	1857-1936
William T.	Taliaferro	1826-66

PEEKS

John C.	Stewart	1850-90

PEEL

John Sr.	Jefferson	1816
Richard	Jefferson	1793-1806

PEEPLES

Abram M.	Camden	1795-1829
David	Greene	1794-1810
J. A. Sr.	Camden	1795-1829
Joseph	Walton	1834-9
William J.	Gwinnett	1852-86

PEGG		
G. Y.	Sumter	1838-55 bond
William	Sumter	1838-55 bond

PEIRSON		
John	Jones	1812-23
William	Pike	1844-76

PELLETEER		
Basite	Camden	--

PELOT		
John F.	Wilkes	1857-77

PEMBERTON		
Anne	Muscogee	1838-1924
Aston	Burke	1853-70

PEMBLETON		
Esther	Lowndes	1871-1915

PENCE		
Absalom	Gilmer	1836-53

PENDAL or Pendall		
Sarah	Lincoln	1796-1808
Sarah	Wilkes	1779-92

PENDARVIS		
Joseph	Wayne	1822-70

PENDERGRASS		
Edwin	Jackson	1802-60

PENICK		
Joseph P.	Morgan	1830-60
Robert	Morgan	1814-30

PENN		
John	Elbert	1824
John W.	Chattooga	1856-1924
Thomas H.	Bartow	1836-85
Wilson	Elbert	1811

PENNINGTON		
J. E.	Polk	1857-1936
John	Sumter	1838-55 bond
(minors of E.)		
Nathan	Glynn	1844-53
Nathan	Oglethorpe	1807-26
Sion	Jefferson	1822
Thomas	Jasper	1825-31
Thomas	Meriwether	1831-59
William B.	Jasper	1826-31

PENNON		
Francis	Floyd	1852-61 minor
Rebecca	Floyd	1852-61 minor
William	Coweta	1849-92

PENNY		
Calvin	Dooly	1847-1901

PENROSE		
John	Colonial	1754

PENROW		
William	Burke	1853-70

PENTECOST		
F. T.	Floyd	1852-61

PEPPER		
Daniel P.	Bibb	1823-55
James M.	Floyd	1861-71

PERDUE		
Alfred	Pike	1844-76
William	Jefferson	1823

PERKERSON		
James H.	Cobb	1879 minor
T. D.	Cobb	1876i

PERKIN		
Henry	Troup	1832-48

PERKINS		
Archibald	Colonial	1766
Archibald	Jasper	1826-31
Brinson L.	Burke	1853-70
Constantine	Morgan	1814-30
Constantine	Morgan	1830-60
David	Burke	1853-70
David	Lincoln	1796-1808
David S.	Burke	1853-70
James	Stewart	1850-90
Jefferson	Randolph	1845-94
John	Colonial	1766
John	Taliaferro	1826-66
Mithe A.	Burke	1853-70
Moses	Jasper	1823-33
Newton	Burke	1853-70
Newton M.	Burke	1853-70
Peter	Warren	1801
S. Mills	Burke	1853-70
Sarah	Greene	1817-42
Walker	Greene	1817-42
William	Morgan	1830-60
William J.	Stewart	1850-90

PERKINSON		
John	Cobb	1874i
Nancy S.	Cobb	1876 minor

PERRY		
A. R.	Cobb	1872i
C. H.	Early	1856-1927 L/A
Elizabeth	Early	1856-1927
Green	Putnam	1823-56
J. Walker	Chattooga	1856-1924
James	Tattnall	1836-40i
James R.	Bibb	1823-55
John G.	Stewart	1850-90
Josiah	Newton	1823-59
Lottie	Washington	1852-1903
Martha	Newton	1823-59
Oscar H.	Chattooga	1856-1924
Peter	Clarke	1802-22
W. F.	Gwinnett	1852-86
Walter	Wilkes	1819-36
William	Jasper	1825-31
William	Meriwether	1831-59
William C.	Lumpkin	1845-1923
William M.	Harris	1850-75
William P.	Upson	1826-1910

PERRYMAN		
Anthony M.	Franklin	1786-1813
David	Franklin	1786-1813
James	Marion	1846-1915
Mary	Marion	1846-1915
Robert	Putnam	1808-22

PERSONS		
Robert B.	Talbot	1862

PERVIS		
Martha	Early	1856-1927

PETEE		
Jane	Wilkes	1819-36

PETEET		
Chenoth	Wilkes	1837-77
Elizabeth	Wilkes	1837-77
Richard	Wilkes	1837-77

PETERS

Edmund	Morgan	1830-60
John	Walton	1827-39
John	Wilkes	1779-92
Joseph C.	Macon	1856-1909
Lewis M.	Macon	1856-1909
Lovicy	Macon	1856-1909

PETERSON

Ann	Early	1834-1920
Jacquelin	Hancock	1824
John	Baldwin	1806
Mallone	Montgomery	1806-63
Robert B.	Early	1834-1920
Thomas B.	Early	1834-1920
William	Putnam	1808-22

PETIT

Benjamin	Wilkes	1792-1801

PETTICROW (Pettygrow)

John	Colonial	1758

PETTIGREW

John	Colonial	1775

PETTIJOHN

Jacob	Jackson	1802-60

PETTIT

Betsey	Henry	1834-69
Levi H.	Polk	1857-1936

PETTUS

Ann	Wilkes	1837-77
John	Wilkes	1837-77
S. G. Sr.	Wilkes	1837-77
Sarah G.	Wilkes	1837-77
Stephen G.	Wilkes	1837-77

PETTWAY

H. B.	Jones	1812-23

PETTY

Adah	Jackson	1802-60

PEUREY

Green	Dooly	1847-1901

PEURIFOY

Stanley	Upson	1826-1910

PFIFFER

A. K.	Screven	1810-1929
B.	Screven	1810-1929
L. F.	Screven	1810-1929

PHARR

Ephraim	Oglethorpe	1793-1807
Ephraim	Wilkes	1792-1801
Francis	Elbert	1803
Francis	Jackson	1802-60

PHELPS

David	Wilkes	1779-92
Lucinda	Jasper	1823-33
Thomas	Jasper	1831-9
Washington	Jasper	1822-26

PHIFER (Phifner)

Daniel	Colonial	1737

PHILEMAN

B. B.	Early	1856-1927 L/A
B. D.	Early	1856-1889 L/A

PHILIPS

Ambrose	Harris	1850-75
Asa A.	Franklin	1848-67

PHILIPS (continued)

John	Campbell	1825-1900
Mark	Wilkes	1779-92
Wilder	Harris	1850-75
Zachariah	Coweta	1828-48

PHILLIPS

A.	Henry	1834-69
Albert	Coweta	1849-92
Ashley	Early	1856-1927 bonds
Benjamin	Morgan	1814-30
Benjamin	Screven	1810-1929
David	Wilkes	1819-36
George	Greene	1817-42
Elijah	Meriwether	1831-59
Elizabeth	Pike	1823-29
Elizabeth	Wilkes	1810-16
George D.	Habersham	1847-1900
H. C.	Henry	1834-69
Hilery	Jasper	1826-31
Hiram	Polk	1857-1936
Isaac	Jasper	1812-17
Isham	Henry	1834-69
J. H.	Polk	1857-1936
J. T.	Screven	1810-1929
James	Bartow	1836-85
James	Jasper	1831-39
James	Newton	1823-51
John	Oglethorpe	1807-26
John	Taliaferro	1826-66
Leonard	Campbell	1825-1900
Leonard	Early	1834-1920
Lucretia	Montgomery	1806-63
Lucy	Screven	1810-1929
Lula Mrs.	Polk	1847-1936
M. M.	Cobb	1900i
M. T.	Cobb	1878i
Maria	Early	1834-1920
Mark	Greene	1817-42
Mark	Laurens	1809-40
Mark	Montgomery	1806-63
Martha	Muscogee	1838-62
Mary	Early	1834-1920
Mary	Jones	1812-28
Mary	Washington	1852-1903
Micajah	Montgomery	1806-63
Nancy	Montgomery	1806-63
Nancy L.	Richmond	1840-53
Pierce A.	Muscogee	1838-62
Richard	Screven	1810-1929
Ryal Bud	Emanuel	1836
Sarah	Harris	1850-75
Sherod	Emanuel	1868i
Singleton	Walton	1834-9
Solomon	Meriwether	1831-59
Solomon H.	Marion	1846-1915
Spencer R.	Polk	1857-1936
Susannah	Washington	1852-1903
T.	Clayton	1859-1921
Thomas	Jackson	1802-60
Tom	Pulaski	1816-50
William	Early	1834-1920
William	Putnam	1808-22
William R.	Ware	1879-1915
Winifred	Polk	1857-1936
Zachariah	Walton	1834-9

PHILPOT

Charlott Mrs.	Polk	1857-1936

PHILSON

Eliza Mrs.	Glynn	1844-53

PHINIZY

Jacob	Oglethorpe	1833-66

PHIPPS

Aaron	Wilkes	1792-1801
Joseph	Lincoln	1808-32

PICHETT		
Priscilla	Pike	1823-29
PICKENS		
Israel F.	Muscogee	1838-62
John	Jackson	1802-60
John B.	Cobb	1866 minor
M. C.	Cobb	1877 minor
M. J.	Cobb	1877 minor
R. H.	Cobb	1868i
PICKETT		
Betsey	Baldwin	1826
James	Murray	1840-72
James C.	Sumter	1838-55 bond
Jeptha Sr.	Stewart	1850-90
Jepthy B.	Sumter	1838-55 bond
Nancy	Morgan	1814-30
William	Baldwin	1813
PICKLES		
Richard	Early	1856-1929
PIERCE		
Barney W.	Screven	1810-1929
Edmund	Colonial	1757
H. S.	Lumpkin	1845-1923
James	Wilkinson	1883
Jesse	Early	1856-1927 L/A
John C.	Lumpkin	1845-1923
Mary A.	Lumpkin	1845-1923
Thomas	Jefferson	1845
Thomas	Screven	1810-1929
PIERSON		
Elizabeth	Lumpkin	1845-1923
PIGGS		
William	Jones	1810-28
PILCHER		
Lewis	Washington	1852-1903
PILINTON		
Isaac	Upson	1826-1910
PILKINGTON		
Robert	Pike	1844-76
PILMAN		
Nimrod	Washington	1829-71
PINDER		
Ellen	Screven	1810-1929
PINE		
Tamsey T.	Baldwin	1824
PINEHARD		
James	Stewart	1837-49
PINKARD		
C. E. Mrs.	Upson	1826-1910
Enoch	Bartow	1836-85 retns
James C.	Paulding	1850-77 appr
Thomas C.	Coweta	1828-48 retn
PINKERTON		
O.	Bartow	1836-85
PINKSTON		
Green B.	Stewart	1850-90
John	Hancock	1799
Shadrach	Stewart	1837-49
PINSON		
Boyd	Oglethorpe	1833-66
Charles	Bartow	1836-85
James	Jasper	1812-17

PINSON (continued)		
James	Madison	1842-96
William B.	Coweta	1849-92
Winney	Warren	1798
PINYAN		
Stokes	Lumpkin	1845-1923
PIPKINS		
Moses	Dooly	1847-1901
PIPPARD		
William	Bartow	1836-85
PIPPINS		
Clayton	Jones	1826-50
PITT		
Louisiana	Bibb	1823-55
PITTARD		
Elijah	Gwinnett	1852-86
PITTMAN		
Elbert	Sumter	1838-55 bond
Haring	Randolph	1845-94
James	Wilkinson	1883
James N.	Lincoln	1831-69
John E.	Polk	1857-1936
M. A. M. Mrs.	Washington	1852-1903
Mary	Sumter	1838-55 bond
R. M.	Cobb	1873i
PITTS		
Aaron	Jones	1812-23
Asa	Coweta	1828-48
George	Pulaski	1816-50
H. W.	Carroll	1852-96
Hardy	Warren	1840
Henry	Muscogee	1835
Isaac	Dooly	1847-1901
Jesse	Houston	1855-96
John	Baldwin	1817
John	Jones	1826-50
Lunsford	Houston	1855-96
M. V.	Cobb	1895i
Polly Ann	Cobb	1872i
Robert P.	Polk	1857-1931
Samuel	Harris	1850-75
Sarah	Carroll	1852-96
Thomas N.	Marion	1846-1915
(from Pike Co.)		
William	Warren	1811
PLACE		
Seth	Colonial	1757
PLANT		
George B.	Houston	1855-96
William	Meriwether	1831-59
PLASTER		
Benjamin	DeKalb	1840-69
PLATILLO		
Elizabeth	Troup	1832-48
PLATT		
George	Jasper	1812-17
Jonathan	Union	1877-1942
PLAYER		
Joseph E.	Wilkinson	1920
PLEDGE (or Pledger)		
Joseph	Clayton	1859-1921
Simeon	Elbert	1834
Thomas	Elbert	1829-60

PLETTER

John	Colonial	1773

PLUMMER

James W.	Gwinnett	1852-86

POGUE

Andrew	Hancock	1797

POLHILL

Nathaniel	Colonial	1756
Nathaniel	Jefferson	1844
Rebecca	Jefferson	1838

POLLARD

Clarence Alice	Ware	1879-1915
Marina	Floyd	1852-61
Richard	Jasper	1823-33
Thomas	Taliaferro	1826-66
William P.	Harris	1850-75

POLLEN

Charlotte	McIntosh	1873-1915

POLLOCK

Jesse	Houston	1827-55
Lewis	Houston	1855-96
Thomas	Houston	1855-96

POLSTON

Jonathan	Carroll	1852-96

POMCEY

Lucian T. C.	Camden	1830-67
Victor	Camden	1830-67

POMEROY

Edgar	Cobb	1891

PONDER

Abner	Oglethorpe	1807-26
Ephraim	Jefferson	1836
George R.	Chattooga	1856-1924
J. H.	Cobb	1904
James	Oglethorpe	1807-26
Jane G.	Oglethorpe	1807-26
John H.	Morgan	1830-60
Maiden Word Mrs.	Chattooga	1856-1924

PONDS

John M.	Henry	1834-69

POOL

A. J. H.	DeKalb	1840-69
Aaron	Jefferson	1803
B. G.	Bartow	1836-85
Dudley	Wilkes	1819-36
Elizabeth	Jefferson	1847
Elzy W.	Cobb	1898
James	Henry	1834-69
James	Houston	1855-96
John S.	Paulding	1850-77
Middleton	Washington	1829-71 divs
Philip	Warren	1801
Samuel	Jackson	1802-60
Stovall	Wilkes	1837-77
T. J.	Carroll	1852-96
Temperance	Henry	1834-69

POOLE

Clabourn	Hall	1819-37
Walter	Franklin	1848-67
William	Franklin	1848-67

POPE

Alexander	Wilkes	1837-77
Ann E.	Stewart	1850-90
Barnaby	Hancock	1794
Burwell	Clarke	1822-42

POPE (continued)

Burwell	Wilkes	1779-92
Fleet	Laurens	1809-40
Henry	Oglethorpe	1807-26
Hunter C.	Wilkes	1837-77
J. F.	Carroll	1852-96
J. H.	Clayton	1859-1921
James	Houston	1827-55
Jesse	Hancock	1818
John	Randolph	1845-94
John	Wilkes	1819-36
John H.	Wilkes	1837-77
Lewis	Oglethorpe	1793-1807
Mary Mrs.	Burke	1853-70
Mary	Wilkes	1837-77
Mary F. (nee Palmer)	Cobb	1875i
Middleton	Oglethorpe	1833-66
Middleton	Washington	1852-1903
Olive	Oglethorpe	1833-66
W. A.	Cobb	1875 minor
Wiley H.	Morgan	1830-60
Willy M.	Randolph	1845-94
Wylie	Wilkes	1819-36

POPHAM

Amstead	Habersham	1847-1900

POPWELL

James P.	Wayne	1822-70i

PORLE

Maggie C.	Polk	1857-1936

PORTER

B. S.	Lumpkin	1845-1923
Benjamin	Macon	1856-1909
Benjamin	Wilkes	1819-36
Catherine	Jasper	1825-31
Cecelia	Wilkes	1819-36
Douglas M.	Morgan	1814-30
Elizabeth	Jasper	1823-33
Elizabeth	Morgan	1830-60
Jedethan	Franklin	1848-67
Joel F.	Stewart	1850-90
Joel S.	Early	1834-1920 bonds
John	Morgan	1830-60
John Sr.	Dooly	1847-1901
John P.	Clayton	1859-1921
Joseph	Lumpkin	1833-52
Joseph	Lumpkin	1845-1923
Oliver	Greene	1817-42
William	Stewart	1850-90

PORTERFIELD

James	Madison	1842-96
W. H. C.	Madison	1842-96

PORTREE

James P.	Pike	1823-29

POSEY

Bennett	Troup	1832-48
Henry	Washington	1852-1903
Jane C.	Coweta	1849-92
John H.	Putnam	1823-56
Marcus	Warren	1831
Thomas	Warren	1824

POSNER

Joseph Gabriel	Jefferson	1812

POSS

William	Wilkes	1837-77

POST

Gordon W.	Lee	1854-1955
Joseph M.	Troup	1832-48

POSTELL		
J. C.	Houston	1855-96
POSTON		
Jefferson S.	Washington	1852-1903
POTTER		
E. D.	Chattooga	1856-1924
Ira L.	Stewart	1850-90
Washington	Sumter	1838-55 bond
POTTS		
Henry	Jackson	1802-60
Moses	Wilkes	1792-1801
Stephen	Jasper	1826-31
Stephen	Jasper	1831-39
Thomas O.	Coweta	1849-92
William	Jackson	1802-60
POTS		
Avis	DeKalb	1840-69
POU		
James	Jasper	1831-39
POUND		
Joel	Hancock	1842
John L.	Gwinnett	1852-86
Merryman	Putnam	1823-56
William	Taliaferro	1826-66
POWELL		
Barney	Walton	1834-9
Benjamin	Wilkes	1819-36
Charity	Warren	1807
Charles	Clarke	1802-22
Coleman	Early	1856-1889 L/A
Coleman	Early	1856-1927 L/A
Edward Jr.	Oglethorpe	1793-1807
Edward Sr.	Oglethorpe	1793-1807
George	Upson	1826-1910
Hiram	Early	1856-1927
Hiram	Early	1856-1927 L/A
Hiram	Talbot	1851
James	Coweta	1828-48
James	Jefferson	1803
James B.	Early	1856-1889 L/A
Jason	Jefferson	(no date)
John	Coweta	1849-92
John	Oglethorpe	1793-1807
John	Oglethorpe	1807-26
John Dr.	Jefferson	1826
Lewis	Screven	1810-1929
Martha	Glynn	1844-53
Mary	Colonial	1776
Mary	Wilkes	1819-36
Mary	Wilkes	1837-77
Moses	Jasper	1820-23
Nelson	Wilkes	1819-36
Reuben	Jefferson	1823
Sampson	Houston	1827-55
Sarah J.	Clayton	1859-1921
Seymore	Oglethorpe	1807-26
Stephen	Jefferson	1802
Theophilus	Jefferson	1824
Thomas	Chattooga	1856-1924
Thomas	Talbot	1866
Thomas S.	Randolph	1845-94
W. L. B.	Polk	1857-1936
W. O.	Rabun	1863-88
William	Decatur	1828-38
William	Jasper	1812-17
William	Marion	1846-1915
William R.	Elbert	1829-60
Zacheus	Jasper	1812-17
POWER		
David	Madison	1812-41
F. E.	Madison	1842-96

POWER (continued)		
Francis	Madison	1812-41
Francis	Madison	1842-96
J. D.	Madison	1842-96
James	Madison	1812-41
William	Madison	1812-41
William W.	Madison	1842-96
POWERS		
Agnes P.	Bibb	1851-71
Clem	Effingham	1829-59
Edward	Muscogee	1838-62
John	Dooly	--
John	Effingham	1829-59
John	Greene	1806-18
Julia A.	Bibb	1851-71
Lewis	Hall	1837-67
Michael	Walton	1827-31
Milton H.	Effingham	1829-59
Sarah J.	Early	--
POYNER		
John	Henry	1834-69
POYTHRESS		
Cleton	Screven	1810-1929
H. C.	Screven	1810-1929
PRATHER		
Benajah	Wilkes	1837-77
Elias J.	Wilkes	1837-77
John	Gilmer	1836-53
Nathaniel	Stewart	1850-90
Richard	Cobb	1879
Thomas	Wilkes	1819-36
William C.	Stewart	1837-49
PRATT		
James	Houston	1855-96
Leonard	Harris	1850-75
N. A.	Cobb	1879
PRAY		
Ann	Wilkes	1819-36
PRENIERES (Pruniere)		
Joseph	Colonial	1768
PRESBY		
John	Henry	1834-69
PRESCOTT		
Anderson	Burke	1853-70
Ann C.	Early	1834-1920 bonds
Benjamin	Screven	1810-1929
George	Early	1834-1920 bonds
Jesse P. Sr.	Lowndes	1871-1915
Ransom	Lowndes	1871-1915
Richard	Houston	1827-55
Samantha	Appling	1877-1925
PRESKITT		
N. Harris	Burke	1853-70
PRESTON		
David	Crawford	1835-52
George W.	Crawford	1835-52
Gilliam	Butts	1826-41
Thomas	Clarke	1822-42
PREWETT		
Japheth	Franklin	1786-1813
Samuel	Franklin	1786-1813
PRICE		
A. C.	Chattooga	1856-1924
Edward	Hancock	1799
C. C.	Carroll	1852-96
Daniel	Wilkes	1810-16

PRICE (continued)

Francis	Fayette	1828–97
H. F.	Bartow	1836–85
Harriett	Washington	1852–1903
James	Clarke	1822–42
John	Lincoln	1808–32
L. B. Jr.	Washington	1852–1903
Meredith	Hancock	1796
Moor	Washington	1852–1903
O. S.	Fayette	1828–97
Percy A.	Lee	1854–1955
Richard	Washington	1829–71 divs
Thomas S.	Floyd	1861–71
W. P.	Lumpkin	1845–1923
W. P. Sr.	Lumpkin	1845–1923
William	Lumpkin	1833–52
Zemulia	Putnam	1823–56

PRICHARD

Presley	Putnam	1823–56

PRICKETT

Jesse	Henry	1834–69
John	Jasper	1822–26

PRIDE

Francis W.	Randolph	1845–94

PRIEST

William	Colonial	1737

PRIMROSE

Lucy	Henry	1834–69

PRINCE

Noah	Walton	1834–9

PRINGLE

Coleman S.	Pike	1844–76

PRIOR

Anna Mrs.	Polk	1857–1936
Asa	Polk	1857–1936
Dennis	Polk	1857–1936
Elizabeth H. C.	Morgan	1830–60
J. M.	Polk	1857–1936
John	Morgan	1814–30
Robert	Jefferson	1820
Sarah Ann A.	Polk	1857–1936
Spencer minors of Robt.	Sumter	1838–55 bond
William	Screven	1810–1929

PRITCHARD

James H.	Glynn	1844–53
Mamie Mrs.	Cobb	1877i
Nancy	Cobb	1877i
Richard	Glynn	1844–53

PRITCHETT

Christopher	Muscogee	1838–62
Elizabeth	Early	1856–89 bonds
George	Franklin	1786–1813
Gilbert	Gilmer	1836–53i
Joseph	Hancock	1817

PROCTOR

James	Thomas	1837–45i
John A.	Upson	1826–1910
Joshua	Thomas	1837–45
Richard	Camden	1795–1829
William	Camden	1868–1916
William	Wilkes	1819–36
William	Wilkinson	1821

PROTHERO (or Prothro)

Evan	Elbert	1822
Nathaniel	Elbert	1823
Solomon	Colonial	1775

PRUETT

Henry	Muscogee	1845
Itai	Cobb	1890
Jacob	Muscogee	1839

PRUITT

Maston	Hancock	1810
Michael	Hall	1819–37
Robert W.	Madison	1842–96

PRUNIERE

Amie	Colonial	1755

PRYCE

Elizabeth	Colonial	1759

PRYER

Marlow L.	Baldwin	1825

PRYOR

John Sr.	Pike	1844–75
Sheppard G.	Lee	1854–1955
William	Pike	1844–76

PUCKETT

E. D. Jr.	Bartow	1836–85
Martin	Morgan	1830–60
Rhoda Ann	Wilkes	1779–92
Robert M.	Randolph	1845–94
W. M.	Bartow	1836–85

PUGESLY

John I.	Washington	1852–1903
Tabitha G.	Washington	1852–1903

PUGH

Able	Hancock	1832
J. G.	Houston	1855–96
Shadrach	Thomas	1826–36 declar for pension
William	Hall	1837–67

PULHAM

Nelson	Upson	1826–1910

PULLEN

George Sr.	Wilkes	1837–77
James	Wilkes	1837–77
James T. Sr.	Polk	1857–1936
John M.	Wilkes	1837–77
Mary	Wilkes	1837–77
Mary Ann	Wilkes	1837–77
Mildred R.	Meriwether	1831–59
Silas M.	Wilkes	1837–77
Thomas	Laurens	1809–40

PULLIAM

William	Elbert	1829–60

PULLIN

Elias	Decatur	1824–52 Mts
Henry	Emanuel	1842

PURCELL

Darius E.	Franklin	1848–67

PURDOM

T.	Wayne	1822–70
Thos.	Wayne	1822–70

PURDY

John	Marion	1846–1915
Samuel	Marion	1846–1915

PURIFOY

Arington	Jasper	1825–31
S. M.	Jasper	1826–31
Sarah	Putnam	1823–56

PURKINS		
Robert	Clarke	1802-22
PURPLE		
Samuel B.	Muscogee	1838-62
PURSLEY		
James M. Sr.	Chattooga	1856-1924
PURY		
John Rodolph	Colonial	1756
PUTMAN		
Thomas	Hall	1819-37
PUTNAM		
Katie	Ware	1879-1915
PURVIS		
Charles C.	Montgomery	1806-63
PYE		
Andrew	Bibb	1851-71
Jesse	Putnam	1823-56
John	Colonial	1755
Mary H.	Putnam	1823-56
PYLES		
Everitt V.	Early	1856-1889 L/A
PYRON		
Lewis	Meriwether	1831-59
QUARTERMAN		
Elijah	Liberty	1772-1881
John	Colonial	1763
John	Colonial	1767
Thomas	Liberty	1772-1881
William	Liberty	1772-1881
QUEARNS		
John	Wilkes	1810-16
QUEENS		
J.	Forsyth	1833-44
M.	Union	1877-1942
QUIGLEY		
Charles	Wilkes	1837-77
QUILLIAN		
B. B.	Gilmer	1836-53i
QUIMBY		
David Sands	Lumpkin	1845-1923
QUINN		
C. A.	Lowndes	1871-1915
Hampton	Appling	1877-1925
William	Lincoln	1831-69
RABEN		
Lilly J. Mrs.	Clayton	1859-1921
RABUN		
Matthew	Hancock	1811
RADFORD		
Elijah	Morgan	1830-60
Henry	Clarke	1802-22
John	Morgan	1830-60

RADFORD (continued)		
Reuben	Morgan	1814-30
RAE		
William	Walton	1834-9
RAFFERTY		
Richard	Oglethorpe	1793-1807
RAGAN		
Asa	Jasper	1823-33
Cynthia	Muscogee	1847
D. H.	Lee	1854-1955
Daniel	Pulaski	1816-50
David	Oglethorpe	1833-66
Hambleton	Walton	1834-9
James	DeKalb	1840-69
James W.	Sumter	1838-55
Jane	Sumter	1838-55
Jonathan	Oglethorpe	1807-26
Nathaniel	Lincoln	1808-32
Sarah	Harris	1850-75
William	Sumter	1838-55
		minors of
William G.	Sumter	1838-55i
admr. Wm.		
RAGEN		
William E.	Clayton	1859-1921
RAGLAND		
Eva	Upson	1826-1910
Irby	Camden	1795-1829
J. H.	Chattooga	1856-1924
John R.	Elbert	1803
Robert	Meriwether	1831-59
Sarah	Henry	1834-69
Stephen	Wilkes	1779-92
William	Henry	1834-69
RAGSDALE		
Elijah	Paulding	1850-77
Mary	Clayton	1859-1921
Mary	Paulding	1850-77
RAHN		
Cletus	Effingham	1829-59
Conrad	Colonial	1773
Jonathan	Effingham	1829-59
RAIFORD		
Baldwin	Muscogee	1838-62
John	Jefferson	1822
Morris	Jefferson	1826
RAILEY		
Abner	Bibb	1855-71
RAIN		
Cornelius	Camden	1795-1829
RAINES		
Edmund	Upson	1826-1910
G. W.	Bibb	1851-71
Griffin	Dooly	1847-1901
J. B.	Jefferson	1802
John G.	Upson	1826-1910
RAINEY		
Absalom	Jasper	1831-9
Albert	Coweta	1849-92
Mathew	Oglethorpe	1833-66
O. H.	Cobb	1862i
Thomas F.	Campbell	1825-1900
William	Franklin	1786-1813
RAINWATER		
James	Campbell	1825-1900

RAKESTRAW		
Ann S.	Wilkes	1837-77
Garrison T.	Gwinnett	1852-86
William	Cobb	1866i

RALEN		
John C.	Effingham	1829-59

RALLINS		
Samuel I.	Burke	1853-70

RALLS		
Jacob	Coweta	1849-92
Robinson	Putnam	1823-56

RALSTON		
David	Gilmer	1836-53i
Lewis	Murray	1840-72

RAMEY		
Silas	Stewart	1850-90

RAMSEY		
Alexander	Jasper	1813-19
Benjamin	Lee	1854-1955
Burwell	Laurens	1809-40
C. William	Henry	1822-34
Henry	Jasper	1812-17
Mary	Bibb	1851-71
Mary	Henry	1834-69

RANDAL		
Elizabeth	Burke	1853-70
Oney	Franklin	1848-67

RANDALL		
Francis M.	Polk	1857-1936
Sarah J.	Polk	1857-1936

RANDLE		
--	Hancock	1802
Irvin	Coweta	1828-48 minor
Rosanna	Hancock	1827
Thomas	Coweta	1828-48 minor
William	Morgan	1830-60

RANDOLPH		
Dorothy	Wilkes	1837-77
Eliza M.	Bibb	1823-55
John	Cobb	1867i
Peter	Clarke	1802-22
Richard	Wilkes	1819-36
Richard H.	Bibb	1823-55
Robert	Camden	1795-1829
W. L.	Jackson	1802-60

RANKIN		
William	Muscogee	1838-62

RANSOM		
Reuben	Clarke	1822-42

RANSON		
Reubin	Walton	1834-9
W. M.	Chattooga	1856-1924

RAPE		
Allen	Henry	1834-69
Margaret	Henry	1834-69

RAPER		
J. H. Adam	Lumpkin	1833-52

RASBERRY		
Joseph	Walton	1827-31
Joseph	Walton	1834-9

RASBURY		
Philip	Wilkes	1779-92

RASBURY		
William	Wilkes	1779-92

RATCHFORD		
Robert	Jackson	1802-60

RATCLIFF		
Benjamin	Wayne	1824-55
James	Glynn	1844-53
James	Wayne	1824-55
Richard	Wayne	1824-55
William B.	Glynn	1844-53

RATLIFF		
Allen	Thomas	1826-36 gdn
Joseph E.	Chattooga	1856-1924
Robert	Lincoln	1796-1808

RATSFORD		
Michael	Crawford	1852-94

RAWLINES		
Ezekiel W.	Washington	1852-1903

RAWLINS		
Samuel Capt.	Gwinnett	1852-86

RAWLS		
John	Decatur	1824-52 Mts
John	Decatur	1828-38
Nancy	Hancock	1827

RAY		
Carrie A. Mrs.	Appling	1877-1925
Elizabeth	Henry	1834-69
Emanuel	Cobb	1874
Florence	Cobb	1868 minors
George	Decatur	1828-38
George A.	Meriwether	1831-59
George W.	Upson	1826-1910
John	Cobb	1866i
John	Coweta	1849-92
John	Henry	1834-69
John	Macon	1856-1909
John	Oglethorpe	1793-1807
John	Wilkes	1819-36
Mary	Wilkes	1737-77
Mary Mrs.	Dooly	1847-1901
Solomon	Jasper	1813-19
W. A.	Lowndes	1871-1915
William	Cobb	1863i
William	Cobb	1879 minors
William	Hancock	1826
William	Jackson	1802-60
William A.	Taliaferro	1826-66
William C.	Murray	1840-72
William J.	Murray	1840-72

REA		
David	Greene	1794-1810
James	Bibb	1851-71

READ		
Abner	Stewart	1850-90
Asa	Putnam	1823-56
Benjamin	Hancock	1814
James	Taliaferro	1826-66
Joseph	Putnam	1808-22
William	Macon	1856-1909

READY		
John	Baldwin	1806-19

REAGANS		
James	Pike	1844-76

REAGIN		
R. L.	Cobb	1894

REASE
Alexander   Jones   1812-23

REAVES
Benjamin   Franklin   1786-1813
Elizabeth E. Mrs.   Polk   1857-1936
Simon   Morgan   1814-30
William   Hancock   1826
William B.   Polk   1857-1936

RED
Maria S.   Burke   1853-70
Thomas   Colonial   1772

REDD
William   Muscogee   1838-62 (1838)

REDDICK
David   Marion   1846-1915
J. J.   Screven   1810-1929
Peter   Screven   1810-1929

REDDING
A. W.   Harris   1850-75
Charles   Baldwin   1806-19
Rowland   Dooly   1847-1901
William Sr.   Baldwin   1806-19

REDMAN
Martha   Stewart   1850-90
William   Butts   1826-41

REDWINE
Jacob   Campbell   1825-1900
Jacob   Coweta   1828-48
John   Campbell   1825-1900
John M.   Campbell   1825-1900
Lewis   Coweta   1849-92
Sarah Hutchenson   Campbell   1825-1900
W. P.   Fayette   1828-97
William   Hall   1837-67

REECE
Eliza from Q. H.   Union   1877-1942

REED
Isabella   Jefferson   1803
James   Lincoln   1831-69
Jesse   Lincoln   1796-1808
Joel B.   Cobb   1880
Joseph   Hall   1837-67
Sarah   Appling   1877-1925
William Sr.   Gilmer   1836-53

REEL
Sterling   Richmond   1840-53

REES
Eliner   Putnam   1823-56
Isham Sr.   Jones   1812-23
Jane   Newton   1823-51
William   Putnam   1823-56
William J.   Harris   1850-75

REESE
A. C.   Carroll   1852-96
Eaton   Morgan   1814-30
James   Hancock   1820
Joel   Putnam   1808-22
John   Jefferson   1816
W. J.   Marion   1846-1915

REEVES
Abner   Jasper   1812-17
Asa   Meriwether   1831-59
Henry O.   Appling   1877-1925
J. H.   Clayton   1859-1921
James   Meriwether   1831-59
James W.   DeKalb   1840-69

REEVES (continued)
Jeremiah   Harris   1850-75
Jeremiah   Wilkes   1792-1801
Jonathan   Meriwether   1831-69
Joseph   Pulaski   1816-50
Mary Mrs.   Carroll   1852-96
Q. B.   Pike   1823-29
Susan   Screven   1810-1929
Thomas   Lumpkin   1833-52
William   Wilkes   1818-19

REGAN
Catherine   Pike   1823-29
John   Pike   1823-29

REID
Alexander   Jasper   1812-17
Alexander   Putnam   1823-56
Andrew J.   Cobb   1865
C. M. Mrs.   Union   1877-1942
Daniel   Cobb   1869i
Eliza M.   Cobb   1900
Felisity Mary   Richmond   1840-53
Henry   Upson   1826-1910
James H.   Union   1877-1942
John   DeKalb   1840-69
Joseph   Union   1877-1942
Margaret   Oglethorpe   1833-66
Mathew   Carroll   1852-96
Robert J.   Lincoln   1831-69

REINIER
John Francis   Colonial   1775
Mary   Colonial   1776

REINSTETLER
John Matthias   Colonial   1776

REISSER
David   Effingham   1829-59

REMSON
Rem P.   Lincoln   1831-69

RENDER
James   Meriwether   1831-59
Joshua   Wilkes   1818-19
Joshua   Wilkes   1819-36
Robert T.   Meriwether   1831-59

RENEU
Timothy   Sumter   1838-55

RENFROE
Elisha   Houston   1827-55
Enoch   Warren   1802
Nathan   Muscogee   1847
Sarah   Crawford   1852-94

RESPASS
Churchwell   Jasper   1812-17
Churchwell   Jasper   1813-19
John   Hancock   1800
Richard   Upson   1826-1910
Robert D.   Stewart   1831-5

REVIERE
Herber B.   Wilkes   1837-77
Polly   Wilkes   1837-77
Richard   Upson   1826-1910
Richard   Wilkes   1818-19

REYNOLDS
A.   Cobb   1892
Benjamin   Bartow   1836-85
George   Wilkes   1810-16
Hezekiah   Cobb   1905
J. E. Mrs.   Lee   1854-1955
James   Baldwin   1806-19

REYNOLDS (continued)		
James	Greene	1817-42
James	Jones	1826-50
Jesse	Henry	1822-34
Josiah	Henry	1822-34
Mary Ella	Lee	1854-1955
Spencer	Henry	1822-34 bond
T. O.	Bibb	1851-71
Thomas	Paulding	1850-77
Thomas	Walton	1834-9
orphs John J., Mary, David		
Thomas, Mahala, orph	Walton	1834-91
Thomas (of Burke Co.)	Warren	1829
W. L.	Floyd	1852-61i
William	Jackson	1802-60
William F.	Lincoln	1808-32

RHENEY		
John W.	Burke	1853-70

RHILY		
Elizabeth	Richmond	1840-53

RHINE		
Amanda C.	Chattooga	1856-1924

RHINEHART		
A.	Chattooga	1856-1924
Marion D.	Union	1877-1942
Powell	Chattooga	1856-1924

RHODES		
Absolom	Richmond	1840-53
Benjain	Greene	1806-18
Benjamin	Troup	1832-48
Bettie Mrs.	Polk	1857-1936
Eustice H.	Lincoln	1831-69
J. U.	Paulding	1850-77
James M.	Butts	1826-41
John	Dooly	1847-1901
Mattie E. Mrs.	Lee	1854-1955
Nancy A.	Paulding	1850-77
Samuel	Wilkes	1837-77
Selah	Taliaferro	1826-66
William	Butts	1826-41

RHYMES		
Elizabeth	Meriwether	1831-59
Elizabeth	Morgan	1830-60
John R.	Putnam	1802-22
Willis J.	Morgan	1830-60

RICE		
Ann	Elbert	1829-60
Edward	Franklin	1786-1813
Elizabeth	Floyd	1852-61
Ellen Tate	Polk	1857-1936
G. L. D.	Houston	1855-96
George L.	Madison	1842-96
John	Jasper	1812-17
Leonard	Elbert	1829-60
Mary	Greene	1817-42
Susan	Baldwin	1819-64

RICH		
James	Elbert	1829-60
John	Elbert	1814
Sarah	Elbert	1829-60
Solomon	Union	1877-1942
William	Elbert	1829-60
William Jr.	Elbert	1829-60

RICHARD		
William	Putnam	1823-56

RICHARDS		
G. B.	Camden	1795-1829

RICHARDS (continued)		
John R.	Gwinnett	1852-86
Thomas G.	Pike	1844-76

RICHARDSON		
Armstead	Polk	1857-1936
Baird	Henry	1822-34
Daniel	Hancock	--
Daniel	Stewart	1850-90
Edmund	Camden	1830-67
Elizabeth	Campbell	1825-1900
Everard Dr.	Polk	1857-1936
George	Jasper	1823-33
Harriett	Chattooga	1856-1924
Isham	Wilkes	1818-19
James R.	Elbert	1822
Jane	Hancock	1838
John	Stewart	1837-49
John L.	Campbell	1825-1900
Jorden R.	Henry	1834-69
Mary A.	Gwinnett	1852-86
Obediah	Hancock	1808
Sarah	Jones	1826-50
Thomas	Chattooga	1856-1924
Thomas	Wilkes	1777-78
Thomas A.	Upson	1826-1910
Walker	Elbert	1822
William	Wilkes	1806-08
William B.	Lee	1854-1955

RICHER		
James D.	Early	1856-1927 L/A

RICK		
William	Franklin	1786-1813

RICKMAN		
B.	Harris	1850-75

RICKS		
S. A. Mrs.	Lowndes	1871-1915

RIDDLE		
Cator	Washington	1829-71 divs

RIDER		
Benjamin	Jasper	1802-60
Mary	Forsyth	1833-44i
William	Lumpkin	1845-1923

RIDGWAY		
James	Elbert	1829-60
John	Muscogee	1838-62

RIDLEY		
John Sr.	Wilkes	1819-36

RIESER		
Badasar	Colonial	1775
Michael	Colonial	1775

RIGBY		
Nicholas	Colonial	1754

RIGGINS		
Stephen	Sumter	1838-55
Thomas	Sumter	1838-55

RIGHTMIRE		
Anita	Camden	--
M. R.	Camden	--

RIGLEY		
William Sr.	Troup	1832-48

RILEY		
H. W.	Lumpkin	1845-1923
Martha E.	Franklin	1848-67
Thomas	Greene	1817-42

ROYAL

Hardy D.	Dooly	1847–1901
James H.	Burke	1853–70
John	Houston	1827–55
John J.	Dooly	1847–1901
Sarah T.	Dooly	1847–1901
Simon	Dooly	1847–1901

ROYSTON

George D.	Muscogee	1838–62
Robert	Clarke	1822–42

ROZAL

John C.	Dooly	1847–1901
Lucy A.	Dooly	1847–1901

ROZAR

John	Pulaski	1816–50
Robert S.	Wilkinson	1834

RUARK

Belitha	Warren	1842

RUCKER

A. S.	Pike	1844–76
Barden	Elbert	1829–60
George	Franklin	1848–67
James	Elbert	1829
Martin	Jasper	1831–9
William	Elbert	1835
Willis	Elbert	1834

RUDDELL

Ann Lee	Wilkes	1837–77

RUDICIL

Philipp	Chattooga	1856–1924
R. Y.	Chattooga	1856–1924

RUDISILLE

Henry	Hancock	1807

RUDOLPH

A.	Lumpkin	1845–1923

RUFF

Daniel	Henry	1834–69
M. L.	Cobb	1876

RUFFIN

R. V. C.	Carroll	1852–96

RUMPH

David	Glynn	1844–53
E. C.	Houston	1855–96
Jacob	Glynn	1844–53
Rebecca	Glynn	1844–53

RUMSEY

Field S.	Cobb	1871i
Rubin	Cobb	1871i
Sarah A. F.	Habersham	1847–1900

RUMSON

James W.	Henry	1822–34

RUNNELLS

Dudley	Clarke	1802–22
Frederick	Wilkes	1779–92
Richard	Wilkes	1779–92
Thomas	Butts	1826–41

RUSE

Joseph	Stewart	1837–47

RUSH

Jackson	Harris	1850–75
John	Fayette	1828–97
Levi	Sumter	1838–55

RUSHIN

E. R. Mrs.	Marion	1846–1915

RUSHING

Eli	Crawford	1835–52
Eli	Screven	1810–1929
Eliza Ann	Screven	1810–1929

RUSS

Reuben	Crawford	1835–52

RUSSE

P.	Henry	1822–34 bond

RUSSELL

A. M.	Lumpkin	1845–1923
Ansley	Coweta	1849–92
Burnett	Morgan	1814–30
Clariann	Lincoln	1808–32
David	Jasper	1822–26
E. B.	Polk	1857–1936
Edward	Glynn	1844–53
Eliza Miss	Glynn	1844–53
D. M.	Polk	1857–1936
G. N.	Madison	1842–96
George B.	Bartow	1836–85
George N.	Madison	1842–96
Harris	Carroll	1852–96
J. M. R.	Henry	1822–34
James	Henry	1822–34
James	Henry	1834–69
James	Lincoln	1808–32
James H.	Glynn	1844–53
James S.	Gwinnett	1852–86
Jesse	Henry	1822–34
John	Glynn	1844–53
John,	Glynn	1844–53
est T. R. Leach		
L. B.	Houston	1855–96
Margaret E.	Madison	1842–96
Martin	Baldwin	1819–64
Mary Mrs.	Glynn	1844–53
Mary A.	Glynn	1844–53
Mary Jane	Morgan	1830–60
Mattie V.	Cobb	1888
Nancy	Bartow	1836–85
R. Henry	Glynn	1844–53
Robert	Oglethorpe	1793–1807
Robert T.	Madison	1842–96
Thomas	Henry	1822–34
Thomas	Walton	1834–9
Thomas L.	Henry	1822–34
William	Colonial	1768
William	Gwinnett	1852–86
William	Lincoln	1796–1808

RUST

Robert W.	Franklin	1848–67

RUTHERFORD

B. H.	Bibb	1851–71
J. T.	Marion	1846–1915
James S.	Campbell	1825–1900
John	Baldwin	1819–64
John	Cobb	1873 minor
John	Wilkinson	1851
Nancy	Baldwin	1806–19
R. A.	Marion	1846–1915
Samuel	Crawford	1852–94
Samuel	Wilkinson	1885
William	Campbell	1825–1900
William	Cobb	1867i

RUTLAND

Blake	Dooly	1847–1901
Redden	Bibb	1823–55
Reddick	Bibb	1823–55

RUTLEDGE		
Albert	Campbell	1825-1900
J. M.	Chattooga	1856-1924
J. M.	Polk	1857-1936
James	Putnam	1808-22
James Sr.	Troup	1832-48
James Sr.	Wilkes	1819-36
James W.	Gwinnett	1852-86
Kioh	Morgan	1830-60
Thomas Sr.	Oglethorpe	1807-26
William O.	Harris	1850-75

RYALLS		
Christina	Effingham	1829-59
William	Effingham	1829-59

RYALS		
Jabey D.	McIntosh	1873-1915
John B.	Montgomery	1806-63
Joseph	Montgomery	1806-63
Ruth	McIntosh	1873-1915
Siphia	Laurens	1809-40
William	Montgomery	1806-63

RYAN		
Philip	Jackson	1802-60
Obedience	Jackson	1802-60

RYE		
Elizabeth	Wilkinson	1892

RYLANDER		
Jack	Bibb	1851-71
John C.	Bibb	1823-55

RYLE		
B. F. Jr.	Wilkinson	1917
John	Wilkinson	1834

RYLER		
James	Hall	1819-37

RYLEY		
James	Franklin	1786-1813

RYNDAL		
Thomas	Walton	1827-31

SABB		
Morgan	Colonial	1760

SABIN		
Resolved	Jasper	1820-23

SACRA		
Candace	Bibb	1851-71

SADLER		
Mary	Camden	1830 67
William F.	Lee	1854-1955

SAFFOLD		
Adam G.	Morgan	1830-60
Isham H.	Washington	1852-1903
Reuben	Wilkes	1818-19
Reuben B.	Wilkes	1837-77
Seaborn J.	Morgan	1830-60

SAILORS		
William	Madison	1842-96

SALE		
Peyton W.	Lincoln	1831-69

SALES		
Lenore	Marion	1846-1915

SALISBURY		
Sarah E.	Ware	1879-1915

SALLARD		
William	Hancock	1819

SALLET		
Robert	Liberty	1772-1881

SALTER		
Anna	Colonial	1753
Ellen Mrs.	Lee	1854-1955
James	Sumter	1838-55
Robert Preston	Lee	1854-1955
Thomas	Colonial	1751
Thomas	Washington	1852-1903

SAMBLE		
Agnes	Talbot	1865

SAMPSON		
Moses	Marion	1846-1915

SAMS		
Lewis	Forsyth	1833-44
Louis	McIntosh	1873-1915
Sanders	Madison	1842-96

SAMSON		
James	Greene	1786-95

SAMUEL		
Benjamin	Lincoln	1831-69
Edmund	Lincoln	1831-69
Elizabeth	Lincoln	1831-69

SANDEFORD		
Hill	Burke	1853-70
John	Jefferson	1821
Priscilla	Jefferson	1830

SANDERS		
Aaron	Franklin	1848-67
Abram	Warren	1817
Aley	Crawford	1852-94
Bethany	Wilkinson	1889
Charles H.	Newton	1823-51
Drusilla	Oglethorpe	1807-26
E. R. Mrs.	Clayton	1859-1921
Flora	Fayette	1828-97
Gilly	Upson	1826-1910
James	Hancock	1804
James E.	Madison	1842-96
James M.	Pulaski	1816-50
Joel	Franklin	1848-67
John	Bibb	1855 (not recorded in vault)
John	Glynn	1844-53
M. D.	Lee	1854-1955
Mark	Hancock	--
Nathan	Hancock	1824
Robert	Lincoln	1796-1808
Thomas J.	Crawford	1852-94
William	Clayton	1859-1921
William T.	Franklin	1848-67

SANDERSON		
T. H.	Appling	1877-1925

SANDIFER		
John S.	Crawford	1852-94
Susan	Wilkes	1837-77

SANDIFORD		
Harris	Wilkes	1837-77
John	Liberty	1772-1881

SCOFIELD		
Philip	Crawford	1852-94

SCOGGINS		
Ellick	Oglethorpe	1807-26
James F.	Cobb	1869
James J.	Carroll	1852-96
John W.	Carroll	1852-96
L.	Chattooga	1856-1924
Levi	Chattooga	1856-1924
Millington	Troup	1832-48
Right	Greene	1817-42
Smith	Baldwin	1806-19

SCOTT		
Alexander	Camden	---
B. W.	Dooly	1847-1901
Benjamin	Wilkes	1779-92
Caroline A.	Bibb	1851-71
Daniel	Newton	1823-51
Emma Miss	Chattooga	1856-1924
Francis	Colonial	1733
Francis	Putnam	1823-56
James	Baldwin	1806-19
James	Chattooga	1856-1924
James W.	Screven	1810-1929
John	Bartow	1836-85
John	Bibb	1823-55
John	Madison	1842-96
John	Sumter	1838-55
Joseph	Jackson	1802-60
Joseph	Morgan	1814-30
Lucy	Screven	1810-1929
Mary	Jefferson	1832
Mary	Pike	1844-76
Mary A.	Cobb	1896
Matthew	Polk	1857-1936
Moses	Bartow	1836-85
Philip	Jefferson	1804
Thomas	Franklin	1848-67
Thomas H.	Screven	1810-1929
William	Bibb	1823-55
William	Coweta	1828-48 retn
William	Jasper	1826-31

SCRIBNER		
Sarah T.	Cobb	1883

SCRUGGS		
James	Butts	1826-41
John F.	Screven	1810-1929
John Q. A.	Union	1877-1942
Richard	Screven	1810-1929
Thomas	Chattooga	1856-1924

SCRUTCHEON		
Josiah	Sumter	1838-55
Thomas	Sumter	1838-55

SCUDDER		
William	Carroll	1852-96

SCUDER		
Elizabeth	Forsyth	1833-44

SCURLOCK		
Joshua	Baldwin	1806-19
Joshua	Hancock	1795
William (nunc)	Muscogee	1838-62

SEABOLT		
Barbara A.	Lumpkin	1845-1923
Mary	Lumpkin	1845-1923
Sarah	Lumpkin	1845-1923

SEAGROVES		
Ann	Camden	1830-67

SEALES		
Daniel	Greene	1806-18
Robert	Lincoln	1808-32

SEALEY		
Peter P.	Pike	1844-76

SEALS		
C. C.	Cobb	1906
George	Elbert	1829-60

SEARS		
Eli	Wilkinson	1857
Silas	Polk	1857-1936
Winnie	Wilkinson	1859

SEATS		
Thomas	Morgan	1814-30

SEAY		
Barnett	Cobb	1875i
James J.	Cobb	1875i
Jemima	Lumpkin	1845-1923
S. B.	Bartow	1836-85

SEBINS		
Benjamin	Washington	1829-71 divs

SECKINGER		
Agnesia	Colonial	1772
Andrew	Colonial	1772

SEGAR		
Ann	Henry	1834-69

SEGLER		
John	Newton	1823-51

SEGUS		
Wiley	Early	1856-1927

SELBY		
William	Coweta	1828-48

SELF		
Adeline	Houston	1855-96
Samuel E.	Elbert	1825
Susan	Floyd	1852-61i

SELLERS		
Anna	Washington	1852-1903
Elizabeth	Appling	1877-1925
John	Henry	1822-34
John H.	Appling	1877-1925
Judith	Hall	1837-67
Lewis	Henry	1822-34
Simeon	Thomas	1837-45i
William	Richmond	1840-53

SELMAN		
J. W.	Cobb	1908
James	Campbell	1825-1929
William	Upson	1826-1910
Willis	Floyd	1861-71

SEMMES		
Andrew G.	Wilkes	1819-36
Ethelbert F.	Wilkes	1819-36
Ignatius	Taliaferro	1826-66
Ignatius	Wilkes	1819-36
Thomas	Wilkes	1819-36

SENN		
Daniel	Randolph	1845-95

SEPIONS		
Andrew	Washington	1852-1903
Benjamin	Washington	1852-1903

SESSONS			
Alexander	Ware	1879-1915	
William W.	Ware	1879-1915	
SEVENT			
John	Washington	1829-71 divs	
SEWELL			
Berry F.	Polk	1857-1936	
C. M.	Polk	1857-1936	
Catherine	Coweta	1849-92	
Oswell	Campbell	1825-1900	
Sarah	Polk	1857-1936	
James	Franklin	1786-1813	
James	Meriwether	1831-59	
James L.	Meriwether	1831-59	
Joshua	Walton	1834-9	
William	Meriwether	1831-59	
SEXON			
Solomon	Jackson	1802-60	
SEXTON			
Emily	Madison	1842-96	
William D.	Gwinnett	1852-86	
SEYMOUR			
Evalbon	Greene	1817-42	
Nathan	Muscogee	1838-62	
R. A.	Putnam	1823-56	
SHACKELFORD			
Edmond Sr.	Elbert	1829-60	
Harriett	Early	--	
Henry	Elbert	1829-60	
James	Early	--	
John	Morgan	1814	
John	Walton	1834-9 orphs	
R. E.	Taliaferro	1826-66	
SHACKLEFORD			
Frances	Hancock	1811	
Howard B.	Polk	1857-1936	
SHAD			
Elias B.	Bibb	1851-71	
Solomon	Colonial	1768	
SHADENGEN			
Sarah J.	Cobb	1868 minors	
SHANER			
Johnell	Sumter	1838-55	
SHANK			
Felix	Wilkes	1837-77	
Henry	Wilkes	1837-77	
William	McIntosh	1873-1915	
SHANKLE			
Eli	Jackson	1802-60	
James W.	Jackson	1802-60	
SHANNON			
David	Franklin	1848-67	
Dicey	Franklin	1848-67	
Patrick	Wilkes	1806-08	
Samuel	Franklin	1848-67	
Thomas	Wilkes	1792-1801	
SHARER			
George	Cobb	1873	
SHARMON			
James	Randolph	1845-94	
William	Lincoln	1808-32	
SHARP			
Hiram Jr.	Carroll	1852-96	

SHARP (continued)			
Hiram Sr.	Carroll	1852-96	
James	Jasper	1826-31	
James	Jasper	1831-9	
John	Tattnall	1800-35 deeds	
John,	Tattnall	1836-40i	
gdn for W. H.			
Moore	Tattnall	1836-40 minor	
Nathan J. W. H.	Jackson	1802-60	
Noah C.	Jackson	1802-60	
SHARPE			
Eley	Stewart	1850-90	
John	Lincoln	1808-32	
SHAW			
Eli D.	Jasper	1823-33	
J.	Coweta	1828-48 retn	
James	Camden	1795-1829	
James	Henry	1822-34 bond	
James	Muscogee	1838-62	
Joseph L.	Cobb	1879i	
Louisa C.	Camden	1830-67	
Nancy	Walton	1834-9	
Robert	Morgan	1814-30	
W. W.	Bartow	1836-85	
William	Cobb	1875i	
William	Jackson	1802-60	
SHEALY			
Andrew	Macon	1856-1909	
Nancy E.	Macon	1856-1909	
SHEAR			
Washington	Houston	1827-55	
SHEARER			
James	Wilkes	1810-16	
SHEARLING			
Isham	Stewart	1837-49 bonds	
SHEARMAN			
Edward J.	Camden	1795-1829	
Elizabeth	Camden	1795-1829	
SHEATS			
Benajah S.	Walton	1870-74	
Nicholas	Clarke	1822-40	
SHEBEE			
Elephair	Washington	1852-1903	
SHEEROUSE			
Emanuel	Effingham	1829-59	
Godlief	Effingham	1829-59	
SHEFFIELD			
Alpheus	Early	1834-1920 bonds	
Barnaby	Jasper	1813-19	
Benjamin	Early	--	
Bryant	Wayne	1822-70	
Drewry	Early	1834-1920 bonds	
Henry N.	Polk	1857-1936	
John, exor	Wayne	1822-70	
Mary	Bibb	1851-71	
Pliney exor	Wayne	1822-70	
R. W.	Early	--	
R. W.	Early	1856-1927	
Robert	Early	1834-1920 bonds	
Robert W.	Early	1856-89	
Vescinny	Early	1834-1920 bonds	
SHEFTALL			
Benjamin	Colonial	1765	
SHEHAN			
Dennis	Bibb	1851-71	

SHELL		
Daniel	Fayette	1828-97
Edmond	Walton	1834-9
Elizabeth	Newton	1823-51
George	Franklin	1848-67
Green	Hancock	1834
Herman	Coweta	1828-48

SHELLMAN		
Thomas H.	Polk	1857-1936

SHELTON		
Elizabeth	Murray	1840-72
Thomas	Wilkes	1779-92

SHEPARD		
Christopher B.	Houston	1827-55
Francis	Burke	1853-70
Gotha	Burke	1853-70
Orlando	Walton	1834-9 orphs

SHEPHERD		
Andrew	Wilkes	1819-36
Ann	Newton	1823-51
Carter	Morgan	1830-60
Dennis	Upson	1826-1910
Jerusalem	Wilkinson	1862
John	Walton	1834-9 orph
John A.	Lincoln	1808-32
Mary	Liberty	1772-1881
Mary	Muscogee	1838-62
Mary A.	Morgan	1830-60
Nathaniel	Wilkinson	1863
Talmon W.	Morgan	1830-60
William	Upson	1826-1910

SHEPPARD		
Charles	Baldwin	1806-19
Charles	Washington	1852-1903
Charles H.	Washington	1852-1903
David	Washington	1852-1903
Elizabeth Mrs.	Liberty	1772-1881
John	Dooly	1847-1901
John	Marion	1846-1915
Mathew	Dooly	1847-1901
Orland Wilson	Screven	1810-1929
T. H.	Screven	1810-1929
W. D.	Screven	1810-1929
William	Screven	1810-1929
William S.	Dooly	1847-1901

SHEPPERD		
Francis	Walton	1819-37
John	Elbert	1805
Orlando	Walton	1819-37

SHERARD		
Benjamin	Emanuel	1836
James L.	Emanuel	1867i

SHERIFF		
Charles	Morgan	1830-60

SHERLING		
James	Washington	1852-1903

SHERMAN		
Robert Sr.	Wilkes	1818-19
Robert H.	Stewart	1850-90

SHERRELL		
Reuben	Wilkes	1779-92

SHERRILL		
David	Greene	1817-42

SHEWBERT		
Charles	Marion	1846-1915

SHIELDS		
James	Clayton	1859-1921
Joseph	Jackson	1802-60
Little B.	Madison	1842-96
Littleberry	Madison	1812-41
Rhoda	Madison	1842-96
Samuel	Morgan	1830-60
William	Morgan	1814-30
William G.	Madison	1842-96

SHIFLET		
Picket	Elbert	1829-60

SHIP		
Benjamin	Hancock	1796
John	Newton	1823-31
Richard	Hancock	1813

SHIPLETT		
W. S.	Polk	1857-1936

SHIPLEY		
John	Franklin	1786-1813
Martha	Franklin	1786-1813
Nathaniel	Franklin	1786-1813
Robert	Franklin	1786-1813

SHIPP		
David	Marion	1846-1915
James	Pike	1844-76
Mark Sr.	Lincoln	1831-69
Rhoda	Pike	1844-76

SHIPPEY		
Joseph	Muscogee	1838-62

SHIPWRIGHT		
John Newcomb	Liberty	1772-1881

SHIRLEY		
Young J.	Habersham	1847-1900

SHIRLING		
William B.	Stewart	1850-90

SHIVER		
Abraham	Pulaski	1816-50
Fleming	Houston	1827-55

SHIVERS		
Jonas	Pike	1823-29

SHOCKLEY		
Aquila	Franklin	1786-1813
Richard	Franklin	1786-1813

SHOEINBEIN		
Frederick	Baldwin	1819-64

SHOEMAKER		
James	Madison	1842-96

SHOOK		
John	Rabun	1863-88

SHORT		
Andrew Jackson	Campbell	1825-1900
F. W.	Polk	1857-1936
Howell	Marion	1846-1915
Laben	Pike	1844-76
Nathan P.	Marion	1846-1915

SHORTER		
Sarah	Wilkes	1818-19
Sophia H.	Muscogee	1838-62

SHOTWELL		
Harvey	Bibb	1823-55
Nathaniel	Jasper	1802-60

SHOWS
Daniel   Warren   1838

SHROPSHIRE
M. L. Mrs.   Fayette   1828-97
Wesley   Chattooga   1856-1924

SHRUDER
Thomas   Colonial   1775

SHUFFELD
Bryant   Wayne   1824-55i

SHUMATE
Catherine   Wilkes   1737-77
Mason   DeKalb   1840-69

SHUMWAY
J. E. Mrs.   Cobb   1906

SHURLEY
John W.   Randolph   1845-94
William   Warren   1841

SHURLING
James   Washington   1829-71 divs
James H.   Washington   1852-1903
William F.   Washington   1852-1903

SIBBALD
Jane   Clarke   1822-42

SIDWELL
David   Morgan   1814-30
John   Morgan   1830-60

SIGFRITZ
George   Colonial   1775

SIKES
Darling   Lee   1854-1955
Johnathan   Houston   1827-55

SILES
John   Chattooga   1856-1924

SILAVANT
Daniel Sr.   Liberty   1772-1881

SILMAN
Benjamin F.   Walton   1834-9 orph of
                                     John
George C.   Walton   1834-9
John   Walton   1834-9
John (Col)   Walton   1834-9
Joseph L.   Walton   1827-31
Mary M.   Walton   1834-9
William W.   Coweta   1828-48

SILVA
Sylvester   Camden   1830-67

SILVEY
Abram   Oglethorpe   1807-26
Stephen   Oglethorpe   1833-66

SIMMONS
Abraham   Madison   1842-96
Abraham   Wilkes   1819-36
Adam   Oglethorpe   1807-26
Benjamin   Hancock   1813
Bennett   Madison   1842-96
C. D.   Coweta   1849-92
Catherine   Crawford   1835-52
Charles   Oglethorpe   1833-66
Eliza T.   Gwinnett   1852-86
G. H.   Sumter   1838-55 bond
Harvey M.   Madison   1812-41
Hugh F.   Morgan   1814-30

SIMMONS (continued)
James P.   Gwinnett   1852-86
Jesse   Meriwether   1831-59
John   Clarke   1802-22
John   Hancock   1828
John   Jones   1826-50
John   Lumpkin   1845-1923
John   Madison   1842-96
John   Sumter   1838-55
John Sr.   Elbert   1835
John F.   Marion   1846-1915
John W.   Camden   1868-1916
M. A. E.   Bibb   1851-71
Mary Jane   Crawford   1852-94
Otheoplus   Appling   1877-1925
Richard   Floyd   1861-71
Richard   Oglethorpe   1793-1807
Ritter   Polk   1857-1936
Samuel   Screven   1810-1929
Sarah   Hancock   1815
Stern   Lincoln   1808-32
William   Madison   1812-41
William   Morgan   1814-30
William   Oglethorpe   1807-26
William   Sumter   1838-55
  admr of Chas. H.
Zaddock   Wilkinson   1821

SIMMS
Britain Sr.   Coweta   1849-92
John   Coweta   1849-92
John   Greene   1806-18
John   Wilkes   1792-1801
Littleberry   Sumter   1838-55
Robert   Hancock   1815

SIMONTON
Emily   Gwinnett   1852-86
James   Cobb   1866 minors
Joel   Greene   1817-42
Margaret   Wilkes   1779-92
Robert   Greene   1817-42
Theophilus   Clarke   1802-22

SIMPLER
William   Warren   1831

SIMPSON
Hester   Wilkes   1819-36
James   Morgan   1814-30
Juda   Wilkes   1819-36
Leonard A.   Cobb   1866i
  (Rebecca, wid)
Leroy   Wilkes   1819-36
Lizzie   Polk   1857-1936
Mary Ann H.   Cobb   1902
Susan W.   Madison   1842-96
W. T.   Lee   1854-1955
William   Colonial   1766
  (Chief Justice)
William   Colonial   1772
  (St. John's Par.)
William   Stewart   1837-49

SIMS
Amy   Stewart   1850-90
Bartlett Sr.   Warren   1802
Benjamin   Richmond   1840-53
Bennett   Madison   1842-96
Charles   Madison   1812-41
Charley   Clarke   1822-42
Elisha   Coweta   1849-92
Fannie Mrs.   Clayton   1859-1921
George   Henry   1834-69
H. L.   Forsyth   1833-44
Henry L.   Lumpkin   1833-52
Isham   Walton   1834-9
James   Oglethorpe   1807-26
Jimmy   Oglethorpe   1833-66

SIMS (continued)
Joel	Oglethorpe	1793-1807
John	Pike	1823-29
John	Walton	1827-31
L.	Coweta	1828-48 retn
Lenard	Clarke	1822-42
Lenard	DeKalb	1840-69
P. D.	Marion	1846-1915
Philip	Hancock	1833
Robert	Clarke	1822-42
Sherod	Pike	1844-76
Susan	Bibb	1851-71
W. T.	Clayton	1859-1921
William	Baldwin	1806-19
William A. Sr.	Lowndes	1871-1915

SINCLAIR
Jesse	Stewart	1850-90

SINGER
Johann George	Stewart	1850-90
John	Stewart	1850-90

SINGLETARY
M. K.	Houston	1855-96
Nathan P.	Sumter	1838-55

SINGLETON
Henry	Jasper	1812-17
Hezekieh	Putnam	1823-56
Ishmael	Bartow	1836-85
J. Lawton	Screven	1810-1929
James	Putnam	1808-22
John	Jasper	1812-17
Thomas	Liberty	1772-1881
William	Early	1856-89 L/A

SIRING
Henry	Wilkes	1779-92

SIRMANS
Jacob	Early	1856-1927 L/A
Johnson	Early	1856-1927 L/A
Lazarus	Early	1856-1927 L/A

SISSON
James et al	Lumpkin	1833-52

SISTRUCK
Green B.	Lincoln	1831-69
John	Lincoln	1831-69
S. H. J.	Houston	1855-96
Samuel	Jasper	1826-31

SITTON
John	Lumpkin	1833-52

SIZEMORE
Isom	Tattnall	1836-40i

SKAGGS
Charles	Putnam	1823-56

SKALES
Thomas	Walton	1819-37

SKELLIE
W. A.	Houston	1855-96

SKELTON
John	Elbert	1829-60
John Jr.	Elbert	1829-60
W. T.	Cobb	1873i

SKIDMORE
Jett T.	Morgan	1830-60
Samuel	Morgan	1830-60
William S.	Floyd	1861-71

SKINE
Benjamin	Washington	1829-71 divs
Mary E.	Ware	1879-1915
William A.	Washington	1829-71 divs

SKINNER
Archer	Elbert	1813
Lockey	Burke	1853-70
Oliver	Hancock	1817
William W.	Burke	1853-70
Willis	Muscogee	1838-62

SKIPWITH
Peyton	Camden	1795-1829

SLACK
Jesse	Wilkes	1819-36
Joseph B.	Morgan	1830-60

SLADE
J.	Dooly	1847-1901
Jane	Morgan	1830-60
Jeremiah	Decatur	1824-52 Mts
Nicholas	Wilkes	1792-1801
Samuel	Pike	1844-76

SLAPPEY
G. H.	Macon	1856-1909
Henry	Jasper	1820-23
Jacob C.	Macon	1856-1909
Reuben H.	Houston	1855-96

SLATER
James P. Sr.	Appling	1877-1925

SLATHAM
William	Lincoln	1808-32

SLATON
Littleberry	Harris	1850-75
Uriah	Jackson	1802-60

SLATTER
Nancy	Jones	1826-50
Solomon	Jones	1812-23

SLAUGHTER
Ezekiel	Greene	1786-95
Henry	Jasper	1820-23
Henry	Jasper	1822-26
John	Greene	1794-1810
John	Greene	1817-42
Martin	Putnam	1808-22
Monroe	Harris	1850-75
Robert W.	Bartow	1836-85
Samuel	Baldwin	1806-19
Sarah	Cobb	1890

SLAYDEN
Arthur	Wilkes	1806-08

SLAYTON
Isaac D.	Oglethorpe	1833-66

SLEDGE
Cresy Ann	Upson	1826-1910
John	Hancock	1798

SLEETER
James	Thomas	1837-45

SLIGHT
John	Macon	1856-1909

SLINCHCOMB
Absalom	Elbert	1833

SLOAN
David U.	Clayton	1859-1929

SMITH (continued)

John	Hall	1819-31 Mts
John	Henry	1822-34
John	Houston	1827-55
John	Jones	1812-23
John	Jones	1826-50
John	Washington	1829-71 divs
John	Wilkes	1792-1801
John	Wilkes	1806-08
John Sr.	Clarke	1822-42
John A.	Campbell	1825-1900
John A.	Coweta	1849-92
John B.	Lee	1854-1955
John C.	Jones	1812-23
John C.	Warren	1828
John E.	Washington	1852-1903
John H.	Baldwin	1806-19
John H.	Macon	1856-1909
John M.	Houston	1827-55
John S.	Dooley	1847
Joseph	Colonial	1764
Joseph	Greene	1786-95
Joseph	Oglethorpe	1807-26
Joseph	Walton	1827-31 orph
Joweph T.	Clayton	1859-1921
Laddison	Early	1834-1920 bonds
Lavina	Washington	1852-1903
Louisa H.	Washington	1852-1903
Lovett -	Sumter	1838-55i
Jackson L. Smith, admr		
Lucy	Richmond	1840-53
Lucy	Wilkes	1819-36
Margaret	Camden	1830-67
Margaret	Elbert	1829-60
Mark	Coweta	1828-48
Marshall	Baldwin	1806-19
Martha	Campbell	1852-96
Martha	Macon	1856-1909
Martha E.	Houston	1855-96
Martha Jane	Washington	1852-1903
Martha M. Mrs.	Screven	1810-1929
Mary	Colonial	1763
Mary Mrs.	Houston	1855-96
Mary	Jackson	1802-60
Mary	Jefferson	1799
(of Lincoln Co.)		
Mary (Polly)	Upson	1826-1910
Mary Elizabeth	Lee	1854-1955
Mary F., minor	Cobb	1862i
Mary P.	Cobb	1903
Mathew	Dooly	1847-1901
Mathew	Lee	1854-1955
Mathew H.	Coweta	1828-48
Minerva	Cobb	1899
Mollie E.	Wilkinson	1916
Mongin	Cobb	1866i
Moses	Oglethorpe	1833-66
Munsell J.	Tattnall	1836-40i
N.	Polk	1857-1936
Nancy	Greene	1817-42
Nancy Mrs.	Washington	1852-1903
Nancy Sr.	Bartow	1836-85
Nathan	Wilkes	1818-19
Nathan H.	Coweta	1828-48
Nathaniel	Elbert	1802
Nathaniel	Wilkes	1779-92
Alexander		
Needham	Houston	1855-96
Noah B.	Campbell	1825-1900
O. S.	Burke	1853-70
Oliver	Upson	1826-1910
Owen	Lowndes	1871-1915
P. W.	Henry	1834-69
Peter	Oglethorpe	1807-26
Peter B.	Walton	1834-9 orph
Peter P.	Washington	1852-1903
Peyton	Greene	1817-42
Peyton S.	Baldwin	1806-19
Peyton T.	Greene	1806-18

SMITH (continued)

R. F.	Burke	1853-70
R. T.	Dooly	1847-1901
R. W.	Cobb	1903
Rebecca	Wayne	1822-70
Reddick	Harris	1850-75
Reuben	Greene	1817-42
Richard	Floyd	1852-61i
Richard	Houston	1827-55
Richard	Morgan	1814-30
Richard	Washington	1829-71 divs
Richard J.	Baldwin	1825
Robert	Oglethorpe	1833-66
Robert	Paulding	1850-77 appr
Robert	Wayne	1824-55 orph
Robert T.	Oglethorpe	1833-66
S. B.	Habersham	1847-1900
Samuel	Coweta	1828-48 orphs of
Samuel	Jones	1826-50
Samuel F.	Washington	1829-71 divs
Samuel H.	Lumpkin	1845-1923
Sarah	Campbell	1825-1900
Sarah	Cobb	1866
Sarah	Jasper	1831-9
Sarah	Morgan	1830-60
Sarah	Oglethorpe	1807-26
Sarah	Oglethorpe	1833-66
Sarah	Walton	1834-9i
orph of Joseph		
Sarah	Washington	1829-71 divs
Sarah E.	Carroll	1852-96
Sarah E.	Cobb	1879 minor
Sarah F.	Campbell	1825-1900
Simeon	Lumpkin	1833-52
Simon	Tattnall	1800-35 deeds
Simon	Tattnall	1836-40i
Stephen	Fayette	1849
Stephen	Madison	1812-41
Stephen G.	Marion	1846-1915
Sterling W. Sr.	Jones	1826-50
T. J.	Montgomery	1806-63
T. P.	Appling	1877-1923
Tabitha	Clayton	1859-1921
Temperance	Campbell	1825-1900
Theresa M. Mrs.	Ware	1879-1915
Thomas	Bartow	1836-85
Thomas	Early	1834-1920 bonds
Thomas	Houston	1827-55
Thomas	Jasper	1831-9
Thomas	Pulaski	1816-50
Thomas	Warren	1796
Thomas J.	Dooly	1847-1901
Tillman	Cobb	1887
V. H.	Coweta	1849-93 retn
Vivian,	Tattnall	1836-40i
Chas. exor		
W. A. F.	Washington	1852-1903
W. M.	Madison	1842-96
W. N.	Marion	1846-1915
W. Russell	Henry	1822-34
W. T.	Floyd	1852-61
Wesley	Carroll	1852-96
William	Camden	1830-67
William	Clarke	1822-42
William	Early	1834-1920 bonds
William	Floyd	1852-61i
William	Franklin	1848-67
William	Greene	1817-42
William	Houston	1827-55
William	Madison	1812-41
William	Washington	1852-1903
William	Wilkinson	1848
William C.	Hancock	1826
William C.,	Sumter	1838-55i
Simpson B. Smith, admr		
William H.	Houston	1855-96
William Jackson	Wilkinson	--
Winfred H.	Washington	1852-1903
Z. A.	Cobb	1875

SMITHWICK

Reuben	Stewart	1850-90

SNEAD

Hamilton	Lumpkin	1833-52
John	Fayette	1828-97
Rebecca	Pike	1823-29

SNEED

Dudley	Lee	1854-1955
Elijah	Cobb	1866i
H.	Oglethorpe	1807-26

SNELL

Daniel P.	Pulaski	1816-50
David	Pulaski	1816-50

SNELLINGS

George	Elbert	1818
John	Morgan	1830-60
John (second)	Morgan	1830-60
Richard J.	Stewart	1850-90
Tabitha	Morgan	1830-60
Virginia B.	Morgan	1830-60

SNELSON

Nathaniel	Wilkes	1837-77

SNIDER

Barnett	Warren	1820
Catharine	Effingham	1829-59
Fletcher	Screven	1810-1929
J. T.	Newton	1823-51
James J.	Bibb	1851-71
Margaret T.	Bibb	1851-71

SNIGHTON

Wyatt	Pike	1844-76

SNOOKS

Daniel P.	Effingham	1829-59

SNOW

Henry	Jackson	1802-60

SOCKWELL

Thomas L.	Polk	1857-1936

SOLOMON

Berry	Screven	1810-1929
David	Wilkinson	1874
Henry	Bibb	1823-55
Jane	Bibb	1880
Willis L.	Laurens	1809-40

SOMERVILLE

Edward	Colonial	1762
Jane	Colonial	1779
John	Colonial	1773

SORRELL

Charles L.	Madison	1842-96
George	Greene	1796-1806
J. T.	Polk	1857-1936

SORROW

John	Oglethorpe	1793-1807
Samuel	Oglethorpe	1793-1807
William	Oglethorpe	1793-1807

SOSEBEE

L. Daniel	Lumpkin	1845-1923
Thomas J.	Habersham	1847-1900

SOUELLA

Henry	Cobb	1909

SOUTHERN

John	Union	1877-1942

SOUTHWELL

George W.	Sumter	1838-55

SOWELL

Mary E. Mrs.	Screven	1810-1929
Pearce	Screven	1810-1929
W. F.	Screven	1810-1929

SOWERBY

Henry	Liberty	1772-1881

SPALDING

Queer	McIntosh	1873-1915
Thomas	McIntosh	1873-1915

SPARKS

Ann	Franklin	1786-1813
Anna	Franklin	1786-1813
George W.	Washington	1852-1903
Henry	Washington	1829-71 divs
James	Franklin	1786-1813
Jeremiah	Franklin	1786-1813
Jeremiah	Morgan	1830-60
John	Washington	1852-1903
Leo Sr.	Polk	1857-1936
Morgan M.	Washington	1829-71 divs
Morgan M.	Washington	1852-1903
Samuel	Laurens	1809-40

SPARROW

Daniel	Pulaski	1816-50

SPAULDING

Isham	Camden	1795-1829
Lucy	Camden	1830-67

SPEAK

Margaret T.	Butts	1826-41

SPEAR

David	Laurens	1809-40
Joseph	Butts	1826-41 orph

SPEARS

John	Burke	1853-70
Joseph G.	Walton	1819-37
Joseph G.	Walton	1827-31
William	Burke	1853-70

SPECKLER

John	Macon	1856-1909

SPEED

Terrell	Morgan	1830-60

SPEEN

Permela	Bartow	1836-85

SPEER

Guilford	Upson	1826-1910
John W.	Fayette	1828-97

SPEIGHT

Thomas	Early	1834-1920 bonds

SPEIGHTS

John	Baldwin	1819-64

SPEIGNOR

Deborah	Early	1856-1927

SPENCE

John	Troup	1832-48
Thomas	Wilkinson	1847

SPENCER

Amanda	Henry	1822-34
Anna	Muscogee	1838-62
Charity	Jones	1812-23

SPENCER (continued)		
E. T.	Jasper	1822-26
L.	Jasper	1822-26
Levi	Bartow	1836-85
M. E.	Jasper	1822-26
Richard	Colonial	1767
Samuel	Liberty	1772-1881
Sarah	Liberty	1772-1881
William	Colonial	1776

SPERRY		
Makus E.	Macon	1856-1909

SPICE		
Henry C.	Fayette	1828-97

SPIERS		
Joseph	Cobb	1868i
William	Jefferson	1831

SPINKS		
Ephraim	Warren	1832
Henry M.	Jones	1826-50
John	Lincoln	1796-1808
Marian F.	Houston	1855-96
Rolley	Jones	1826-50

SPIRES		
Martha	Lincoln	1831-69
William S.	Lincoln	1831-69
Zachariah	Lincoln	1796-1808

SPIVER		
John	Union	1877-1942

SPIVEY		
G. A.	Lincoln	1809-40
Henry	Putnam	1825-56
Jethro Benton	Lincoln	1809-40
Littleton	Houston	1827-55
William	Putnam	1808-22
William	Putnam	1825-56
William	Upson	1826-1910

SPLOTT		
Edward	Colonial	1773

SPRAGGINS		
D. Mrs.	Cobb	1871i
Frances	Cobb	1866 minors
Thomas E.	Cobb	1869i

SPRATLIN		
Jesse M.	Fayette	1828-97
William	Coweta	1849-92
William	Morgan	1814-30

SPRATLING		
Francis A.	Madison	1842-96
James	Wilkes	1810-16

SPRAYBERRY		
Benjamin	DeKalb	1840-69

SPRIGG		
John	Lumpkin	1845-1923

SPRIGGS		
Cathrine	Camden	1830-67
Gilead	Bartow	1836-85

SPRINGER		
Ann	Wilkes	1819-36
John	Wilkes	1792-1801
Martha	Morgan	1830-60

SPRUCE		
John	Henry	1834-69

SPRUELL		
John F.	Carroll	1852-96
M. B. (nunc)	Carroll	1852-96

SPRY		
Mary	Colonial	1771
Royal	Liberty	1772-1881

SPULLOCK		
Owin	Clarke	1822-42

SPUR		
John	Clarke	1802-22

SPURLIN		
James M.	Fayette	1828-97

STAFFORD		
Anderson	Pike	1844-76
E. A.	Wayne	1822-70
James	Wayne	1822-70
Robert	Camden	1795-1829
Robert	Camden	1868-1916
Robert	Wayne	1822-70
Robert	Wayne	1824-55i
Robert Jr.	Wayne	1824-55i
Samuel	Floyd	1852-61
Samuel S.	Early	1856-1927 L/A
Sarah	Pike	1844-76
Thomas	Camden	1795-1829
William	Wayne	1822-70
William	Wayne	1824-55i

STAINBACK		
Francis	Warren	1817

STALEY		
Elizabeth Ann	Dooly	1847-1901
J. C.	Houston	1855-96
Jane	Houston	1827-55
Samuel	Houston	1827-55

STALLINGS		
Charlotte	Muscogee	1838-62
J. G.	Bartow	1836-85
James	Oglethorpe	1807-26
Malachi	Greene	1796-1806
William	Morgan	1830-60

STAMPER		
Robert	Morgan	1814-30
Spencer	Pike	1844-76

STAMPS		
J. S.	Upson	1826-1910
James	Coweta	1849-92
Moses W.	Coweta	1849-92

STANBACK		
J. V.	Cobb	1905
Luella	Cobb	1908

STANCIL		
William E.	Lumpkin	1845-1923

STANDARD		
Daniel	Wilkes	1837-77
Kimbro	Lincoln	1796-1808
Kimbro	Wilkes	1819-36

STANDERFORD		
Tilman	Hall	1837-67

STANDIFER		
Luke	Madison	1842-96

STANDLEY		
Charles V.	Randolph	1845-94 inv, appr

STANDLEY (continued)
| Robert | Tattnall | 1836 |

STANFIELD
| Elias | Ware | 1879-1915 |
| Henry T. | Clayton | 1859-1921 |

STANFORD
Jesse	Warren	1828
Joseph	Warren	1827
Joshua	Warren	1825

STANLEY
Edward N.	Houston	1855-96
James	Gwinnett	1852-86
Joseph	Colonial	1770
Martin	Jasper	1823-33
Richard R.	Wilkinson	1899
Sherwood	Greene	1817-42

STANLY
| John | Clayton | 1859-1921 |

STANSELL
| David | Cobb | 1866i |
| James N. | Cobb | 1869 minors |

STANTON
| B. S. | Newton | 1823-51 |
| Jordan | Gwinnett | 1852-86 |

STAPLER
John R.	Lowndes	1871-1915
Robert	Jackson	1802-60
Ruth	Jackson	1802-60
Thomas	Jackson	1802-60

STAPLES
David	Elbert	1822
Fanney	Elbert	1829-60
John	Wilkes	1837-77
John F.	Carroll	1852-96
Stephen	Wilkes	1806-08

STARGEL
| John | Lumpkin | 1845-1923 |

STARK
| Francis L. | Lumpkin | 1845-1923 |
| Sauel | Butts | 1826-41 |

STARKE
| Thomas | Greene | 1845-1923 |

STARKEY
| John | Oglethorpe | 1807-26 |

STARLING
Benjamin F.	Upson	1826-1910
Francis	Camden	1795-1829
L.	Chattooga	1856-1924
William C.	Upson	1826-1910

STARNES
Adam	McIntosh	1873-1915
Ebenezer	Wilkes	1792-1801
Elizabeth	Jasper	1822-26
George D.	Paulding	1850-77 appr
Samuel	Jasper	1826-31
Thomas	Wilkes	1792-1801

STARR
Asa D.	Wilkes	1819-19
D. R.	Montgomery	1806-63
Henry	Morgan	1814-30
Hiram	Wilkinson	1821
Joshua	Wilkes	1819-36

STATEN
| C. E. A. Mrs. | Lowndes | 1871-1915 |
| Solomon | Tattnall | 1800-35 deeds |

STATHAM
Charles Woodson	Polk	1857-1936
Jane	Wilkes	1819-36
William	Houston	1827-55

STATHEN
| John | Elbert | 1823 |

STATON
| Willis | Lumpkin | 1845-1923 |

STAUNTON
| David B. | Ware | 1879-1915 |
| William | Camden | 1795-1829 |

STEAGALL
| Elizabeth | Coweta | 1849-92 |

STEDELER
| Peter | Colonial | 1769 |

STEDHAM
| Martin | Bartow | 1836-85 |

STEED
| S. P. | Coweta | 1849-92 |

STEEDLY
| Lawrence P. | Ware | 1879-1915 |

STEEL
| Elizabeth | Baldwin | 1806-19 |
| John | Lincoln | 1796-1808 |

STEELE
| Robert | Henry | 1834-69 |
| Robert A. | Newton | 1823-51 |

STEELMAN
| William H. | Bartow | 1836-85 |

STEERMAN
| Henrich | Colonial | 1769 |

STEERNES
| John T. | Talbot | 1864 |

STEGALL
Blackwell	Bartow	1836-85
Samuel	Henry	1834-69
William W.	Coweta	1849-92

STEGER
| R. M. | Pike | 1844-76 |

STEINHIBS
| Anna Yvels Christian | Colonial | 1748 |

STELL
| E. Fletcher | Henry | 1822-34 |
| John | Henry | 1822-34 |

STEMBRIDGE
John	Crawford	1852-94
Thomas	Crawford	1835-52
William	Putnam	1823-56

STEPHENS
A.	Walton	1827-31
Abram	Putnam	1823-56
Andrew B.	Taliaferro	1826-66
Carman	Union	1877-1942
David Sr.	Clarke	1822-42
Dorothy Mrs.	Cobb	1904

STOKES		
E. S.	Early	1856-1927 gdn bond
George	Clarke	1802-22
Joel	Stewart	1837-49
Judith	Coweta	1849-92
Lucretia	Lincoln	1808-32
Nancy H.	Lincoln	1831-69
Richard H.	Lincoln	1808-32
Sarah	Madison	1812-41
Sarah	Wilkes	1837-77
Thomas	Elbert	1816
William	Elbert	1794
William	Lincoln	1808-32
William Sr.	Lincoln	1808-32
William W.	Lincoln	1831-69
Young S.	Coweta	1828-48

STONE		
Daniel R.	Stewart	1850-90
Erastus	Crawford	1835-52
George	Early	1856-1927 gdn bond
James	Jefferson	1841
James	Wilkes	1818-19
Jefferson	Macon	1856-1909
John	Wilkes	1806-08
Joseph	DeKalb	1840-69
Marble	Jefferson	1788
Osborn	Wilkes	1819-36
Uriah	Clarke	1802-22
William	Jones	1810-28
William	Putnam	1823-56
William	Wilkes	1837-77
William A.	Wilkes	1837-77

STONEHAM		
Henry	Jackson	1802-60

STONNUM		
Bryan	Hancock	1816

STOREY		
Thomas	Franklin	1786-1813
Thomas	Jackson	1802-60

STORY		
Benjamin W.	Marion	1846-1915
Charles	Colonial	1763
Edward	Coweta	1849-92
Edward M.	Coweta	1849-92
Josiah	Marion	1846-1915
M. F. Mrs.	Marion	1846-1915
Peter	Pike	1844-76
R. C.	Houston	1855-96
Samuel	Warren	1838
Thomas	Franklin	1786-1813
William M.	Chattooga	1856-1924

STOTESBURY		
Arthur	Bibb	1851-71
George W.	Screven	1810-1929
Louisa Mrs.	Bibb	1851-71

STOUTAMIRE		
Newell	Greene	1817-42

STOVALL		
David	Newton	1823-51
George S.	Greene	1817-42
George T.	Floyd	1852-61
Henry Bishop	Lee	1854-1955
James M.	Franklin	1848-67
John	Jackson	1802-60
Joseph	Baldwin	1819-64
Josiah	Lincoln	1796-1808
Lewis	Lincoln	1808-32
Mary	Franklin	1848-67
Stephen	Lincoln	1831-69

STOWE		
B. E.	Putnam	1823-56

STRANGE		
A. A.	Chattooga	1856-1924
James W.	Cobb	1882
Martha	Washington	1829-71 divs
Seth	Franklin	1848-67
Theodosia W.	Washington	1852-1903

STRAWN		
Absalom	Campbell	1825-1900
L. P.	Murray	1840-72

STREET		
George L.	Forsyth	1833-44
John	Colonial	1768
Samuel	Jackson	1802-60
Thomas	Jefferson	1846

STREETER		
Willey	Morgan	1830-60

STREGLE		
George	Colonial	1767

STREGLUS		
F. P.	Screven	1810-1929

STRETCHAM		
Charles	Houston	1855-96

STRIBLER		
George W.	Bartow	1836-85

STRIBLING		
Anthony	Harris	1850-75
Dorothy	Wilkes	1819-36
Edward A.	Meriwether	1831-59
Francis	Wilkes	1792-1801
Thomas	Wilkes	1837-77

STRICKLAND		
Abel	Thomas	1837-45i
Abigail	Thomas	1837-45i
Abraham	Tattnall	1836-40i
B. F.	Lowndes	1871-1915
Cary	Pike	1844-76
Charles	Lowndes	1871-1915
David	Hancock	1804
Elizabeth	Jackson	1802-60
Elizabeth	Thomas	1837-45i
Enoch	Paulding	1850-77
Ezekiel	Meriwether	1831-59
H. A.	Henry	1834-69
Hilliard	Henry	1822-34
Jacob	Elbert	1804
Jacob	Franklin	1786-1813
Jacob	Forsyth	1833-44i
James H.	Coweta	1849-92
John	Macon	1856-1909
John	Thomas	1837-45i
John M.	Butts	1826-41
Kinchen	Madison	1842-96
Lewis	Tattnall	1836-40i
Lewis M.	Screven	1810-1929
Nancy	Madison	1842-96
O.	Forsyth	1833-44
Rebecca	Tattnall	1836-40i
S. L., admr of H. W. Harris	Paulding	1850-77
S. L. admr of C. R. Walker	Paulding	1850-77
Sarah	Thomas	1837-45i minor
Sarah A.	Screven	1810-1929
Solomon	Henry	1834-69
Solomon	Madison	1842-96
Tolbert	Madison	1812-41
Willis	Madison	1842-96

TATE (continued)

Robert	Hall	1837-67
T. A.	Lumpkin	1845-1923
Thomas J.	Wilkes	1819-36
P. T.	Lumpkin	1845-1923
William	Lumpkin	1845-1923
Zemri	Elbert	1826

TATOM

Allen M.	Sumter	1838-55 bonds
Isaac	Lincoln	1795-1808
Jane	Lincoln	1795-1808
John	Lincoln	1795-1808
John	Lincoln	1808-32
John Sr.	Wilkes	1792-1801
William	Wilkes	1779-92

TATTERSELL

Michael	Colonial	1775

TATUM

Abel	Lincoln	1795-1808
M. A. Mrs.	McIntosh	1873-1915
Nathaniel	Hancock	--

TAYLOR

A. J.	Macon	1856-1909
Alfred	Washington	1829-71 divs
Anna	Jasper	1822-26
Bartholomew	Meriwether	1831-59
Benjamin	Screven	1810-1929
Berzilla S.	Appling	1877-1925
Caleb	Habersham	1847-1900
Catherine	Oglethorpe	1833-66
Charles	Franklin	1786-1813
Charles	Hancock	1814
Christopher	Harris	1850-75
Clarke	Oglethorpe	1833-66
Elizabeth	Elbert	1831
Elizabeth	Franklin	1786-1813
Elnora L.	Houston	1855-96
G.	Chattooga	1856-1924
George D.	Wilkes	1819-36
Gracie A.	Washington	1852-1903
Henry	Washington	1852-1903
Hugh	Hancock	1826
Isaac	Houston	1827-55
J. J.	Chattooga	1856-1924
J. J.	Early	1856-1889 L/A
Jacob	Houston	1827-55
James	Carroll	1852-96
James	Early	1856-1889 L/A
James	Early	1857-1927 L/A
James	Greene	1796-1806
James	Jones	1826-50
James	Tattnall	1836-40i
James	Wilkes	--
James E.	Washington	1852-1903
James M.	Pulaski	1816-50
James R.	Washington	1829-71 divs
Jane Alice	Camden	1795-1829
Jesse	Houston	1855-96
Jesse	Tattnall	1836-40i
John	Morgan	1014-30
John M.	Butts	1826-41
Joseph	Clarke	1822-42
Joseph G.	Jones	1812-23
Josiah W.	Newton	1823-51
Kinchen	Washington	1852-1903
M. H.	Appling	1877-1925
Mary	Butts	1826-41
Milly	Washington	1852-1903
Noah	Butts	1826-41
O.	Bartow	1836-85
Peter S.	Screven	1810-1929
Richard	Franklin	1786-1813
Seth K.	Sumter	1838-55
Simeon	Houston	1855-96
Simeon L.	Dooly	1847-1901

TAYLOR (continued)

U. E.	Pike	1844-76
W. N.	Carroll	1852-96
Walter	Morgan	1814-30
William	Early	1834-1920 bonds
William	Randolph	1845-94
William	Upson	1826-1910
William A.	Marion	1846-1915
William D.	Upson	1826-1910
William F.	Washington	1852-1903
William P.	Washington	1829-71 divs
William R.	Washington	1829-71 divs
William S.	Washington	1852-1903
Winney	Elbert	1825

TEASDALE

John	Colonial	1752

TEASLEY

Benager	Elbert	1829-60
Isham Sr.	Elbert	1834
James Sr.	Elbert	1829-60
William	Elbert	1824

TEAT

James	Floyd	1861-71

TELFAIR

Jacob	Colonial	1760
Jane	Richmond	1840-53

TEMPLE

Nancy	Hancock	1822

TEMPLES

James Sr.	Wilkinson	1893
John Sr.	Wilkinson	1859

TEMPLETON

Andrew	Cobb	1868 minor

TENANT

George A.	Early	1856-1927 L/A

TENNILLE

Frances	Washington	1829-71 divs

TERCHUNE

Anna L.	Floyd	1861-71

TERONDET

Daniel	Wilkes	1779-92
Daniel	Wilkes	1792-1801

TERREL

Joel	Wilkes	1779-92
William	DeKalb	1804-69

TERRELL

Charles	Wilkes	1818-19
David	Crawford	1835-52
David	Greene	1817-42
Elizabeth	Greene	1817-42
Elizabeth	Wilkes	1837-77
Henry	Franklin	1786-1813
Henry	Morgan	1830-60
Henry	Wilkes	1837-77
Hezekieh	Franklin	1786-1813
J. T.	Polk	1857-1936
Jeremiah	Elbert	1811
Joel H.	Polk	1857-1936
Joel H.	Taliaferro	1826-66
Joel W.	Coweta	1828-48i
John	Henry	1822-34
John	Wilkes	1819-36
John D.	Franklin	1788-1813
Joseph	Franklin	1786-1813
Mary Ann	Henry	1822-34
Peter	Wilkes	1792-1801

THOMPSON (continued)

L. Jane	Forsyth	1833–44
L. Q. C.	Polk	1857–1936
Lucy	Warren	1813
Malinda	Emanuel	1868 minor
Paul	Taliaferro	1826–66
Peter	Upson	1826–1910
Priscilla	Taliaferro	1826–66
Richard	Colonial	1767
Robert	Emanuel	1866i
Sallie B.	Lee	1854–1955
Samuel	Campbell	1825–1900
Samuel	Fayette	1828–97
Samuel R.	Campbell	1825–1900
Seth	Meriwether	1831–59
Sherrod	Jackson	1802–60
Thomas	Houston	1855–96
W. D.	Pike	1844–76
William	Elbert	1811
William	Floyd	1861–71
William	Madison	1840–60
William	Madison	1842–96
William G.	Jasper	1825–31

THOMSON

Guy	Sumter	1838–55
W. H.	Burke	1853–70

THORNTON

A. B.	Washington	1852–1903
Annie C. Mrs.	Appling	1877–1925
Benjamin Sr.	Elbert	1829–60
Daniel	Elbert	1829–60
Daniel Sr.	Elbert	1829–60
David	Walton	1819–37 minor
Dred	Walton	1819–37
Dred	Walton	1827–31
Elijah	Cobb	1876i
Elizabeth	Elbert	1829–60
Elizabeth	Oglethorpe	1807–26
George	Hall	1837–67
Harrison L.	Oglethorpe	1833–66
Heywood	Fayette	1828–97
Hudson A.	Muscogee	1838–62
Isaac	Walton	1819–37 minor
John H.	Stewart	1837–49
Joshua	Oglethorpe	1793–1807
Kittie C.	Fayette	1828–97
Mark	Jackson	1802–60
Mark	Meriwether	1831–59
Narcissa	Walton	1819–37
Patsy	Walton	1819–37 minor
Rachel	Oglethorpe	1833–66
Redman	Greene	1817–42
Reuben	Elbert	1829–60 (1810)
Reuben	Franklin	1786–1813
Richard	Oglethorpe	1807–26
Robert C.	Stewart	1850–90
Roger	Hancock	1796
Sally	Greene	1817–42
Solomon	Wilkes	1810–16
William	Wilkes	1779–92
Wyatt	Walton	1819–37 minor

THRASH

Andrew	Putnam	1823–56
Christopher	Meriwether	1831–59
Jacob	Putnam	1808–22
W. M.	Lee	1854–1955

THRASHER

Benjamin	Franklin	1786–1813
Robert	Franklin	1786–1813
William	Gwinnett	1852–86
Zeney	Morgan	1814–30

THRELKELD

J. B.	Madison	1842–96

THRIFT

Elizabeth	Ware	1879–1915
William	Ware	1879–1915

THROWER

M. F.	Pike	1844–76

THURMAN

Absalom	Wilkes	1792–1801
Elisha	Wilkes	1779–92
Emily E.	Polk	1857–1936
Richard	Carroll	1852–96
Stephen	Coweta	1849–92
William Sr.	Carroll	1852–96

THURMOND

Felix	Lincoln	1795–1808
Fountain M.	Jasper	1825–31
Harris F.	Walton	1834–9
Harrison	Jackson	1802–60
James	Jackson	1802–60
James M.	Walton	1834–9
Martha	Bartow	1836–85
Martin	Walton	1827–31
Phillip	Bibb	1823–55
William	Jackson	1802–60
William Sr.	Wilkes	1810–16

THWEATT

James	Hancock	1814
Thomas	DeKalb	1804–69

TIGNER

H. H.	Meriwether	1831–59

TILGHMAN

Aaron	Fayette	1828–97

TILLER

John P.	Oglethorpe	1833–66
Joseph	Baldwin	1806–19
Mitchell D.	Oglethorpe	1833–66

TILLERY

Henry	Putnam	1808–22
Joshua	Morgan	1814–30

TILLEY

Elizabeth	Stewart	1850–90

TILLMAN

J. C.	Appling	1877–1925
James	Appling	1877–1925
John	Meriwether	1831–59

TILLORY

Thomas	Lincoln	1831–69

TILLOTSON

Blaford	Houston	1855–96

TILSON

Thomas B.	Pike	1844–76

TIMMONS

James	Gilmer	1836–53i
John	Montgomery	1806–63
William	Carroll	1852–96

TIMMS

John	Gwinnett	1852–86

TINDALL

Alfred	Randolph	1845–94
Elizabeth	Henry	1822–34
Jonathan	Henry	1822–34
William	Clarke	1822–42

TINER
Jackson	Sumter	1838-55 bonds

TINLEY
David	Richmond	1840-53
John	Colonial	1760

TINNEY
Isaac	Gwinnett	1852-86

TINSLEY
Ira N.	Bartow	1836-85
Lucy	Jasper	1825-31
Mary	Cobb	1863I
Philip	Randolph	1845-94
William	Sumter	1838-55
William B.	Baldwin	1819-64

TIPPEN
D. J.	Cobb	1892

TIPTON
James	Baldwin	1806-19

TISON
Eason	Lee	1854-1955
Elizabeth	Montgomery	1806-63
Hammel	Effingham	1829-59
Job	Glynn	1844-53
Moses	Sumter	1838-55 bonds
Moses B.	Lee	1854-1955
Stephen	Emanuel	1839
W. W. Dr.	Polk	1857-1936

TITSWORTH
Isaac	Jackson	1802-60

TOBEY
Frederic	Muscogee	1838-62

TOBIN
Mary	Bibb	1851-71

TODD
Benjamin Sr.	Jones	1826-50
Hardy	Warren	1801
Henry	McIntosh	1873-1915
Henry W.	Greene	1817-42
James	Wilkinson	1850
John	Colonial	1756
John	Houston	1827-55
John	Laurens	1809-40
John	Liberty	1772-1881
John	Putnam	1808-22
Richard	DeKalb	1804-69
S. W.	Early	1856-1927 L/A
Samuel W.	Early	1856-1927 L/A
William	Tattnall	1800-35 deeds
William	Wilkinson	1866

TOLBERT
William	Franklin	1786-1813
William	Walton	1834-9

TOLE
James	Wilkes	1810-16

TOLER
Amelia	Wilkinson	1920

TOLLIS
James M.	Marion	1846-1915

TOLLISON
Susannah	Cobb	1876i

TOMBERLIN
John	Campbell	1825-1900
John	Irwin	1821-64

TOMBLIN
Owen	Marion	1846-1915

TOMKINS
John	Jefferson	1836

TOMLIN
Zilpha	Burke	1853-70

TOMLINSON
David	Lincoln	1795-1808
E. H.	Lowndes	1871-1915
Elizabeth	Putnam	1823-56
Jared	Sumter	1838-55 bonds
John	Baldwin	1806-19
L. H.	Fayette	1828-97
Nathan	Putnam	1823-56

TOMPKINS
Humphrey	Oglethorpe	1807-26
John	Camden	--
Susannah	Oglethorpe	1807-26
Wiley J.	Baldwin	1819-64

TONDEE
Peter	Colonial	1775

TONEY
Sarah R.	Marion	1846-1915

TOOKE
Allen	Houston	1827-55
Arthur	Pulaski	1816-50
Austin	Houston	1855-96
William	Greene	1806-18
William Sr.	Macon	1856-1909

TOOKOM
Seth	Henry	1834-69

TOOLE
Susannah	Richmond	1840-53

TOOLEY
William	Jones	1812-23

TOOMBS
Dawson	Wilkes	1792-1801
Gabriel	Wilkes	1792-1801
Robert	Wilkes	1818-19

TOOMER
Henry	Houston	1855-96
John S.	Houston	1855-96

TORRANCE
Clara	Muscogee	1838-62
Mansfield	Muscogee	1838-62

TORRENCE
John	Warren	1825
William H.	Baldwin	1819-64

TOUCHSTONE
Daniel	Glynn	1844-53

TOWERS
Isaac	DeKalb	1834-69
Larkin	Bartow	1836-85

TOWLER
James	Lincoln	1795-1808
Martha	Morgan	1830-60

TOWNS
Bartley	Greene	1806-18
Drury	Elbert	1807
Elisha	Elbert	1803
George W.	Bibb	1851-71

TOWNS (continued)		
James	Madison	1840-60
John G.	Jasper	1823-33
Leonard	Bartow	1836-85
Rebecca	Taliaferro	1826-66

TOWNSEND		
John	Floyd	1852-61
John	Oglethorpe	1793-1807
N. W.	Meriwether	1831-59
Silas B. F.	Irwin	1821-64 ind
Thomas	Lumpkin	1833-52

TOWNSLEY		
Sarah Mrs.	Houston	1855-96

TOWRY		
James M.	Lumpkin	1845-1923

TOWSON		
James	Randolph	1845-1894
Myhack	Greene	1796-1806

TRACY		
B.	Lee	1854-1955
Edward D.	Bibb	1823-55

TRAMMELL		
Daniel	Jones	1810-20
David	Stewart	1850-90
L. N.	Cobb	1900
Pulaski L.	Harris	1850-75
Thomas	Lincoln	1808-32
Thomas	Pike	1823-29
Thomas	Wilkes	1819-36
Woodward	Wilkes	1819-36

TRAPP		
Daniel	Paulding	1850-77
		gdn bond

TRAVIS		
Asa	Tattnall	1800-35 deeds
Jesse	Henry	1834-69
William	Warren	1805

TRAWICK		
Francis	Hancock	1813
Henry	Hancock	1821
Jane	Hancock	1837

TRAYLOR		
Bassal	Oglethorpe	1793-1807
Edward	Upson	1826-1910
John S.	Upson	1826-1910
Washington	Troup	1832-48
Wiley	Troup	1832-48
William	Jasper	1826-31

TRAYWICK		
Jasper	Pulaski	1816-50

TREADWELL		
Isaac Sr.	Clarke	1822-42

TREPPE		
Turner H.	Bartow	1836-85

TREZEVANT		
Margaret G.	Houston	1855-96

TRIBBLE		
Dicy	Oglethorpe	1807-26
Joel	Oglethorpe	1833-66
Martha	Washington	1852-1903

TRIBLE		
Benjamin	Oglethorpe	1807-26
Spilisby	Madison	1842-96

TRICE		
Benjamin	Baldwin	1806-19
Elisha	Jones	1812-23
James	Jones	1812-23
John	Jones	1810-28
William	Upson	1826-1910

TRIMBLE		
Ruth	Morgan	1830-60

TRIPLETT		
William	Wilkes	1819-36
William P.	Oglethorpe	1807-26

TRIPP		
James	Pulaski	1816-50
John J.	Stewart	1850-90
William	Jasper	1812-17

TRIPPE		
E. M.	Dooly	1847-1901
Henry	Greene	1786-95
John	Hancock	1794

TROTMAN		
Cullen	Stewart	1850-90
Jacob	Stewart	1850-90

TROTTER		
Mary	Polk	1857-1936

TROUP		
Robert L.	Montgomery	1806-63

TROUT		
Nathaniel	Jackson	1802-60
Sarah	Jackson	1802-60

TRUAN		
David	Colonial	1775

TRUETT		
Riley	Jasper	1822-26
Samuel	Harris	1850-75
William P.	Harris	1850-75

TRUITT		
Purnal	Wilkes	1837-77

TRULL		
John	Pulaski	1816-50

TRULOCK		
Sutton	Pulaski	1816-50

TRULUCK		
James	Early	1834-1920 bonds
John	Dooly	1847-1901
Mary	Early	1834-1920 bonds
Sutton	Early	1834-1920 bonds

TUBB		
William	Burke	1853-70

TUCK		
Benjamin	Wilkes	1837-77
Josiah	Wilkes	1837-77
Martha F.	Wilkes	1837-77

TUCKER		
Ann Mrs.	Baldwin	1819-64
Cinthia Caroline	Oglethorep	1833-66
Daniel	Elbert	1818
Daniel	Wilkes	1806-08
Eli, admr Reuben	Sumter	1838-55 bonds
Elizabeth E.	Houston	1855-96
Godfrey	Elbert	1827
Isaiah	Warren	1821
J. S.	Chattooga	1856-1924

UNDERWOOD

George W.	Bartow	1836-85
Isaac	Putnam	1823-56
John	Coweta	1849-92
Joseph	Elbert	1822
Reuben	Washington	1852-1903
Thomas	Wilkinson	1850
William	Tattnall	1836-40i

UNSELD

David	Colonial	1770

UNTHREY

John L.	Campbell	1825-1900

UPCHURCH

Eaton	Henry	1822-34
H. H.	Gwinnett	1852-86
Harbard	Henry	1822-34
J. W.	Campbell	1825-1900

UPSHAW

Adkin	Carroll	1852-96
G. W.	Carroll	1852-96
George	Elbert	1832
James	Bartow	1836-85
John	Elbert	1834
John Jr.	Elbert	1815
John A.	Bartow	1836-85
Leroy	Elbert	1829-60
M. C. Mrs.	Polk	1857-1936

UPTON

Benjamin	Warren	1813

URQUHART

David	Richmond	1840-53
Nolland	Carroll	1852-96

USERY

Elizabeth	Laurens	1809-40

USHER

Abner	Jasper	1823-33
Maud H.	Screven	1810-1929
Oliver	Jasper	1823-33
Sarah A.	Bibb	1851-71

USRY

Ada P. Mrs.	Lee	1854-1955
John Rober	Lee	1854-1955

USSERY

John	Jones	1826-50

VALENTINE

Levi	Wilkinson	1823
Thomas	Wilkinson	1858

VANCE

Leavin	Harris	1850-75

VANDERPLANK

Mary	Colonial	1758

Van DURANDER

E. H. Mrs.	Polk	1857-1936

Van LANDINGHAM

William	Wilkinson	1873

VANNER

David N.	Pike	1844-76
John F.	Henry	1834-69
Matthew Sr.	Oglethorpe	1833-66

VANSANT

Garrot	Jones	1826-59
Shadrack	Coweta	1849-92

VARNUM

William M.	Lumpkin	1845-1923

VASON

John	Morgan	1830-60
Rebecca	Morgan	1830-60

VASSER

Jane	Elbert	1829-60
John	Hancock	1825

VAUGHAN

Abner	Franklin	1786-1813
Benjamin	Franklin	1786-1813
Betty	Hancock	1795
Elizabeth	Oglethorpe	1833-66
James	Bartow	1836-85
James	Oglethorpe	1792-1807
Joshua	Franklin	1848-67
William	Madison	1842-96
William	Oglethorpe	1833-66

VAUGHN

Isaac	Richmond	1840-53
(not recorded)		
Jesse	Wilkinson	1825
John	Bibb	1823-55
		Returns "D"

VAVIN

Samuel	Washington	1829-71 divs

VAWTER

Johanna	Elbert	1805
Richard	Elbert	1829-60
William	Elbert	1828

VEAL

Alexander	Paulding	1850-77
Edward	Washington	1829-71 divs
Luther S. Sr.	Troup	1832-48
Nathan	Sumter	1838-55
Rubin R.	Troup	1832-48
William	DeKalb	1804-69
William	Macon	1856-1909
William Madison	Washington	1852-1903

VEASEY

James	Greene	1786-95
Thomas	Baldwin	1819-64

VEATCH

John	Chattooga	1856-1924

VEAZEY

Caleb	Carroll	1852-96
Ezekiel	Greene	1817-42
John	Taliaferro	1826-66
Zebulon	Taliaferro	1826-66

VENABLE

James L.	Bartow	1836-85
Richard	Hall	1819-37 Mts
Robert	Jackson	1802-60

VERDEL

Anthony	Wilkes	1779-92

VERDERY

Adell P.	Richmond	1840-53

VERDIN

William	Upson	1826-1910

VERDON
Egeniar   Warren   1808

VERNER
David   Franklin   1848-67

VERNON
Robert   Elbert   1829-60

VEZEY
James   Hancock   1795

VICKERS
Edmund   Pulaski   1816-50
Nancy   Baldwin   1806-19
R. H.   Wilkes   1837-77
Thomas   Hancock   1819

VIGAL
George   Bibb   1823-55

VINCENT
Elijah   Wilkinson   1834
Nancy   Greene   1817-42
Thomas   Colonial   1766
William   Greene   1817-42

VINEYARD
Nancy H. Mrs.   Clayton   1859-1921

VINING
A. G.   Murray   1840-72
John   Jefferson   1805
Nancy   Jefferson   1827
Shadrack   Jefferson   --
T. J.   Upson   1826-1910

VINSON
Benjamin   Houston   1855-96
David H.   Washington   1852-1903
E. C.   Baldwin   1806-19
Elijah   Houston   1855-96
Elisha   Henry   1834-69
Eliza   Houston   1855-96
George   Houston   1827-55
James   Houston   1827-55
Josiah   Houston   1855-96
Wesley   Muscogee   1838-62

VINT
William   Oglethorpe   1807-26

VINTON
John Rogers   Richmond   1840-53

VISSCHER
D. W.   Houston   1855-96

VOLLOTTON
Francis   Burke   1853-70

VOYLES
Sarah E.   Polk   1857-1936

WADDELL
Medora N.   Cobb   1880

WADDLE
William   Meriwether   1831-59

WADE
Akree   Wilkes   1792-1801
Benjamin   Jasper   1823-33
Edward   Greene   1786-95
George   Dooly   1847-1901

WADE (continued)
Hudson   Jasper   1826-31
James   Jasper   1826-31
John   Henry   1834-69
John   Morgan   1830-60
John   Polk   1857-1936
John M.   Early   1856-1927
Julius A.   Early   1856-89 L/A
Peyton L.   Screven   1810-1929
William   Early   --
William   Jasper   1826-31
William F.   Morgan   1830-60
William H.   Early   1856-1927 L/A

WADKINS
Mary   Muscogee   1838-62

WADSWORTH
Archibald   Pike   1844-76
John   Pike   1844-76
Thomas   Lincoln   1796-1808

WAFFOLD
Absalom   Jackson   1802-60

WAGES
Richard   Richmond   1840-53

WAGGONER
George   Warren   1797
S. J.   Clayton   1859-1921

WAGNER
Samuel   Colonial   1736

WAILS
Mark   Bartow   1836-85

WAINWRIGHT
Neville   Colonial   1754

WAITS
John   Jasper   1812-17

WAKEFIELD
Charles   Gilmer   1836-53
Orrin W.   Early   1834-1920 bonds
Sarah Ann   Coweta   1828-48 minor

WAKEMAN
James   Bibb   1851-71

WALDEN
Elisha   Clayton   1859-1921
Lewis   Jones   1812-23
Linson   Wilkinson   1873
Reuben   Pulaski   1816-50
Richard   Jones   1812-23

WALDHAUSER
Israel F.   Lowndes   1871-1915
John C.   Lowndes   1871-1915

WALDON
Samuel   Jefferson   18-9

WALDROPE
Solomon   Jasper   1831-9

WALDROUP (Waldrop)
Abraham   Butts   1826-41
Benjamin   Fayette   1828-97
John   Fayette   1828-97
Matthew   Henry   1822-34
Reuben M.   Coweta   1849-92
Samuel   Montgomery   1806-63 receipt
V. M.   Union   1877-1942

WALEA		
James	Emanuel	1837

WALES		
Isaac	Hancock	1825
John	Fayette	1828-97
Samuel A.	Muscogee	1838-62

WALKER		
Benjamin	Harris	1850-75
Betsey	Houston	1827-55
C. R.	Paulding	1850-77
Charles	Liberty	1772-1881
Charles W.	Marion	1846-1915
D. C. Blake	Houston	1855-96
Daniel	Walton	1834-9
David	Morgan	1814-60
Edwin T.	Greene	1817-42
Eliza	Richmond	1840-53
Elizabeth	Baldwin	1806-19
Elizabeth	Jefferson	1795-1834
Emily	Early	1834-1920 bonds
Enoch	Morgan	1814-30
Francis J.	Burke	1853-70
George	Houston	1827-55
George	Jones	1826-50
Green B.	Troup	1832-48
Henry	Jackson	1802-60
Isaac	Morgan	1830-60
Isham	Wayne	1824-55i
James	Butts	1826-41
James	Upson	1826-1910
James Freeman	Washington	1852-1903
James T.	Early	1834-1920 bonds
Jeremiah	Elbert	1792
Joel	Houston	1855-96
Joel	Liberty	1772-1881
Joel	Putnam	1814-64
John	Henry	1834-69
John	Lincoln	1796-1808
John D.	Pulaski	1816-50
John F.	Talbot	1866
John H.	Early	1834-1920 bonds
John H.	Walton	1834-9
John H.	Washington	1852-1903
Jonathan A.	Morgan	1830-60
Jonathan A.	Union	1877-1942
Joseph	Carroll	1852-96
Joseph Sr.	Wilkes	1819-36
Lankford	Lincoln	1808-32
Larkin	Carroll	1852-96
Luther	Early	1856-1927 L/A
Luther S.	Early	1856-1927 L/A
Margaret	Crawford	1835-52
Mary	Randolph	1845-94
Memorable	Elbert	1803
Moses	Burke	1853-70
Moses	Jasper	1831-9
Nancy	Cobb	1873 minors
Oliver, est of J.	Sumter	1838-55 bond
S. S.	Murray	1840-72
Samuel	Muscogee	1838-62
Samuel	Putnam	1823-56
Sanders	Oglethorpe	1793-1807
Tabitha	Stewart	1850-90
Thacker V.	Harris	1850-75
Thomas	Colonial	1753
Thomas D.	Pulaski	1816-50
Thomas G.	Screven	1810-1929
Thomas M.	Coweta	1849-92
Valentine Gen.	Richmond	1840-53
William	Greene	1806-18
William	Oglethorpe	1807-26
William	Oglethorpe	1833-66
William D.	Washington	1852-1903
William H.	Screven	1810-1929

WALL		
Anna R.	Cobb	1879

WALL (continued)		
Elizabeth	Jones	1812-13
James J.	Washington	1829-71 divs
Robert	Burke	1853-70
Robert	Sumter	1838-55
William D.	Montgomery	1806-63

WALLACE		
Ann C.	Macon	1856-1909
Balim	Pulaski	1816-50
Benjamin	Wilkes	1837-77
Drucilla	Emanuel	1866 minor
Eliza	Emanuel	1866 minor
Epps	Pulaski	1816-50
Harris	Emanuel	1866 minor
James	Lincoln	1808-32
James	Morgan	1830-60
John J.	Hancock	1811
Levi	Jackson	1802-60
Martha D.	McIntosh	1873-1915
Mary Mrs.	Marion	1846-1915
Nancy	Emanuel	1866 minor
Oliver	Clarke	1802-22
Rachael	Jackson	1802-60
Thomas	Lincoln	1808-32
W. J.	McIntosh	1873-1915
William	Burke	1853-70
William	Cobb	1865i
William	Hancock	1814
William	Lincoln	1796-1808
William	Lincoln	1831-69
William	Newton	1823-51
William	Putnam	1808-22

WALLER		
James	Hancock	1816
John	Hancock	1798
John	Hancock	1807
John	Hancock	1815
Joseph Jr.	Baldwin	1806-19
Joseph Sr.	Baldwin	1806-19
Nathaniel	Hancock	1816
Nimrod	Wilkes	1837-77

WALLING		
Michael	Jackson	1802-60

WALLIS		
Bland Sr.	Marion	1846-1915
Nancy	Greene	1817-42
Reuben	Clayton	1859-1921
Richard	Clayton	1859-1921
Thomas	Newton	1823-51
W. D.	Clayton	1859-1921
William	Newton	1823-51

WALLRAVEN		
John	Bartow	1836-85

WALSTON		
John	Troup	1832-48

WALTER		
Peter W.	Morgan	1830-60

WALTERS		
Enoch	Crawford	1852-94
George	Muscogee	1838-62
Jack (Col)	Lee	1854-1955
John	Franklin	1786-1813
John	Thomas	1826-36i
Madison	Wilkinson	1862
Moses	Franklin	1848-67
Richard	Washington	1852-1903
Robert	Franklin	1786-1813

WALTERSON		
John H.	Clayton	1859-1921

WALTHALL

Edward	Jasper	1822-26
Garard Jr.	Elbert	1801
Garred	Elbert	1803-06
J. H.	Coweta	1849-92
Susan	Polk	1857-1936
Susanna	Elbert	1805

WALTON

Bryant	Morgan	1830-60
E. L. Mrs.	Marion	1846-1915
Elizabeth	Wilkes	1837-77
Hugh	Burke	1853-70
Isaiah	Houston	1855-96
Jesse	Coweta	1849-92
Jesse	Franklin	1786-1813
John H.	Lincoln	1808-32
John S.	Lincoln	1831-69
Joseph W.	Morgan	1830-60
Killis	Franklin	1786-1813
Mary	Franklin	1786-1813
Nancy	Elbert	1829-60
Newell	Lincoln	1808-32
Noah	Lincoln	1808-32
Overton H.	Houston	1855-96
Richard T.	Wilkes	1837-77
Robert	Franklin	1786-1813
Robert	Lincoln	1831-69
Robert J.	Jasper	1812-17
Robert J.	Putnam	1808-22
Thomas	Burke	1853-70
Thomas	Meriwether	1831-59
Thomas Sr.	Lincoln	1796-1808
Thomas J.	Richmond	1840-53
V. E.	Houston	1855-96

WANSLOW

John Sr.	Elbert	1835
Thomas	Elbert	1829-60

WARBURTON

Thomas	Morgan	1814-30

WARD

Abner	Stewart	1850-90
Amos	Putnam	1823-56
Bryan	Camden	1795-1829
David T.	Dooly	1847-1901
Francis Sr.	Burke	1853-70
Frank	Lowndes	1871-1915
J. L. D.	Bartow	1836-85
James	Burke	1853-70
James	Henry	1822-34
James	Wilkinson	1864
John	Baldwin	1819-64
John	Jones	1812-23
John L.	Carroll	1852-96
Mary B.	Stewart	1850-90
Peyton	Baldwin	1819-64
Richard	Elbert	1826
Ridley	Baldwin	1819-64
Samuel	Oglethorpe	1833-66
Sara A.	Wilkinson	1901
Sarah	Emanuel	1825
		deed of gift
Seth	Oglethorpe	1807-26
Thomas C.	Sumter	1838-55
Thomas J.	Early	1856-89 L/A
Walter H.	Elbert	1827
William	Floyd	1852-61
William W.	Hall	1837-67
Wyatt	Pike	1844-76

WARDLAW

James (of S. C.)	Richmond	1840-53
John B.	Macon	1856-1909

WARDS

Albrittain	Henry	1834-69

WARE

Bennett M.	Troup	1832-48
Cato	Madison	1842-96
Edward	Floyd	1852-61
Edward	Madison	1812-41
Elisha	Madison	1842-96
Henry	Jasper	1822-26
Henry	Lincoln	1796-1808
Henry	Lincoln	1808-32
J. M.	Paulding	1850-77 bond
James	Henry	1822-34
James,	Henry	1822-34
M & C McLendon		
James	Morgan	1814-30
James,	Paulding	1850-77
adm of T. Crumpton		
John	Franklin	1786-1813
Julia C.	Coweta	1849-92
Nicholas	Morgan	1814-30
Samuel H.	Madison	1842-96
Shadrack	Macon	1856-1909
William J.	Campbell	1825-1900

WARNACK

Robert	Oglethorpe	1793-1807

WARNER

Benjamin	Jefferson	1820
Elijah	Jefferson	1822
Elizabeth W.	Screven	1810-1929

WARNOCK

James	Jefferson	1804

WARREN

Aaron	Houston	1827-55
Amanda	Screven	1810-1929
Dread	Macon	1856-1909
Eli	Houston	1855-96
Elizabeth	Hancock	1833
G. W.	Glynn	1844-53
Henry	Morgan	1814-30
J. V.	Carroll	1852-96
Jackson	Macon	1856-1909
James	Emanuel	1867i
James N.	Houston	1855-96
Jeremiah	Hancock	1831
Jesse	Carroll	1852-96
Jesse Sr.	Hancock	1826
John	Jefferson	1797
Lott	Lincoln	1796-1805
Stephen	Morgan	1814-30
Thomas Y.	Carroll	1852-96
Valentine	Hall	1819-37 Mts

WARTHEN

F. J.	Washington	1829-71 divs
Richard	Washington	1829-71 divs
Richard	Washington	1852-1903
Sarah Mrs.	Washington	1852-1903
Thomas	Washington	1852-1903

WARWICK

Patrick	DeKalb	1840-69

WASH

William Sr.	Randolph	1845-94

WASHINGTON

George (Col)	Lee	1854-1955
J. H. R.	Bibb	1851-71
Robert B.	Baldwin	1819-64
William	Hancock	1796

WATERMAN

Asaph	Richmond	1840-53

WATERS

Abner	Gilmer	1836-53i

WEST (continued)

Name	County	Date
Elizabeth	Hancock	1822
Elizabeth R.	Polk	1857-1936
Emma K.	Ware	1879-1915
Ephraim	Hancock	1812
Fort	Stewart	1850-90
George	Hancock	1809
George W.	Polk	1857-1936
Henry	Lincoln	1796-1808
Irena	Cobb	1870
Irene Mrs.	Polk	1857-1936
James	Morgan	1814-30
Jane C.	Polk	1857-1936
John Jr.	Greene	1817-42
John M.	Wilkes	1819-36
John Q.	Wilkes	1837-77
Joseph	Baldwin	1819-64
Levin	Harris	1850-75
Martha E.	Polk	1857-1936
Mary A.	Stewart	1850-90
Mary Alice	Randolph	1845-94
Moses S.	Baldwin	1819-64
P. Mrs.	Polk	1857-1936
Philip	Sumter	1838-55
Roxanna	Polk	1857-1936
Sarah A. E.	Randolph	1845-94
William	Morgan	1814-30
William	Stewart	1850-90
William Stanley	Lowndes	1871-1915
Windance	Fayette	1828-97

WESTBROOK

Name	County	Date
J. H.	Gwinnett	1852-86
Thomas	Franklin	1848-67
William R.	Campbell	1825-1900

WESTBURY

Name	County	Date
Thomas	Colonial	1773

WESTER

Name	County	Date
Hardy	Warren	1795
Henry	Montgomery	1806-63
Richard	Tattnall	1836-40i

WESTFIELD

Name	County	Date
Eliza	Cobb	1888

WESTMORELAND

Name	County	Date
James	Pike	1823-29
Reuben	Coweta	1828-48
Reuben	Pike	1823-29
Robert	Pike	1823-29

WESTON

Name	County	Date
Grace	Camden	1868-1916
Stephen	Stewart	1837-49

WHALEY

Name	County	Date
E.	Walton	1819-37
James	Pike	1823-29
Matilda	Clayton	1859-1921
Nathaniel	Upson	1826-1910
William	Greene	1786-95

WHALING

Name	County	Date
Bryan Hope	Lee	1854-1955

WHATLEY

Name	County	Date
Archey	Troup	1832-48
Dorton	Oglethorpe	1793-1807
James	Pike	1844-76
James G.	Upson	1826-1910
John	Greene	1806-18
John B.	Jasper	1812-17
Michael	Greene	1794-1810
Ornam	Oglethorpe	1793-1807
Simeon A.	Coweta	1849-92
W. O. B.	Polk	1857-1936
Wiley	Polk	1857-1936

WHATLEY (continued)

Name	County	Date
William H.	Pike	1844-76
Willis	Hancock	1799

WHATTLEY

Name	County	Date
Willis	Jasper	1812-17

WHEAT

Name	County	Date
Augustus Walter	Campbell	1825-1900
Harvey	Lincoln	1831-69
Mary	Lincoln	1831-69

WHEATLEY

Name	County	Date
Joseph	Wilkes	1837-77
Nancy	Wilkes	1837-77
Othrel	Wilkes	1837-77

WHEELASS

Name	County	Date
Elizabeth	Talbot	--
Hardy	Talbot	1859
Levi	Talbot	--

WHEELER

Name	County	Date
Benjamin	Warren	1817
Green M.	Sumter	1838-55
Hezekiah Gideon	Butts	1826-41
Isaac	Camden	1795-1829
Isham	Warren	1836
James	Gwinnett	1852-86
James	Jackson	1802-60
James B.	Lincoln	1808-32
John	Houston	1827-55
Josiah	Dooly	1847-1901
Mary	Franklin	1786-1813
Rebecca	Burke	1853-70
Thomas	Elbert	1829
William	Franklin	1786-1813

WHELCHEL

Name	County	Date
Davis Sr.	Hall	1837-67
Francis	Hall	1837-67
Francis	Lumpkin	1845-1923
James M.	Lumpkin	1845-1923
M. F.	Lumpkin	1845-1923

WHELESS

Name	County	Date
Pardy	Jones	1812-23

WHELON

Name	County	Date
Michael	Oglethorpe	1807-26

WHETSTONE

Name	County	Date
James M.	Houston	1827-55

WHIDBY

Name	County	Date
Irene	Ware	1879-1915

WHIDENER

Name	County	Date
James	Early	1856-1927

WHIGHAM

Name	County	Date
John	Jefferson	1823
William	Jefferson	1848

WHIPPLE

Name	County	Date
Elizabeth	Wilkinson	1881
George Knight	Wilkinson	1861
Stephen	Wilkinson	1847

WHITAKER

Name	County	Date
Benjamin	Jefferson	1820
David E.	Jefferson	1833
Elizabeth	Putnam	1808-22
Ensign	Jasper	1831-9
George W. H.	Washington	1852-1903
Hudson	Lee	1854-1955
Isaac	Franklin	1786-1813
John B.	Jasper	1831-9
Polley	Franklin	1786-1813

WICKER

Margaret Mrs. S.	Washington	1852-1903
Thomas	Washington	1852-1903
Thomas A.	Washington	1852-1903
William H.	Early	1856-89

WIDEMAN

Henry	Troup	1832-48

WIGGINS

Allen	Macon	1856-1909
Christopher H.	Henry	1834-69
Elias	Jefferson	1837
George	Washington	1852-1903
John	Emanuel	1866 senile
(Michael, gdn)		
Joseph	Wayne	1822-70
Joseph	Wayne	1824-55i
Richard	Warren	1832
Richard L.	Washington	1829-71 divs
Sarah	Houston	1827-55
Sarah	Richmond	1840-53
(formerly McCollier)		
Whittington	Stewart	1850-90
William	Houston	1827-55
William	Washington	1829-71 divs
William J.	Marion	1846-1915
Willis	Marion	1846-1915

WIGHT

Martin	Cobb	1897

WIGLEY

James	Oglethorpe	1807-26

WILBORN

Thomas	Putnam	1823-56

WILBORNE

William	Wilkes	1792-1801

WILBURN

Margarete	Henry	1822-34

WILCOX

George	Irwin	1821-64
James	Wilkinson	1827
John	Telfair	1869-1921
T. D.	Telfair	1869-1921
W. A.	McIntosh	1873-1915

WILDE

Richard Henry	Richmond	1840-53

WILDER

Dred	Wilkes	1806-08
E. W.	Crawford	1852-94
Reuben	Ware	1879-1915
William	Jones	1826-50
William L.	Bibb	1823-55

WILDON

Isaac	Jasper	1831-9

WILEY

Ann	Bibb	1851-71
George	Early	1834-1920 bonds
George	Early	1856-89 L/A
George	Greene	1796-1806
Jacob	Early	1834-1920 bonds
John B.	Bibb	1851-71
L. M.	Bibb	1851-71
Mary	Hancock	1831
Moses	Baldwin	1806-9
Pope	Talbot	1857
William	Hancock	1827

WILHIGHT

Penelope	Meriwether	1831-59

WILHIGHT (continued)

Ricks	Meriwether	1831-59

WILHITE

Calvin F.	Elbert	1829-60
John	Madison	1812-41
Philemon R.	Elbert	1829-60

WILKENS

Henry	Early	1856-1927

WILKERSON

Mary E.	Lee	1854-1955
William R.	Campbell	1825-1900

WILKES

Jesse	Montgomery	1806-60
Samuel	Oglethorpe	1833-66

WILKEY

John	Wilkes	1792-1801

WILKINS

Clement	Elbert	1829-60
Clement	Franklin	1786-1813
Drury	Jasper	1831-9
Francis	Pike	1844-76
James	Hancock	1809
John	Henry	1822-34
John Sr.	Elbert	1828
John R.	Henry	1822-34
Leroy	Wilkes	1819-36
Nancy	Elbert	1839
Nathaniel	Lumpkin	1845-1923
William N.	Oglethorpe	1833-66

WILKINSON

A. M.	Harris	1850-75
Alexander	Meriwether	1831-59
Ann	Wilkes	1819-36
B. H.	Macon	1856-1909
Benjamin	Wilkes	1810-16
Eley (or Elie)	Camden	1868-1916
Ezekiel	Hancock	--
Hammon	Jasper	1825-31
John	Murray	1840-72
John	Wilkes	1837-77
Reuben	Screven	1810-1929
Robert	Campbell	1825-1900

WILL

Robert,	Sumter	1838-55 bond
minor of Jesse		

WILLARD

Roswell	Jasper	1826-31
Royal	Henry	1834-69

WILLBANKS

Elosie	Coweta	1828-48i
Hosea	Gwinnett	1852-86

WILLBORN

Alfred	Meriwether	1831-59
David	Newton	1823-51

WILLBORNE

James	Jackson	1802-60

WILLEY

Solomon	Jefferson	1823

WILLIAMS

A. E.	Lowndes	1761-1915
Andrew J.	Sumter	1838-55
Anthony	Screven	1810-1929
B.	Walton	1827-31
B. N.	Appling	1877-1925
Barbara	Oglethorpe	1833-66

WILLIAMSON (continued)

William	Baldwin	1806-19
William	Franklin	1786-1813
William	Jackson	1802-60
William	Wilkes	1806-08

WILLIBY

William	Clarke	1822-42

WILLIFORD

Hans	Crawford	1852-94
J. B.	Stewart	1850-90
John	Stewart	1850-90
Lucy	Madison	1812-41
William	Wilkinson	1889

WILLING

David Thomas	Upson	1826-1910

WILLINGHAM

A.	Polk	1857-1936
Charles H.	Newton	1823-51
Harriet	Jackson	1802-60
Mary	Oglethorpe	1833-66
Reuben S.	Lincoln	1831-69
William B.	Walton	1834-9

WILLIS

Albinia Fletcher	Talbot	--
Anna	Upson	1826-1910
Arthur	Jasper	1825-31
Elizabeth	Henry	1822-34
Harriett C.	Upson	1826-1910
James	Wilkes	1810-16
Joseph	Franklin	1786-1813
Louis	Wilkes	1818-19
Mary	Franklin	1786-1813
Nancy	Upson	1826-1910
William J.	Upson	1826-1910

WILLMAKER

J. H.	Pike	1844-76

WILLOUGHBY

William	Walton	1834-9 minors

WILLS

Jacob H.	Screven	1810-1929

WILLSON

Anderson	Forsyth	1833-44
David	Warren	1827
Elizabeth	Richmond	1840-53
(alias Betsey)		
James L.	Jefferson	1807
(of Richmond Co.)		
John	Jasper	1825-31
Keating (Col)	Richmond	1840-53

WILSHIRE

Benjamin	Wilkes	1792-1801

WILSON

Achilles	Jasper	1831-9
Barbara	Colonial	1770
Boley	Madison	1842-96
Columbus B.	Early	1856-1927
David	Washington	1829-71 divs
Elijah	Jasper	1831-9
Elihu	Effingham	1829-59
Elizabeth	Randolph	1845-94
George	Jackson	1802-60
Henry	Newton	1823-51
Henry M.	Effingham	1829-59
Isaac	Meriwether	1831-59
James	Coweta	1828-48
James	Effingham	1829-59
James	Putnam	1823-56
James	Upson	1826-1910

WILSON (continued)

John	Elbert	1802
John	Greene	1817-42
John	Jefferson	1801
John	Meriwether	1831-59
John	Taliaferro	1826-66
John F.	Campbell	1825-1900
John W.	Madison	1846-1915
Joseph	Macon	1822-26
Leighton	Glynn	1844-53
Lucy	Jackson	1802-60
M. G.	Telfair	1869-1921
M. W.	Glynn	1844-53
Martha F.	Upson	1826-1910
Martha J.	Murray	1840-72
Matthew	Houston	1827-55
Michael	Jackson	1802-60
Moses	Carroll	1852-96
Richard	Hall	1837-67
Robert	Hancock	1798
S. W.	McIntosh	1873-1915
Saloma	Early	--
Samuel	Hancock	1799
Samuel	Jackson	1802-60
Samuel	Muscogee	1838-62
Samuel	Washington	1852-1903
Samuel D.	Polk	1857-1936
Sarah	Jasper	1831-9
Sarah	Lincoln	1808-32
Sarah Jane	Upson	1826-1910
Thomas	Greene	1817-42
Thomas	Hall	1819-37 Mts
Thomas	Ware	1879-1915
William	Baldwin	1806-19
William	Early	1856-1927
William	Franklin	1786-1813
William	Greene	1796-1806
William	Greene	1817-42
William	Hall	1837-67
William	Jefferson	1801
Zacheus	Oglethorpe	1793-1807

WILT

O. H.	Washington	1852-1903

WIMBERLY

Charlotte A.	Burke	1853-70
Ezekiel	Bibb	1851-71
Henry	Houston	1827-55
Lewis	Jones	1826-50
Rebecca C.	Bibb	1823-55

WIMBISH

Cyntha C.	Bibb	1851-71

WIMBLE

Egbert	Washington	1829-71

WIMPEY

John B.	Floyd	1852-61i

WIMPY

A. G.	Lumpkin	1845-1923
John A.	Lumpkin	1845-1923
Nancy W.	Lumpkin	1845-1923
S. G.	Lumpkin	1845-1923

WINDHAM

Chapman	Madison	1842-96

WINDSOR

Alexander	Lee	1854-1955
Anderson	Gwinnett	1852-86

WINDSTON

John	Early	1856-89
		admrs bonds

WOOD (continued)

John M.	Campbell	1825-1900
John N.	Liberty	1772-1881
John S.	Dooly	1847-1901
Jordan A.	Carroll	1852-96
Keziah	Early	1834-1920 bonds
Lewis	Early	1834-1920 bonds
Lewis B.	Bibb	1851-71
Martha	Coweta	1849-92
Mary Mrs.	Dooly	1847-1901
Milton B.	Jackson	1802-60
Robert M.	Lumpkin	1845-1923
Thomas	Walton	1819-37
Thomas	Walton	1827-31
Thomas, orphs of	Walton	1834-9
Timothy	Walton	1834-9
William M.	Jackson	1802-60
William P.	Polk	1857-1936
William T.	Washington	1852-1903

WOODALL

Dollie Miss	Marion	1846-1915
John	Morgan	1830-60
John	Wilkes	1792-1801

WOODARD

Asa	Houston	1855-96
Isaac	Houston	1855-96
Jesse	Carroll	1852-96
L. T.	Harris	1850-75
Martha	Greene	1817-42
Young	Laurens	1809-40

WOODLAND

James	Camden	1795-1829
Thomas	Houston	1827-55

WOODLEY

James B.	Carroll	1852-96

WOODLIFF

Isabella	Forsyth	1833-44i

WOODMAN

Job	Jefferson	1822

WOODRUFF

Clifford	Oglethorpe	1833-66
S. W.	Marion	1846-1915

WOODS

David	Macon	1856-1909
Elizabeth	Lumpkin	1845-1923
Harriett R. Mrs.	Lowndes	1871-1915
Martha	Tattnall	1800-35 deeds
Middleton	Elbert	1807
Robert	Madison	1812-41
Samuel	Hall	1819-37 Mts
T. J.	Chattooga	1856-1924
W. W.	Screven	1810-1929
William Sr.	Lincoln	1831-69
William J.	Chattooga	1856-1924
Wyley E.	Chattooga	1856-1924

WOODSON

Benjamin	DeKalb	1840-69
Creed T.	Houston	1855-96
W. L.	Upson	1826-1910

WOODWARD

Julia W.	Polk	1857-1936
Osmma	Macon	1856-1909
Thomas	Franklin	1786-1813
William	Liberty	1772-1881

WOODY

John	Carroll	1852-96

WOOLBRIGHT

Andilla Mrs.	Lee	1854-1955
John	Lee	1854-1955

WOOLFOLK

John	Muscogee	1838-62
Thomas	Bibb	1851-71

WOOLLEY

Ezekiel	Hall	1837-67
George M.	Camden	1830-67
Mary A.	Bartow	1836-85

WOOTEN

Adison A.	Butts	1826-41
Elizabeth	Jasper	1831-9
James	Butts	1826-41
James	Hancock	1830
James Sr.	Butts	1826-41
Jessie C.	Coweta	1849-92
Joseph	DeKalb	1840-69
Josiah M.	Baldwin	1819-69
Paschal H.	Sumter	1838-55
Seaborn L.	Butts	1826-41
Shadrack	Decatur	1824-52 Mts
Simeon	Butts	1826-41

WOOTTEN

James	Wilkes	1819-36
John A.	Lumpkin	1845-1923
Richard B.	Wilkes	1792-1801

WORD

Joshua	Franklin	1848-67
Thomas A.	Carroll	1852-96
William	Carroll	1852-96

WORKMAN

Charles	Franklin	1786-1813
Jonathan	Franklin	1786-1813

WORLEY

James H.	Lumpkin	1845-1923
W. J. Mrs.	Lumpkin	1845-1923
William J.	Lumpkin	1845-1923

WORNUM

William	Putnam	1823-56

WORRELL

Exum	Stewart	1850-90

WORRILL

Eleanor	Elbert	1829-60
James W.	Randolph	1845-1894
Jesse	Marion	1846-1915
Solomon	Newton	1823-51
William	Newton	1823-51

WORSHAM

Archer	Baldwin	1806-19
John R.	Crawford	1852-94
Lud	Jackson	1802-60

WORTHAM

William C.	Coweta	1849-92

WORTHEY

Thomas	Troup	1832-48

WRAY

John	Oglethorpe	1793-1807
Laura L.	Polk	1857-1936
Malvena	Polk	1857-1936
W. A.	Polk	1857-1936
W. V.	Polk	1857-1936

WRENN

Susannah	Emanuel	1835
		deed of gift

WRIGHT

Abednigo	Hancock	1822
Abraham S.	Pike	1844-76
Amos	Warren	1810
Ann A.	Oglethorpe	1833-66
Apple White	Walton	1870-74
Charlotte	Lincoln	1831-69
D. B.	Cobb	1893
Dodson B.	Cobb	1867i
Elizabeth	Lincoln	1831-69
Gabriel	Elbert	1817
Henry	Chattooga	1856-1924
Henry	Clayton	1859-1921
Henry	Dooly	1847-1901
James G.	Wilkinson	1908
James H.	Crawford	1835-52
James N.	Camden	1795-1829
Jarrett	Greene	1817-42
John	Clarke	1822-42
John	Franklin	1786-1813
John	Jackson	1802-60
John	Lincoln	1808-32
John	Lincoln	1831-69
John	Polk	1857-1936
John M.	Washington	1852-1903
John Norton	Colonial	1749
John S.	Baldwin	1806-19
John W.	Clayton	1859-1921
Joseph	Colonial	1771
L. Sr.	Wilkes	1819-36
L. B.	Cobb	1873i
L. D.	Wilkes	1837-77
M. J.	Chattooga	1856-1924
Martha	Harris	1850-75
Mary	Clarke	1822-42
Mary Elizabeth	Polk	1857-1936
Mrs.		
Mary F.	Lincoln	1831-69
Nancy	Jefferson	1843
Nathan	Lincoln	1831-69
Nathan Sr.	Lincoln	1831-69
Nicodemus K.	Hall	1837-67
Obadiah	Franklin	1786-1813
Parson	Putnam	1808-22
Pleasant	Morgan	1830-60
Spencer	DeKalb	1840-69
Stephen S.	Crawford	1852-94
Susan	Lincoln	1808-32
Rebecca	Glynn	1844-53
Robert	Colonial	1773
Robert	Greene	1817-42
Robert M.	Chattooga	1856-1924
Robert M.	Crawford	1835-52
Sally	Oglethorpe	1833-66
Samuel	Glynn	1844-53
Stephen	Coweta	1849-92
Susannah	Newton	1823-51
Tabitha	Bibb	1851-71
Thomas	Franklin	1786-1813
Thompson T.	Harris	1850-75
William	Clarke	1802-22
(Preacher)		
William	Colonial	1756
William	Decatur	1824-52 Mts
William	Decatur	1828-38
William	Jefferson	1814
William	Lincoln	1808-32
William Dr.	Clarke	1802-22
William Sr.	Walton	1827-31
William B.	Polk	1857-1936
William J.	Chattooga	1856-1924
Zacheus	Greene	1817-42
Zebulon	Greene	1817-42

WRYE

Elizabeth	Pike	1823-29

WYATT

Collier	Hancock	1826
J. M.	Chattooga	1856-1924
John	Chattooga	1856-1924
John J.	Carroll	1852-96
John P.	Henry	1822-34
Peyton	Lincoln	1796-1808
Rhodamantha	Chattooga	1856-1924
Thomas B.	Newton	1823-51
Thomas H.	Morgan	1830-60
Thomas H.	Richmond	1840-53
Samuel	Henry	1822-34 bond
William H.	Henry	1822-34

WYCHE

George	Elbert	1829-60
John T.	Montgomery	1806-63
L.	Thomas	1837-45i
Littleton	Thomas	1826-36i
Peter	Jones	1812-23
R. D.	Montgomery	1806-63

WYLIE

Elizabeth	Wilkes	1792-1801
Nicholas	Wilkes	1837-77
Peter	Oglethorpe	1793-1807

WYLLY

Alexander	Glynn	1844-53
Campbell		
Thomas	Effingham	1829-59
Webster Ann	Glynn	1844-53

WYNN

Ann E.	Wilkes	1837-77
Daniel	Madison	1842-96
Green	Jones	1812-23
John	Putnam	1823-56
John	Wilkes	1819-36
John H. C.	Wilkes	1837-77
Jones	Putnam	1823-56
Julius A.	Polk	1857-1936
Robert	Baldwin	1806-19
Robert	Polk	1857-1936
Thomas	Wilkes	1792-1801
Thomas Sr.	Hancock	1807

WYNNE

Benjamin	Warren	1839
Clement	Warren	1825
John	Oglethorpe	1833-66
Peter Sr.	Colonial	1770
Susannah	Oglethorpe	1833-66

YANCEY

Thomas	Oglethorpe	1833-66

YARBOROUGH

E. W.	Polk	1857-1936
Henry	Bartow	1836-85
John	Campbell	1825-1900
Sarah E.	Bartow	1836-85

YARBROUGH

Elijah	Wilkinson	1880
Groves	Franklin	1786-1813
Groves	Franklin	1848-67
Harriet S.	Randolph	1845-94
Henry S. &	Pike	1844-76
John A.		
Lewis	Randolph	1845-94
Wade L.	Lumpkin	1833-45

YARWOOD

J.	Paulding	1850-77 appr

YATES

James E.	Washington	1852-1903
Joseph	Franklin	1786-1813
Mary E.	Washington	1852-1903
Nancy	Washington	1852-1903

YAWN

Lewis	Appling	1877-1925

YEARLY

Thomas	Bibb	1851-71

YEARWOOD

Starling	Habersham	1847-1900

YEOMANS

Daniel	Emanuel	1867 minor
Eliza L.	Emanuel	1867 minor
James	Sumter	1838-55
John	Emanuel	1867 minor
Mary M.	Emanuel	1867 minor

YONGE

Philip	Upson	1826-1910

YORK

Jeffery	Rabun	1863-88
Jeremiah	Rabun	1863-88
W. S.	Rabun	1863-88
Wesley	Bartow	1836-85

YOUBANKS

Jane	Dooly	1847-1901

YOUMANS

James E.	Appling	1877-1925

YOUNG

A. M.	Wilkinson	1911
Augustine	Polk	1857-1936
C. O.	Lee	1854-1955
Elizabeth	Elbert	1824
Enos	Dooly	1847-1901
George	Oglethorpe	1833-66
Giles	Oglethorpe	1833-66
Isaac	Colonial	1766
Isaac M.	Irwin	1821-64
J. C.	Randolph	1845-94
James	Franklin	1786-1813 petition
James	Newton	1823-51
James	Warren	1794
James N.	McIntosh	1873-1915
John J.	Lee	1854-1955
Owen W.	Laurens	1809-40
R. M.	Bartow	1836-85
Ramer	Lowndes	1871-1915
Robert	Colonial	1734
Robert	Hall	1837-67

YOUNG (continued)

Robert L.	Polk	1856-1936
Roxey A. Mrs.	Lowndes	1871-1915
Thomas	Wilkes	1810-16
William	Colonial	1776
William	Wilkes	1792-1801
William W.	Sumter	1838-55

YOUNGBLOOD

J. T.	Washington	1852-1903
Mary S.	Washington	1852-1903
Winfred M.	Washington	1852-1903

YOW

Thomas A.	Franklin	1848-67

ZACHRY

Abner	Morgan	1830-60
Asa C.	Morgan	1830-60
Clementina R.	Morgan	1830-60
John S.	Jones	1826-50
Sarah	Walton	1827-31

ZEIGLER

William	Crawford	1852-94

ZELLERS

Jacob	Lincoln	1808-32

ZELNER

George Jr.	Lincoln	1808-32
George Sr.	Lincoln	1808-32

ZETTLER

Mathias	Colonial	1768

ZIMMERMAN

Barnard	Wilkes	1819-36
Philip	Lincoln	1808-32

ZIPPERER

C. E.	Lowndes	1871-1915

ZITTERAUER

Ludlief	Effingham	1829-59

ZORN

G. W.	Upson	1826-1910
James	Upson	1826-1910

ZOUBERBUHLER

Bartholomew	Colonial	1766

ZUBER

Abraham	Oglethorpe	1793-1807
Emanuel	Oglethorpe	1833-66
Jacob	Putnam	1808-22
Martha O.	Randolph	1845-94

www.ingramcontent.com/pod-product-compliance
Lightning Source LLC
Chambersburg PA
CBHW050716280326
41926CB00088B/3043